THE ART OF
PROFILING

READING PEOPLE RIGHT THE FIRST TIME

— EXPANDED SECOND EDITION —

ALSO BY

————————

DAN KOREM

————————

SNAPSHOT
READING AND TREATING PEOPLE
RIGHT THE FIRST TIME

RAGE OF THE RANDOM ACTOR
DISARMING CATASTROPHIC ACTS
AND RESTORING LIVES

SUBURBAN GANGS
THE AFFLUENT REBELS

THE ART OF
PROFILING

READING PEOPLE RIGHT THE FIRST TIME

— EXPANDED SECOND EDITION —

DAN KOREM

INTERNATIONAL FOCUS PRESS

RICHARDSON, TEXAS

Published by

International Focus Press

P.O. Box 831587, Richardson, Texas 75083–1587

www.ifpinc.com

ISBN 978–0–9639103–9–4

Library of Congress Catalog Number: 2012900356

For quantity purchases, please contact

International Focus Press

Printed in the United States of America

Sixth Printing May 2020

—For my Sandy,
You read me from the beginning,
And showed me how to love.
Thirty-nine years . . .

CONTENTS

AUTHOR ON THE EXPANDED SECOND EDITION

(Please don't skip)

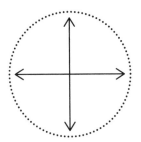

The Art of Profiling was first published in 1997. Its core concepts have stood the test of time as applied by over 40,000 professionals globally who have been trained to use the *Korem Profiling System*® (*KPS*). This expanded second edition contains many refinements from their collective experiences and results for making accurate profiling reads, including two "safety checks" to ensure accuracy, updates on the profiles, a new section in each profile that provides guidance how to lead/motivate, and a new profile—the CAUTIOUS INNOVATOR—the fastest growing profile that few understand. Also, the terms used for two of the gauges have been changed for added clarity. (The ASK–TELL gauge is now ASSERTIVE–NONASSERTIVE and PREDICTABLE–UNPREDICTABLE is now CONVENTIONAL–UNCONVENTIONAL.)

This edition is meant to be read in tandem with its new companion, *Snapshot—Reading and Treating People Right the First Time*, and I recommend that you read it first. Here's why.

Since the publication of *The Art of Profiling*, people from every walk of life produced so many significant results using the *KPS* that I initially considered including many of these cases in this edition. The problem, though, was that it would have expanded to over 450 pages, and most people want something that is short and concise. Additionally, many asked for a book of rapid-fire profiling reads they could make today—immediately—without learning the entire *KPS*. That's when I decided to write *Snapshot*.

Snapshot—Reading and Treating People Right the First Time is now the primer for rapid-fire profiling. It details stories in which people have made reads using just one of the gauges in the *KPS*, rather than whole system, and produced extraordinary results in their personal and professional lives.

I recommend reading it first because you quickly learn how to use the four profiling gauges and how to immediately put them to use. And, it's short—you can read it on a couple of plane rides. It also contains fascinating insights into new trends that affect every facet of our lives, who are the best profilers and why, and more—all based on data I've collected for over twenty years. You can also use *Snapshot* as a quick refresher of key concepts or for introducing rapid-fire profiling to someone you know.

Regardless of how you proceed or how you put the *KPS* to use, please do so for the benefit of others first. As you'll learn why in Chapter 2, honest transparent people have the highest profiling accuracy. It is for these people that the *KPS* was created and for whom I continue to look for new and wonderous ways to treat others right the first time.

Dan Korem
March 2019

FOREWORD

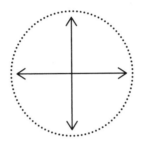

This book is a rare find.

I know of no other text that is even remotely similar.

As a twenty-five-year veteran of the FBI, a former assistant unit chief of the Bureau's Behavioral Sciences Unit, and a criminal personality profiler for a time, I always encouraged new and in-service recruits to try to "read" people in a more accurate way. I was never able, however, to tell them how to do this; I believed it came with some "natural ability" and years of experience.

In *The Art of Profiling—Reading People Right the First Time*, Dan Korem demonstrates that while natural ability and experience may be useful, they are not necessary ingredients. This is a masterful text which proves one does not need a degree in psychology to gain an almost immediate sense of how a person prefers to communicate, perform on the job, and make decisions. The *Korem Profiling System®* offers a simple, direct, and structured system for an activity we find ourselves doing hundreds of times a day reading people.

While there are others who "profile," they are unable to pass these critical profiling skills to others. Thus the importance of this book. It provides you with necessary information and practice sessions to insure success. Learning the *Korem Profiling System®* will separate you from the masses when it comes to reading people right the first time. Dan has lectured on profiling at the FBI Academy to the toughest audience possible, an assembly of the best police psychologists in the country.

This book will serve as a mile-marker for those interested in improving communication skills, exploring and fine-tuning business relationships, gaining better parenting and/or teaching skills, increasing sales, insuring confident hiring, and more. Profiling is a skill everyone needs and yet very few have. The information in this book allows you to avoid making erroneous assumptions about people looking beyond their façades to become a better judge of character, a better predictor of behavior, and a better communicator.

Dan provides you with a "compass" and a "map" for your journey into the art of profiling. This ensures that you will always know where you are and where you are going. Reading this book and following the instructions provided by Dan will result in your being able to do "Snapshot reads," "Fine-tuned reads," and/or "Comprehensive Profiles."

This method of profiling has been presented to educators, medical doctors, psychologists, law enforcement personnel, and representatives of major corporations, and financial institutions. Without exception, its acceptance was immediate and its application proven.

Now you can learn the same skills and techniques used by some of the most effective people and corporations in the world, the *Korem Profiling System*®. It's your next step to a better understanding of people and increased success.

Dr. James T. Reese
Woodbridge, VA

CHAPTER 1

THREE SHORT STORIES

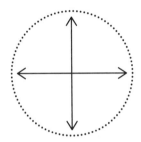

The Next Level

I prepared one question to identify the football coach's profile. Based on his response, I would make a decision whether or not I would enter into a contract. The coach, who we'll call Steve, had been successful at several Division I college programs. He was now in his first year at a storied top-tier program. One of his assistant coaches, who had seen the success possible when coaches used rapid-fire profiling for recruiting and coaching athletes, asked me to talk to his head coach about bringing this skill into the program.

But, there was a problem.

He said his coach was an extremely cautious decision maker. My experience is that when fearful/cautious decision makers are asked to adopt something new, that is foreign to what they've done in the past, successful implementation is unlikely. They'll either reject the new idea outright or, as soon as a bit of doubt creeps in, they'll bring the new initiative to a halt.

That his head coach wasn't decisive, though, sounded off to me. How could a coach win if he wasn't confident? Yet, the assistant described how all the coaches were frustrated with Steve's severe over analyzing of most decisions. They respected that Steve was confident in his *knowledge* of the game, but they didn't think he was decisive enough to win at this level when critical decisions had to be made. I was suspicious. This was probably venting by assistant coaches who wanted to see their schemes and strategic objectives installed, but the coach wanted to go in a different direction.

I agreed to meet with Steve. If he was interested and I determined he was also a confident decision maker, then we'd look at implementation.

About halfway through our meeting, I asked the pivotal question.

"If you were convinced that this profiling system could work for you, how many *additional* new blue chip recruits would you like to recruit a year?"

Blue chippers are the premier athletes who are the most heavily recruited. Have enough of them, and they can define the success of a program.

"I'll have to think about that," was his response. He wasn't being coy or testing me, he meant it.

Every coach who I've posed the same question to, who was a confident decision maker, has answered with something like: *Why does there have to be a limit? Let's recruit them all!*

Steve's assistant coaches were right. He was an extremely cautious decision maker, and coaches who are decisive don't like it. They have to make lightning decisions against the clock without second guessing. If you're not committed, hesitation will kill you.

One time Steve called a trick play, and it worked. At half-time, the on-field television analyst asked him about *that risky play.*

"Yes, but it was calculated," Steve responded. Again, he showed that even fast-moving decisions were made out of caution. A confident decision-making coach would have said something like, *You make your best call and you just move forward. We don't second guess our calls.*

While Steve offered me a trial to incorporate profiling into his system, I declined.

Steve was personable, exceedingly bright, and a positive influence on his players. He was a decent guy who genuinely cared about his players. I was convinced, though, that his coaches were right. He wasn't suited for the top-tier job. Steve didn't survive his move up and went on to coach a much smaller program at a fraction of his $1.5 million salary.

Find 1 out of 1,500 in 30 Minutes . . . Tick, Tick, Tick

Her voice with steady, but pointedly alarmed.

"Dan, I need your help. Can you be here at 7:00 a.m. tomorrow morning?"

The superintendent of a large suburban school district that bordered a major military contractor, Dr. Childers had reason to be concerned. Bomb threats had been escalating at the high school for several months, and it was near the end of spring, when stressors are the highest.

A month before, she heard me give a speech about why the needle was at "10" for a potential school massacre attacks in her area, like the 1999 massacre at Columbine High School in Littleton, Colorado.

Calls like Dr. Childers's were frequent. A year before, the head of intelligence of a major police department had a serious threat in another suburb near Dr. Childers. He asked me to train one of this intel officers *on the phone* how to identify the Random Actor profile—the profile of almost every mass school shooter/bomber, as well as most suicide bombers, postal and company shooters, and serial killers. Within two hours of arriving at a 3,000-student, upscale suburban high school, the officer found not one but *two school massacre plots*—and the threats were successfully mitigated.

When I arrived the next morning to meet with Dr. Childers's administrators, they were huddled around the table in the high school principal's conference room.

They immediately began the meeting by telling me about a half a dozen students who might be making the threats.

"If this isn't a prank, and if the threats truly are escalating, it will probably be one of about 90 students in your school," I started.

"About 6% of your students have the Random Actor profile," I explained.

"And, most who are committing attacks have this profile and usually aren't on anyone's radar. They haven't been arrested or regularly in trouble, like the students you described," I added.

"Here are the two traits in the Random Actor profile.

"First, they're *extremely* unconventional. They like to be *different*. This by itself doesn't mean someone will blow up a school.

"Second, they are *extremely fearful* in their day-to-day decisions. They may be very bright and confident in their competency, but otherwise, most decisions are made out of extreme fear.

"Do any of these students you've just mentioned have these two traits?" I asked. None of them did, but they had been in fights.

"Where is the wall where the threats were written?" I asked.

They described the location on the second floor and, because of the location of the threat, they knew during which period they were scrawled on the wall. The threats were left several times in the same proximity.

"Which classes on the hall are more structured disciplines like history, math, or language arts," I asked "classes that are more *conventional*, as this can alienate a person with the Random Actor profile who is extremely *unconventional*? In other words, theater, video production, shop and classes that are more unconventional won't set them off."

They rattled off three classes.

"Get the roles from those classes," I instructed, "and tell me which students have the Random Actor traits *and* if they did something that was off. You might not have considered it to be important, but it showed paranoia and/or a comment about harming others—even if it seemed flip."

"Yeah, Jeremy, has that profile, and I remember him making a joke about shooting up the school a couple of years ago, but didn't think much of it at the time," one of the administers remembered. Jeremy wasn't on anyone's list for special attention, let alone a suspect for Random Actor violence.

"Can we get some papers he's written in a composition class?" I asked.

We got lucky. He was in a comp class, and within ten minutes we were poring over his papers, which were filled with despair, isolation, anger, and more.

"If Jeremy is the student, I want Mr. Velka [the principal] to bring him down and talk to him. Mr. Velka, I need about another fifteen minutes to give you some do's and don'ts of what to say and how to say it."

It was 7:30 a.m.

By 8:00 a.m., Jeremy was in Mr. Velka's office. As instructed, using non-threatening open-ended questions, Mr. Velka asked Jeremy for his insight about the threats. He explained that he heard Jeremy was astute and might be able to shed light from a student's perspective.

"Well, he's not Hispanic," Jeremy jumped in. "He's going to be white, pretty smart, and his parents probably work at the plant [military contractor nearby]. He's had problems with them and he's angry, but I don't think he's going to do anything right now." In effect, Jeremy was describing himself and in an odd way, was letting Mr. Velka know he wasn't going to act now—without admitting he was guilty. He trusted Mr. Velka and his approach.

"Jeremy, I've done a lot reaching out to various student leaders. Is there anyone else you think I should get to help me to make sure that all students feel a part of our school?"

"Well, who did you talk to?" Jeremy asked.

"You know, student counsel leaders, class leaders, and others," Mr. Velka explained.

"Yeah, but what about us students *in the middle*? Who aren't the tops but also aren't always in trouble?" he added.

"About how many students are we talking about?" Mr. Velka asked.

"About 70 or 80," Jeremy said firmly. Mr. Velka was stunned. It was approximately the same number of students with the Random Actor profile I told the administrators were in Mr. Velka's school—and Jeremy knew it without sophisticated training or mentoring.

That day, the threats stopped. Jeremy became part of Mr. Velka's team to reach *all* students, and he did well the rest of the year.

Out of 1,500 students, Jeremy was identified by administrators equipped with only thirty minutes of training. The result: a threat was mitigated, and a young teen's life was restored. Not all students have to go to jail to make a turn for the good. They just need someone to profile them and *treat and lead them right the first time.*

Closing the Deal

Josh, an entrepreneur in his twenties, was trying to solve a puzzle. A major player wanted to do business with his start-up company, but he couldn't get the VP to sign the contract. It seemed to drag on without a specific reason. They wanted his services, could afford it, and there wasn't another competitor interfering. Frustrated, he called his friend, David, for input because he knew how to profile.

David immediately asked, "Is the VP conventional or unconventional."

"Definitely, unconventional."

"How do you know that?"

"He's always talking about pushing the envelope with new ideas."

"What's more important to him, innovation or seeing his ideas implemented?"

"Seeing his ideas implemented," Josh fired back.

"Then send him an email that you are concerned that if the contract isn't wrapped up soon, he might not be able to implement some of his key ideas."

The email went out. The deal closed that day based upon a read made in seconds.

This is a real case in which David, a young professional, was trained to use the *Korem Profiling System*® and could profile a company or player in a company and quickly identify if a behavioral snag needed to be addressed. In this case, the VP preferred to be unconventional in what he did, rather than conventional. The uptick is that he liked change, innovation, and was open-minded. A potential down-tick was that he might not follow-up on day-to-day details, which for him was tedious.

David made the accurate read based upon Josh's observations, Josh took target specific action, and the deal closed.

Together, these three stories about everyday people are examples of what you're going to be able to achieve as you learn how to rapid-fire profile using the *Korem Profiling System*®.

CHAPTER 2

RAPID-FIRE PROFILING: A POWERFUL TOOL

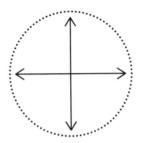

Imagine within just a few minutes of interaction being able to accurately predict how someone is likely to:

- Communicate
- Perform tasks
- Make decisions

These are three of the most valuable pieces of information people would like to know about others professionally or personally. Consider how they affected the outcomes in the three cases you just read in Chapter 1. Obtaining this kind of insight about someone is called behavioral profiling, and the ability to do it on the spot without tests or batteries of questions is called *rapid-fire* profiling. Using the *Korem Profiling System*® (*KPS*), you're going to learn how to make four quick behavioral reads and then identify the profile. This is not a thin line descriptor, but up to three pages of information. And, you don't need years of behavioral sciences training to do it.

The term "profiling" is used in various professions to identify many kinds of information. In law enforcement, a criminal profile might identify how and when a felon is likely to commit his next crime. In the media, reporters do background profiles as a part of feature stories to detail a person's past. I used this skill as an investigative journalist to put people at ease who were victims of crimes, conduct interviews, obtain confessions, assess threats, and even negotiate contracts. Although we didn't call it profiling in the early 1980s, that's what it was, and it helped save lives during life-threatening investigations. Then, in the late 1980s, my career took an unexpected turn.

Members of the Young Presidents Organization (YPO) asked if I could develop a profiling system they could use for high-stakes negotiations abroad. To qualify for membership you had to be the president of a sizable company before the age of forty, and you could remain a member only until you were fifty. Young, aggressive, and often industry leaders, they complained of severe missteps when reading people that had cost them millions of dollars—especially in foreign countries. Intrigued, I asked them specifically what they needed and why.

"For negotiations, we need to size people up quickly like you do without stereotyping or confusing cultural nuances with who a person actually is. For example, someone might appear agreeable at the table, which might be the public, cultural norm, but then you find they are actually extremely forceful in private."

"Why don't you use one of your organizational behavioral experts from HR to help sort it out?" I asked.

"Won't work and would be considered rude. We have to do it ourselves," was their response.

They emphasized that a system had to be tight and compact that would work quickly to develop trust, promote transparent dialogue, and produce a positive outcome for everyone.

"Specifically, what do you want to know?" I probed. Here is what they and hundreds of others I surveyed said.

First, how does someone prefer to communicate? Certainly this was the first priority, as this is how negotiations begin. They gave me many examples where they didn't start off appropriately and the problems and mistrust it caused.

Second, how does someone prefer to operate or perform? This was important so they could do business appropriately and understand and respect someone's comfort zone and potential weaknesses.

Third, how does someone prefer to make decisions? This is also logical because all negotiations have the goal of reaching a decision.

I assumed there was an existing system that could be modified, but there wasn't. All that was available were written tests used for hiring staff. With a clear picture of the three pieces of information that the execs wanted, I recruited corporate and law enforcement behavioral science experts to help me develop the *KPS*. I also added two conditions for using the system that broke new ground.

The first is that the *KPS* gives you the flexibility to profile people before you meet them, which is an invaluable time saver. And second, the *KPS* allows you to profile people without stereotyping even if you can't speak their language. These were two conditions I regularly faced during investigations and which I felt would be indispensable in our speed-driven, tightly knit global community (explained in Chapter 16).

From 1992 to 1995 the system was refined and taught to virtually every type of professional work group in the US and Europe, including leaders of organizations, human resources, audit, sales, law enforcement, and educators. Transferability issues were refined to ensure that anyone could learn and use the system. Then, in January of 1995, I presented the *KPS* to over ninety of the leading police psychologists from the US and Europe at the invitation of the FBI's Behavioral Sciences Unit to flesh out any structural flaws. None were found, and they said the system was structurally, culturally, and instructionally sound.

Although the rapid-fire *KPS* was designed for executives negotiating contracts, since 1992, over 35,000 professionals globally have used their new skill for all kinds of situations as well as in their personal lives when working with kids, being a better parent and spouse, and reaching out to help friends.

Versatile for Many Applications

In the past, profiling skills were only acquired by those with unique professional needs, such as FBI agents, who track serial killers or terrorists, or human resource managers making hiring and personnel-development decisions. There is also a fascination with how profiling can be used for truth detection.

Rapid-fire profiling, though, can benefit anyone for any type of interactions. The reason most people never learn to profile is they lack a simple and direct system. Even in the human resource arena, over 90% don't have a system for profiling people on the spot without the use of a written personality test (based on surveys I conducted of thousands of professionals at human resource conferences in the US).

For some, profiling skills seem too "fuzzy" to be easily learned. Be assured, even if you have a difficult time reading others, with practice, the *KPS* will enable you to significantly increase your accuracy. We've found that the average person when tested has only 25–35% accuracy when shown video clips of real people in real situations. Even those with behavioral sciences backgrounds have the same limited accuracy because they also haven't been trained to rapid-fire profile. This means that most people 65–75% of the time ineffectively start interactions, which is painfully obvious when you video record their interactions. In a day or two of workshop training or two to three months of self-study, however, the average accuracy increases to 75–80% or higher.

If you are blessed with keen intuitive insight, you might ask: *Why do I need to learn to profile? I'm pretty good at reading people.* If this fits you, ask yourself three questions:

1. Can I teach others how to make the same intuitive reads with systematic accuracy?
2. Do I specifically know what I need to do to increase my accuracy?
3. When I misread someone, can I identify the source of the misread, correct it, and ensure that I don't repeat the same mistake?

If you answered with a negative to two of the questions, you have your answer: You need a dependable on-the-spot profiling system. (Additionally, our data shows that most people who think they can read people accurately have the same low accuracy as everyone else.)

My experience is that people usually don't consider learning how to profile until they've had a negative experience—a bad hire, they've been lied to, or to the extreme, someone threatens their life. You may have purchased this book because of a difficult situation, but the more potent way to use profiling is to improve people's lives, provide wiser counsel and leadership, and improve productivity. Be proactive, not reactive. With this in mind, here is a short list where profiling is an indispensable tool for professional and personal needs, followed by specific ways people have used the *KPS*.

PROFESSIONAL APPLICATIONS

- Lead teams/boards
- Negotiate and sell
- Consult clients
- Deliver presentations
- Defuse confrontations
- Teach and educate
- Recruit, hire, and develop staff
- Sharpen communication skills
- Conduct interviews
- Select career path
- Work with diverse cultures
- Provide counsel

PERSONAL APPLICATIONS

- Provide encouragement, motivation, and direction
- Uniquely respond to the needs of spouses, friends, and others
- Reduce conflict
- Understand those whom we love and care about
- Recognize how you are perceived so that you can quickly adapt to difficult situations.
- Nurture and discipline our children to help them reach their potential

Senior Leadership

Communicate Vision and Expectations—All organizations have a profile (as do groups, countries, and regions). Convey big-picture themes, vision, and bottom-line expectations in a way that is target-specific to your audience (a skill often used by leading athletic coaches).
Senior Level Interactions—Efficiently work with a hard-to-read or difficult partner/board member/colleague.
Mergers and Acquisitions—Extremely useful for mergers and acquisitions to ensure seamless transitions.

Lead Teams—Make better selections of who should lead and how a team should be led.

Human Resource Management

Recruiting and Hiring—Excellent check on written self-assessment tests which all have inaccuracy. Chapter 16 describes how to integrate profiling when screening and interviewing candidates.

Team Leadership—Lead diverse personalities and improve interactions while simultaneously reducing unstated biases against specific personality types—"those who are different from us." This enables team players to broaden the range of personality types with whom they can effectively perform.

Personnel Development and Selection—Identify those in an organization best equipped to take on new responsibilities.

Educators and Counselors

Instruction—Teachers, pastors, medical professionals, and social workers can identify an individual's or a group's profile and modify instruction to immediately increase comprehension and retention.

Identify Allies—Teachers, counselors, and probation officers can quickly assess whether a specific parent, guardian, or caregiver will effectively assist in the disciplining and nurturing of a youth.

Avoid and Defuse Conflict—Recognize how you are perceived so that you can quickly adapt to difficult environments.

Cross-cultural Interactions

Separate cultural nuances from a person's actual profile—All cultures have a behavioral profile and specific customs, which can be identified separate from a person's actual profile. This insight can be utilized to quickly establish communication. (Chapter 16)

Law Enforcement, Security, and Safety

Confrontations—Quickly identify how to confront different profiles and defuse potential threats.

Investigations—Better predict criminal strategies and obtain information during interviews.

RANDOM ACTOR Violence Prevention—This volatile profile, which is the profile of most company and school attackers who commit massacres as well as homicide-suicide terrorists, is explained, as well as themes to prevent incidents. (Chapters 9 and 15)

Sales, Negotiators, and Communicators

Close Sales—Determine who makes confident or cautious decisions and modify approach to bring closure.

Reduce Cancellations—Predict who is and isn't likely to keep appointments. (Chapter 8)

Sharpen Presentations—Predict when one should present more or fewer options to a client or audience.

Quickly Establish Trust—Reduce the time to establish.

Office Management

Temporary Help—Quickly identify strengths and weaknesses to optimize performance.

Customer Relations—Modify message, improve customer satisfaction.

Interviewing Skills

Confrontational Interviews—Auditors, law enforcement, and security can decrease the amount of time to collect data and actionable intelligence without inciting hostile retaliation.

Nonconfrontational Fact-gathering—Auditors, journalists, financial analysts, and doctoral students can increase the precision and scope of information gathered during interviews.

Medical Personnel

Structured Follow-up—Identify patients who need more or less structure and guidance to adhere to follow-up recommendations, such as remembering when to take medications, following rehabilitation regimens, etc. (Chapter 8)

Personal Use

Social Contacts—Shorten the time required to establish relationships.
Respecting One's Spouse—Understand and more effectively communicate with your spouse and adapt to his or her weaknesses and strengths.
Raising Children—Direct and instruct children based upon their unique profiles.

These are just a few of the ways in which people have used the *KPS*. The *KPS* and other research I've developed has been used to prevent school massacres, mass company shootings, terrorist attacks, and more. These attacks are usually committed by those with the RANDOM ACTOR profile, which you'll learn about in Chapters 9 and 15 (detailed cases and prevention strategies are found in my book, *Rage of the Random Actor— Disarming Catastrophic Acts and Restoring Lives*). While safety and security are certainly important, the greater good is achieved by using profiling for uplifting others and productivity-building pursuits.

What follows are actual cases in which profiling was the difference between success and failure. Each case will be expanded later in the text. (Because this text is designed for an international audience, the male pronoun will be applied when appropriate as this is the currently accepted convention, although examples will employ both male and female gender.)

Case #1—An outside consultant is working with a creative work group in the audit industry. Every time the consultant makes a proposal the staff wants to initiate, the group's manager throws up illogical roadblocks that nearly derail the project. What course of action did the consultant take to save the project? (Chapter 13)
Case #2—Marc was pursuing a lucrative contract with XYZ Inc., a Fortune 1000 company, when he encountered an unusual challenge. XYZ's CEO requests an exploratory meeting with Frank and tells him that under no conditions can any of Marc's staff make contact with anyone at XYZ before the first meeting. Then, the day of the meeting, the CFO slams the boardroom door shut and screams at his subordinates,

while Marc and his staff stand outside the door within earshot of the CFO's loud barks. What action did Marc take, based upon the CFO's actions, that increased his company's chances of securing a future contract? (Chapter 13)

Case #3—In Zurich, Switzerland, several doctors used the *KPS* to identify more accurately those patients who require more or less regimen for follow-up to treatments, taking medicine, etc. What did the doctors and their nurses profile in each patient that enabled them to uniquely meet the needs of each patient? (Chapter 8)

Case #4—The leader of a cult-like group, who has a criminal record including kidnapping and robbery, knows the police are likely to arrest him on a stolen guns charge. He has threatened to kill others and himself if he is apprehended, reminiscent of other cult leaders like Jim Jones and David Koresh. There is only one opportunity to engage this individual tactically so a bloody siege doesn't take place. What key element was addressed during the confrontation which enabled this dangerous individual to be successfully apprehended and a confession obtained? (Chapter 9)

Profile Information Provided: Three Options

The *KPS* enables you to access up to three pages of profile information, including potential strengths, shortcomings, and suggestions for how to interact. To see how much information is provided, review the SERGEANT–MANAGER profile, the first profile in Chapter 12. (Another half page of "type" information is also provided that will be introduced later.) Since you won't need all the information available for every interaction, you have three choices of how much you want to access.

Snapshot Read—A short two-line description, useful in many short-term, noncritical interactions. (Chapter 10)

Fine-tuned Read—Details of specific positive and negative actions—

useful for critical long-term interactions. (Chapter 10)

Comprehensive Profile—20 profiles provided, useful for long- and short-term interactions. (Chapter 12)

The Profiler's Tools: A Compass and a Map

When people say they want to be able to profile, they're really asking for two pieces of information.

First, they want to identify someone's profile, such as how a person is likely to communicate and perform and make decisions in a given situation. Second, they want to know *what to do* with that information. The *KPS* provides you with a compass and a map that will help you accomplish both. The profile not only provides insight into a person, it also provides suggestions for how to interact with someone based upon your needs.

The Compass: Four questions/wires—A compass points a backpacker in the direction that he should hike. The *KPS* utilizes four questions that will be your profiling compass and point out the profile. You won't ask someone these four questions, rather you'll answer them in your own mind. The questions help identify four of the thinnest wires of human behavior that are found in everyone, regardless of age or culture. The questions, which we'll also refer to as traits, wires or gauges, aren't complicated and can be answered by anyone without specialized training.

Two questions (traits/wires/gauges) identify how a person communicates. We call these the communication or "talk" traits, and they are:

- CONTROL or EXPRESS: Does a person typically control or express his emotions when he communicates? (Chapter 4)

- ASSERTIVE or NONASSERTIVE: Does a person prefer to be assertive or nonassertive when he communicates? (Chapter 5)

If you think about it, everyone displays these actions. We usually prefer to either control or express our emotions, or be assertive or nonassertive when we communicate. Yes, we can vary some, but usually we tilt in one direction or the other.

The last two questions (traits/wires/gauges) identify how people like to operate and make decisions—what we call the performance or "walk" traits. They are:

- CONVENTIONAL or UNCONVENTIONAL: Does a person prefer to be conventional or unconventional? (Chapter 8)

- CONFIDENT or CAUTIOUS/FEARFUL: Does a person make decisions confidently, cautiously, or out of extreme fear? (Chapter 8)

Talk versus walk—An important innovation in the *KPS* is you'll always be able to read how people communicate—their "talk"— *separate* from how people prefer to perform tasks and make decisions— their "walk."

Statistically, the number one source for misreads is a confusing communication trait with a performance trait. The *KPS* works by *always reading them separately*. No exceptions.

All of us have been fooled by someone who talks confidently but, when called on to perform, operates out of fear. The talk looks and sounds great, but the walk is something completely different.

Similarly, it's easy to be fooled by people whose talk is shy and retiring, but when called upon to perform, they perform confidently.

One Tweak Immediately Increases Accuracy 20–30%—Statistically, I found with just one slight modification in how we make our reads, accuracy immediately increases 20–30%—and in any culture. It works like this.

If you ask yourself "Is John CONTROL or EXPRESS," the tendency is to make a subjective decision and your accuracy will vary. Imagine, however, if we put a famous person who represents the extreme end of each wire like Queen Elizabeth II, who typically controls her emotions to the extreme when she communicates, and actor/comic Jim Carrey, who expresses his emotions to the extreme in most of his roles. Now, instead of thinking, Is John CONTROL or EXPRESS, we think: *Does he communicate more like the Queen or Jim Carrey? Which way does he tilt?* It's amazing, but every group in the world in any culture immediately increases their accuracy because they are comparing John to two extremes rather than making a subjective read based upon two descriptors. The details of how this works is explained in Chapter 4 when you learn how to use your first wire.

The COMPREHENSIVE profile Is your map—When backpacking, you need a map to plot out the best route toward your destination, gauge distances, and point out natural obstacles to avoid, such as swamps and impassable gorges. When profiling, your map will be the COMPREHENSIVE PROFILE (Chapter 12) that identifies typical strengths, weaknesses, and tendencies of each person's profile as well as suggestions for interactions. The twenty profiles include strengths, shortcomings, and interaction suggestions such as how to sell and present ideas/products, lead and motivate, and how to defuse a confrontation. Graphically, the relationship between your profiling compass and map is shown below.

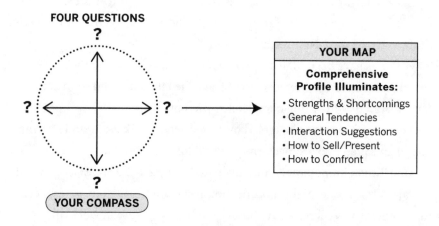

Two safety checks for misreads—You're probably wondering what happens if you misread someone. Another important innovation has been added to the *KPS* that gives you two safety checks. As will be explained in Chapters 6 and 12, it is now possible to quickly identify a misread and then correct the misread on the fly. Additionally, common reasons for misreads and how to avoid them are detailed in Chapter 11.

Rapid-fire Profiling When Tests Fail or Aren't Appropriate

When you look at one of the COMPREHENSIVE profiles in Chapter 12, you might think, "This looks similar to a personality test I took when I applied for a job." The difference is the *KPS* isn't a written or oral test. The profile is identified by rapid-fire profiling. Written tests have their place and I've used them in my business, but they have limitations.

First, someone has to agree to take the test. Second, you have to depend upon the person to provide truthful/accurate answers. Third, you can't make adjustments when the results are off. Some people, for example, have learned how to distort their answers to match a desired profile. Other people don't test well. And for others, results can be skewed by a bad day or life stresses, which I personally experienced with employees.

One of my staff, for example, took the popular DISC test, which I used for hiring. When I reviewed her results, they were off. I knew they weren't a match for her because I'd known her for several years. She agreed to take the test again a week later, and the results were a match. When we discussed the tests, she explained that a distracting personal situation was probably the reason for the severe discrepancy. For people experiencing a life-changing circumstance, their traits may be exaggerated or concealed due to uncharacteristic stress. Today, because of the dramatic increase in social deterioration over the past thirty years, more people are going through life-changing events, which can translate into decreased test accuracy.

Finally, the most obvious limitation with written tests is they aren't appropriate for most situations. Imagine starting a meeting with: "Mr. Johnson, before we negotiate this contract, I want you to fill out this test truthfully so that I will have an accurate bead on your profile." Or, "Ms. Dean, we haven't met, so before we start this audit evaluation, would you mind filling out this test so that I can identify your profile?" With rapid-fire reads, you control when and where you want to profile someone. You don't have to ask for permission or rely upon truthful/accurate answers.

Also, a need for a check on written tests—In light of this instability factor, there was a perceived need in the HR community for a rapid-fire, on-the-spot profiling system that can be used as a check on written tests. The Chicago chapter of the Society of Human Resource Management

(SHRM) asked me to provide training for its members because "you've developed the first reliable and practical check on a written assessment." As word spread through their community, we trained over 1,500 HR professionals nationally, and Korem & Associates was the first to combine rapid-fire reads with behavioral interviewing (Chapter 16).

How the System was Refined

During the early and mid-1980s, as an independent investigative journalist, I investigated a number of individuals and groups that posed a criminal threat. They ranged from youth gangs to cults to sophisticated con artists. I preferred to focus on long-term issues, rather than the latest scam.

Often, I was in critical situations, needing guidance and reassurance I was profiling each person or group with pinpoint accuracy. An inappropriate action because of a misread could put myself or others in harm's way. In fact, several times law enforcement followed my lead because of the unique nature of the individuals or groups I was investigating. The two people I most relied upon for guidance were Hugh Aynesworth and Margaret Singer, Ph.D. They were my profiling mentors.

In 1981, Hugh, a four-time Pulitzer Prize nominee, agreed to help me with my first investigative television documentary, *Psychic Confession*. He had just finished coauthoring *The Only Living Witness*, in which he detailed how serial killer Ted Bundy murdered over thirty women. It was one of the first confessions of a serial killer, and his interview tapes are archived at the FBI's Behavioral Sciences Unit.

For the documentary, we investigated a cult-like individual, James Hydrick from Salt Lake City, who had the same background profile as Waco cult leader David Koresh. Like Koresh, Hydrick was from an abusive home, was obsessed with weapons, threatened to kill others and himself, embraced a contrived religious dogma, and was a pedophile. The investigation culminated in the first confession of a cult-like leader. Hydrick detailed how he deceived millions of people into believing that he had powers and how others wanted to use him to control people. During the eighteen-month investigation, Hugh helped me refine my interviewing skills.

Three years later, the late Margaret Singer, internationally respected for her knowledge of psychopathic behavior, thought reform techniques, and interviewing skills, continued where Hugh left off, further shaping my concepts of profiling. If I could place only one call to one person in a potentially life-threatening situation, Margaret would get the call. She never failed to provide concise, reliable, and easily digested guidance.

During one harrowing investigation in a small logging town in upstate Washington in 1987, my production crew, feeling the pressure, fled. They were spooked by threats made by a couple of former Vietnam vets who had a history of instability. (I didn't have time to prescreen the crew as I hired them with only one day's notice.) Alone, I called Margaret for advice on how to engage the volatile and unstable group. With razor precision, she helped me tailor each interview question so that it would uniquely relate to both the scoundrels, the victims, and the heroes that I interviewed. After hiring a new crew, not only did we successfully capture the story without incident, but as important, no one was hurt after the interviews—when volatile individuals had time to mull over what I had asked. Margaret's profiling insight was what provided me with the tools that enabled me to help others safely.

Investigating cases shaped my perspective of rapid-fire profiling. I always profiled key people or interviews before meeting them, relying on the observations of others, my own unobtrusive observations, their past history, how they handled specific situations in the past, and so on. Obtaining this information is essential because most criminals will not voluntarily divulge needed information. Being prepared reduced risk and improved the quality of the content during interviews. It also enabled me to enlist the help of others. (You'll learn more about how to profile people before you meet them in Chapters 7, 16 and 17.)

All interviews I conducted were video recorded, which meant I could see first-hand if I did or didn't do my job and whether or not I was pre-pared. It's excruciating to watch footage of what happens when you don't treat people uniquely based upon their profile. They don't open up, or, if they do provide insight, their answer looks affected, forced, or unconvincing. More than once I had to scrap an interview that had excellent content, but the person didn't come across as believable or they just looked off. On a practical level, profiling helped us facilitate more interviews a day because people were more cooperative more quickly which kept the budgets in line and gave me more options for how to proceed.

How data was collected—To teach the *KPS*, I've used video clips from my investigations as well as other footage of real people in real situations. Students watch a video clip, are given ten seconds to profile the person(s) in the clip, then enter their response on an interactive keypad tracked by our computer. Fascinating pieces of data emerged which helped refine with precision which strategies worked and didn't work and why. (These findings are explained in *Snapshot* noted below.)

For example, I found that there are people from specific professions, countries, and age groups who, when tested, almost always attain 90% profiling accuracy, and there is a consistent theme across all these groups as to why they can do it. I then found ways to accelerate these themes for almost anyone. Anytime statistics are quoted in this book, the source is the keypad inputs of over 35,000 professionals from dozens of countries who have been trained.

When people are tested, the average
profiling accuracy level is only 25–35%.

This means that most people ineffectively start their
interactions 65% of the time or more.

In a day or two of training or two to three months
of self-study, profiling accuracy increases to 75–80% or higher.

Two Additional Tools

The companion to this book, *Snapshot—Reading and Treating People Right the First Time*, is a quick-read primer of how rapid-fire profiling works, accompanied by extraordinary stories of people who made just one read using the *KPS* with amazing results. If you're a big-picture person, you may prefer to read it first, as you'll be able to immediately produce results without prolonged study. Others will want to read *Snapshot* for its many applications that aren't in this text and as a quick refresher. Whether you read it now or later, references are provided throughout this book of new applications in *Snapshot* for you to review.

App available—After several years of requests, we developed the Pocket PeopleReader®. It automates the entire *KPS* and places all the profiles and suggestions for interaction at one's fingertips. For more information please see the page at the back of this book or visit KoremAssociates.com.

Road Map to This Book

Throughout the book, I will "lift the hood" and show you how the profiling engine works. Theory will be kept to a minimum, and you'll never be in doubt about how the different parts work and work together.

Like any new lifetime skill, it takes a few weeks, depending upon your background, to feel comfortable. That's okay. What makes learning profiling really fascinating is that it starts with your profile. This requires a little reflection. I promise that if you'll just go chapter by chapter, you will discover amazing things about yourself as you profile others. Please don't skip chapters, as each chapter builds on the ones before. Here are those building blocks by chapter (chapter references are also provided throughout the book for ease of navigation):

1. Learn how to read the four "wires" making ten-second reads. (Chapters 4, 5, and 8)
2. Learn how to combine the four wires (questions) to identify the nine different "types." (Chapters 6 and 9)
3. Profiling tips and advanced applications. (Chapters 7, 11, 16, and 17)
4. Additional concepts include:
   • Profiling in a foreign country or new culture—invaluable for those who travel abroad or work with culturally diverse groups. (Chapter 16)

- How to profile and interact with the potentially volatile and even dangerous RANDOM ACTOR profile. (Chapters 9 and 15)

You'll note that specific terms are provided in all-caps format to avoid confusion. The term ASSERTIVE, for example, only designates someone who is assertive when communicating, rather than the broader dictionary definition. I also provide chapter references throughout to remind you where specifics concepts can be quickly located.

If possible, I recommend that you learn to profile with a partner, who can be a sounding board, which can add to your enjoyment, insight, and even help you connect in a fresh way.

Lastly, updates, insights, and errata regarding the *KPS* are posted on the "Live Addendum" for this book on the IFP website (ifpinc.com).

The Goal and Philosophy

The foundation of this book is rooted in the idea of treating others as you would like to be treated. This means working to understand the other person and trying to meet their needs.

Statistically, those who have the highest profiling accuracy when tested are those who are considered honest and transparent by their peers. The reason for this is that people are willing to trust them with more parts of their lives. Thus the transparent person starts with more data points when it comes to profiling people accurately.

Accurately reading people isn't the goal. The goal and philosophy is:

I know who you are.
Good for me, better for you.
It's the art of *treating* people right the first time.

This isn't just a clever saying. It's an attitude about life that's the heartbeat of the best profilers.

WHAT PROFILERS REALLY DO . . .

"Pappa D, what do you do for a living?" my wide-eyed ten-year-old granddaughter asked me.

"Well, what do you think I do?"

"Well, I know you're a profiler," Hannah said.

"But what do you think that is?" I asked, smiling at the wheels turning.

"I guess you file papers for your job," she said, arching her brow.

"Why do you say that?" I asked, wondering what she had seen.

"Well I always see these papers and files everywhere," she said, pointing her finger across the room at the always present stacks "for the next book."

Aha. Pro filer. Well, at least she thought I *was* professional!

CHAPTER 3

SYSTEMATIC ACCURACY

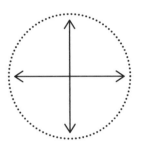

READING PEOPLE:
IT STARTS AS A NATURAL REACTION

Reading people is a natural reaction none of us can avoid. We all spend time reading and interpreting people's actions, trying to predict how they will act in the future. We ask ourselves questions, like:

- What will he do next?
- He has such a good poker face, how do I know what he's really thinking?
- Have I designed this presentation to meet her needs?
- Is he reliable?
- How can I best communicate with him?
- Why am I not getting through to this student?
- Why is she misreading me? How do I get her to move on this? How do I know if it fits her needs?
- How does he make decisions?

We want to know what makes people "tick."

Each time we make an observation that tries to answer one of these questions, we make a read. In the *KPS*, when we make four reads and combine them together, we identify someone's COMPREHENSIVE profile, which provides a more complete picture of a person.

In this short chapter are the three simple and direct rules that will help you develop systematic accuracy when profiling. They aren't complicated, and many will seem like common sense—and they are. Without them, though, you won't achieve systematic accuracy.

The Three Rules of Systematic Accuracy

1. People typically act in consistent, similar ways called TRAITS. When two or more TRAITS are combined together, we have what are called TYPES. Combine two or more TYPES together and you get a PROFILE. (These are the moving parts of the *KPS* profiling engine.)

2. We must always measure different people's traits with the same gauges or questions.

3. Anything worth measuring once is worth measuring at least twice.

Rule #1

People typically act in consistent, similar ways called traits. When two or more traits are combined together, we have what are called types. Combine two or more types together and you identify a profile.

Actions and Traits

ACTIONS are the first building block of the *KPS* engine, and when you observe several similar actions, you identify a TRAIT.

When sizing people up, we usually start with reading their ACTIONS. If we are negotiating, for example, we might try and read whether a person prefers to dominate a conversation or be more in the background. A school career counselor might read whether a student is conventional or unconventional to provide the best counsel regarding a career choice. The term *action* is used to specify observable actions as well as speech, attire, nonverbal actions (popularly called "body language"), and past actions. Even the tone and content of a memo could be interpreted as an action, if the memo helps reveal how a person prefers to communicate or perform in a specific situation.

Rule #1 acknowledges that most people's actions are typically consistent over the long haul. The key word is typical. On a given day we may act out of character or in a unique way, but day in and day out we will typically act and respond in the same way. For example, if Joe usually expresses his emotions when he communicates with others, we can count on the fact that he'll do the same in most situations.

When we observe several similar actions that follow a pattern, we call this a TRAIT, which is the second building block of the *KPS* engine. So if Joe displays the group of actions listed below, we can say he has a trait that allows him to EXPRESS his emotions.

- Outgoing at a party.
- Expressive during a sales presentation.
- Easily expresses emotion when talking with new acquaintances.
- Jubilantly cheers on teammates while playing softball.

If Mary displays the group of actions noted below, we could say that she possesses a trait that allows her to CONTROL her emotions.

- Stoic in most conversations.
- Emotionally restrained.
- Calmly and efficiently interacts with her colleagues.

As described in the last chapter, you'll make your reads by using four different "wires," like the CONTROL-EXPRESS wire, to identify the four *KPS* traits. Each wire has a person on each end that is easy to visualize to represent the extremes of that trait. So for Joe, after making some observations, your read (question that you ask yourself) will be: *Does Joe seem to be more like Queen Elizabeth or Jim Carrey?*

So ACTIONS are the first building block of the *KPS* engine and TRAITS are the second building block. Beginning in the next chapter, you'll learn how to quickly identify a trait.

Traits Reveal Types

TYPES are the third building block of the *KPS* engine.

In the same way that similar actions can identify a trait, when you combine two traits together you can identify what are called TYPES. What's great is that once you identify two traits, the types are already identified for you.

Let's imagine we are profiling Joe, and we observe that he prefers to EXPRESS emotions when he communicates and he also prefers to be ASSERTIVE when he communicates—he likes to show use a little force in his voice. When we combine these two communication traits, we can say that Joe is a specific TYPE of person. An identifier that can be used to describe Joe's combination of traits is a SALESMAN type, shown below. For Joe, he likes to be assertive and express emotions to generate enthusiasm for his ideas, products, or whatever is his focus of attention. Another identifier that could be used is a COMMUNICATOR type, as proficient communicators often possess these two traits.

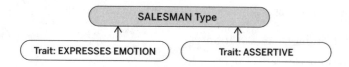

Identifying Joe's type doesn't mean in every situation he will always be assertive or express his emotions when he communicates, but we do know what he prefers to do most of the time.

In the *KPS* there are two categories of types: COMMUNICATION and PERFORMANCE types. COMMUNICATION types show us how someone prefers to communicate, and there are four different COMMUNICATION types. We refer to these as the "talk" types and a dialogue balloon is included in ILLUSTRATION 1 for clarity.

PERFORMANCE types show us how someone prefers to operate and perform tasks, and there are five different PERFORMANCE types. We refer to these as the "walk" types, and a pair of feet is included for clarity.

Reading COMMUNICATION and PERFORMANCE types separately is how we are able to distinguish a person's *talk* separate from his *walk,* which will be explained in more detail later.

For now, the graphic is provided so you can visualize the relationships between actions, traits, types, and profiles.

Illustration 1

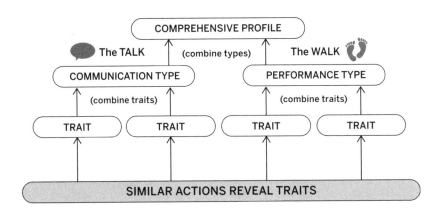

Types Reveal Profiles

Now we come to the fourth building block: the COMPREHENSIVE profile. When we can combine two types together, we can identify someone's COMPREHENSIVE profile, which is at the top of ILLUSTRATION 1.

Here is an example of how actions, traits, and types identify someone's COMPREHENSIVE profile as depicted in ILLUSTRATION 2 on the next page.

Mary, as earlier noted, is a person who CONTROLS her emotions. Let's assume that she also prefers to be ASSERTIVE she communicates. Because she possesses both a CONTROL and an ASSERTIVE trait, we can say Mary is a SERGEANT or COMMANDER type when she *communicates*—someone who can easily direct others while maintaining emotional control. This is her COMMUNICATION type.

Imagine that Mary also has two additional traits: she is CONFIDENT when making decisions and she's CONVENTIONAL in her day-to-day actions.

These two traits when combined together would yield a MANAGER type—her PERFORMANCE type.

Thus, Mary is a SERGEANT type when she communicates (the talk part of her profile) and a MANAGER type when she performs a task (the walk part of her profile).

When we combine the SERGEANT and MANAGER types together, we get a complete picture or a COMPREHENSIVE profile of Mary. The full description of a SERGEANT–MANAGER, about two pages, is provided in Chapter 12 along with the other nineteen COMPREHENSIVE profiles. The graphic representation of Mary's SERGEANT–MANAGER is shown in ILLUSTRATION 2.

Illustration 2

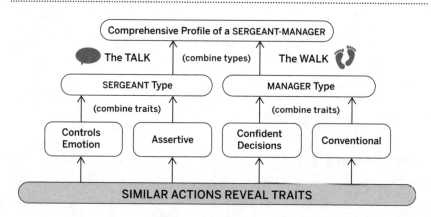

The reason the *KPS* is relatively easy to master is that you only have to identify four traits, like CONTROL or EXPRESS. The rest of the work is done for you. As you can see in ILLUSTRATION 2, the two traits reveal a type, and all the type information is already compiled for you.

And, you also have protection.

If you make a mistake, there are two safety checks you can use to immediately know if you misprofiled someone and what to do to correct your read. For now, though, all you need to remember is that:

1. Similar ACTIONS reveal a TRAIT.

2. Combine two TRAITS together and you get a TYPE of person.

3. Combine two TYPES together and you get a COMPREHENSIVE PROFILE of a person.

Types, Not Stereotypes

The ancient Greeks were some of the first who tried to type people. They believed a person who had a ruddy complexion and appeared warm and outgoing had higher than normal levels of blood in his system. They labeled this person as a "sanguine." Similarly, those who appeared slow were thought to have excessive phlegm in their throats and were called "phlegmatic." The Greeks also believed that sad, "melancholy" people had excessive black bile, while reactive types had too much yellow bile and were accordingly labeled "choleric."

In addition to their mythical body fluids theory, one of the Greeks' greatest errors was they believed there was no differentiation between people who had the *same type*. All sanguine people, for example, were thought to be identical.

Today, we have a word for this: stereotyping, which is the polar opposite of rapid-fire profiling that you'll use in the *KPS*.

To stereotype a SERGEANT type, for example, is to say: (1) all SERGEANTS have the *exact same set of actions and use them exactly the same way*, (2) all SERGEANTS use their traits with the *same degree of intensity*.

Some of the positive and negative actions we see in SERGEANTS, listed in Chapter 6, are: strong, confident, overbearing, unsympathetic, outgoing, egotistical, and assertive. Not every SERGEANT, however, will have the same number of actions. SERGEANT #1 may display every one of these actions, while SERGEANT #2 may only have half of these actions active in his life. The actions for both individuals, though, come from a specific inventory of actions that are common to SERGEANTS and are distinct from other types.

Additionally, not every SERGEANT will use his assertiveness, for example, in exactly the same way. One may be assertive with his tone of voice, another with his tone of voice and choice of words.

Finally, not every SERGEANT will use his actions with the same degree of intensity. For example, two SERGEANTS might both be outgoing, but one may be more outgoing than the other.

When the term "type" is used in this book, we are acknowledging, as in the case of SERGEANTS:

1. A SERGEANT type is likely to operate out of a list of actions—both positive and negative—that is distinct from another type.
2. Not every person who is a SERGEANT type will have the exact same set of actions in his/her life or use them in exactly the same way.
3. Each SERGEANT will use his/her actions with an intensity that may differ from other SERGEANTS.

Rule #2

Always measure different people with the same gauges or questions.

When we ask, "What is the temperature outside?" meteorologists use a gauge, called a thermometer, to measure the temperature. They could try to estimate how cold it is outside by observing what people are wearing, but this wouldn't be as accurate as looking at a thermometer. One person may wear a coat when it's 50 degrees outside while another may only wear a sweater. Attire isn't a consistent or systematic measure of temperature.

For consistent accuracy, meteorologists use the *same* thermometer (because thermometers can vary) and place it in the same location each day. This gives them a method for achieving systematic accuracy. We use the same principle to accurately profile people by using the same gauges for everyone.

Using the same gauge promotes
systematic accuracy and
reduces stereotyping.

When identifying a specific trait, like whether a person CONTROLS or EXPRESSES emotions, we'll use our CONTROL–EXPRESS wire. After a couple of reads of someone's actions, we simply think: *More like the Queen or Jim Carrey?* This promotes accuracy beyond imprecise "gut feeling" or natural instincts—which can fluctuate daily due to anything from personal circumstances to stress. If we don't use the same gauge for everyone, our profiling skills will tend to be biased. (You'll learn the specific details how to use this wire/gauge in Chapter 4.)

Think of it logically. Would you want someone to profile you with a different gauge than he uses to profile everyone else? Even if you don't like someone, profiling solely by instinct isn't in anyone's best interest. The best thing we can do is read people accurately and operate with them based upon their actual profile, rather than upon our own slanted intuition.

The four gauges used in the *KPS* system were selected to help you identify the three pieces of information most people want to know about others. How someone prefers to: communicate, perform tasks, and make decisions.[1]

Rule #3

Anything worth measuring once is worth measuring at least twice.

Everyone can make mistakes. That's why Rule #3 emphasizes that we recheck our initial reads.

Most people meet someone, make a quick assessment, then look for information that will confirm their initial hunches. Research on interviewing has demonstrated that this error, which is called gatekeeping, is one of the single greatest mistakes made by interviewers.

People also make quick, impulsive, and emotional reads and then try to back them up with logic. This is when you can get into real trouble. The perspective toward profiling you'll adopt is just the opposite.

Skilled profilers accept the fact that some reads will be inaccurate.

That's why you'll learn how to make a read and then use specific strategies to test the accuracy of your reads—in addition to the two safety checks you'll learn later. Together, these will help you resist the natural temptation to justify your first read. This doesn't mean you'll be asked to shelve your intuitive ability, but rather you'll test it. In fact, those who have sharp intuitive skills will gain greater insight into *why* their intuition works and *how* to sharpen their intuitive ability to improve their profiling skills.

RECAP OF SYSTEMATIC ACCURACY

1. Similar actions reveal traits; traits when combined together reveal types; types when combined together reveal a profile.
2. We must always use the same "unbiased" questions/gauges for everyone we profile.
3. We must verify our first reads by using our questions/gauges more than once, testing our reads.

Because our natural tendencies and prejudices can derail our profiling efforts, you'll be reminded of these three rules of systematic accuracy throughout the book. Although simple in concept, these rules or principles will each take on a richer meaning as you develop your profiling skills.

Now let's take a look at the first wire/question/gauge that will enable you to profile.

CHAPTER 4

WIRE #1:
CONTROL OR EXPRESS?

CONTROL–EXPRESS

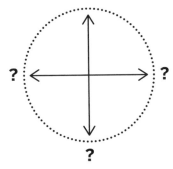

You'll now learn how to personalize and use the first of the two communication wires/gauges/traits and how to answer the question: *Does this person prefer to control or express his emotions when he communicates?*

We'll spend a little more time on the first two communication gauges to be certain you understand how they work. Once you learn how to use them, you'll have completed half the process necessary to profile someone.

WIRE/QUESTION/GAUGE #1:
CONTROL OR EXPRESS EMOTIONS?

Does this person control or express his/her emotions
when he/she communicates?

This is the emotive connector wire. Making a successful read with this wire helps us quickly connect and communicate with people and avoid misinterpreting and second-guessing intent or interest. People who are EXPRESS often think CONTROL people aren't interested, appreciative, or engaged because of a lack of emotion. Conversely, people who are

CONTROL, often stereotype and think a person who shows emotion is weak, lacks substance, oversells, and is naïve. If you know your trait and someone else's trait, you can establish rapport and simultaneously minimize the chance of someone stereotyping you.

Our traits are formed from genetics, how we are raised as children, and our response to life's circumstances. For some people, their traits can change over time, modestly or radically, due to life-changing circumstances and by age and/or station in life. Typically, though, our traits remain consistent.

The CONTROL–EXPRESS wire/gauge, shown in ILLUSTRATION 1, identifies how much we express our emotions, which is why we refer to each question as a gauge. At one extreme, people are extremely expressive, like Jim Carrey. At the other extreme, people are extremely reserved and controlled, like Queen Elizabeth II or Spock from *Star Trek*.

Illustration 1

The endpoints on the gauge, represented by the number 5, are the two extremes: extremely expressive and extremely controlled, while number 1 on the gauge represents low EXPRESS or CONTROL.

Few people are as extreme as Jim Carrey or the Queen. Most of us are somewhere between 1 and 4 on either side of the gauge. POINT A on ILLUSTRATION 2 represents a person who is medium CONTROL, while POINT B plots a person who is high EXPRESS.

That we place extreme examples on each end of the wire doesn't mean that Queen Elizabeth *never* shows emotion or that Jim Carrey *always* expresses emotions to the extreme. Rather, these are excellent examples of people who *typically* use their traits to the extreme.

Illustration 2

Common positive and negative actions that people on both sides of the gauge display are listed in TABLE 1.

Table 1

People Who CONTROL Emotions: Private, controlled, introverted, quiet, suspicious, introspective, indifferent, detailed, thoughtful, and pensive

People Who EXPRESS Emotions: Outgoing, emotional, sensitive, fiery, explosive, passionate, short-fused, moody, dramatic, and expressive

Obviously, not everybody who controls or expresses his/her emotions will display all of the actions listed for each trait. What we do know, however, is that a person's specific actions will typically come from either the CONTROL or EXPRESS pool of actions—and not both. (There is a small minority who can operate out of both pools of actions, and we'll look at this later in the chapter when we discuss the concept of *range*.)

For example, one person who is CONTROL, may display all the positive actions of CONTROL, but only one negative action, such as suspicious. Or another CONTROL person may only display the positive actions of private and detailed and the negative actions of indifferent and suspicious. We each have a unique set of actions, and respecting this factor prevents stereotyping.

What's important is that regardless of the number of actions a specific person shows us, we can predict that the majority of his actions will come from his trait. From a scientific perspective, psychology has established that when we are under pressure we usually show our actual trait, as these are the actions that are most comfortable for us. This is one reason why we can predict a person's possible actions, and we will look more closely at this concept in Chapter 7.

A word of caution about the EXPRESS action *passionate*, which has become a popular buzzword. Comments like *I'm really passionate about what I do* is completely different than *talking* passionately. The first has to do with commitment directed at *what* you do, while the other is simply *talking* passionately. (There's more on this social trend in *Snapshot*.)

Positive and Negative Extremes of the CONTROL–EXPRESS Gauge

Please review ILLUSTRATION 3, which lists individuals and fictional characters, both contemporary and from history, who use their CONTROL and EXPRESS traits both positively and negatively to the extreme (5 plot point on the gauge). If there's someone you aren't familiar with, locate a video clip on the web and watch it.

When people EXPRESS or CONTROL their emotions, they do so through spoken and written words as well as visible actions. One EXPRESS person may infuse emotion by using the tone of his voice for emphasis. Another may use broad sweeps of the hand. While a third EXPRESS person may choose specific words or phrases in order to express emotion, such as "I feel this is the right decision."

Counterpoint this with a CONTROL person who says: "I think that this is the right decision." While another CONTROL person might say, "I feel this is the right decision," but in a tone of voice that does not convey any emotion.

Each of the people selected in ILLUSTRATION 3 have their own unique way of expressing their CONTROL or EXPRESS trait. What is important: The sum total of how they communicate reveals their CONTROL or EXPRESS trait.

Be careful not to confuse emotional reactions with the EXPRESS trait. In all of us, there is a part of our brain called the amygdala. It's often referred to as the fight or flight part of our brain. If you see a rattlesnake, for example, the image goes straight to the amygdala and evokes an emo-

Illustration 3

Positive Extreme CONTROL

- **Queen Elizabeth II**
  (noted for her stoic composure)
- **Spock**
- **Sheldon Patrick**
  (character in *The Big Bang Theory*
  TV show)
- **Tony Dungy**
  (inspiring, soft-spoken coach)
- **Norah O'Donnell**
  (news anchor)

Positive Extreme EXPRESS

- **Jim Carrey**
- **Megyn Kelly**
  (news anchor)
- **Lou Holtz**
  (football coach and commentator
  noted for fiery locker room talks)
- **Joan Rivers**
  (comedienne)

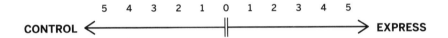

```
        5   4   3   2   1   0   1   2   3   4   5
CONTROL <——————————————————||——————————————————> EXPRESS
```

Negative Extreme CONTROL

- **Heinrich Himmler**
  (Hitler's coldly indifferent
  henchman)
- **A recluse**
- **President Richard Nixon**
  (a complex person, his suspicious,
  dark side)
- **Godfather**
  (Marlon Brando's quiet but ruthless
  portrayal of a mafioso)

Negative Extreme EXPRESS

- **John McEnroe**
  (tennis pro noted for screaming at
  referees; or other tempermental
  athletes or actors/actresses)
- **Lady Gaga**
  (as per her first appearance on *60
  Minutes*)
- **Howard Stern**
  (as brash radio talk show host)
- **Boisterous/offensive sales rep**

tional response. You don't think—you just act to protect. Or, someone sees something funny and laughs. It's an emotive reaction, which we don't want to confuse with how people typically prefer to communicate. Both CONTROL and EXPRESS people can have an emotional reaction: laughing, crying, or acting surprised. When making rapid-fire reads we are reading how people typically prefer to communicate, not how they react out of fright or laugh at something funny.

Is one side of the CONTROL–EXPRESS gauge inherently good or bad?

Neither side of the CONTROL–EXPRESS gauge is inherently good or bad because people can use their traits positively or negatively. For example, one person who expresses emotions might use his trait to motivate those who work for him, while another person might display his EXPRESS trait when screaming at subordinates.

Each person in ILLUSTRATION 3 was selected to provide a simple, visual "snapshot" of the extreme ends of the CONTROL–EXPRESS gauge. Both positive and negative examples of each extreme are provided so that you will remember that people can use their trait positively or negatively.

The only negative is when someone chooses to use a trait in a negative way. When we recognize this fact, we can reduce our built-in prejudices against others.

Profile diversity issues are a greater issue than cultural diversity issues. People tend to see the world from a "self" facing perspective, viewing others from their personal experiences and cultural lens. As the world continues to shrink in terms of accessibility to other cultures, cultural diversity awareness is promoted in most organizations and schools. *Profile diversity* issues though, are even more problematic. This is when we stereotype others who don't have the same traits we do, and because they are different, we view them negatively or in skewed ways, even if they use their traits positively. The reason profile bias is a greater problem than cultural diversity prejudices, is that it exists even *within the same cultural groups.* In most cases, the bias stems from being exposed to a person with a specific trait as a youth who used his trait negatively.

For example, imagine that John had a father who regularly beat his mother when he was a youth. Added to this, his father was extreme EXPRESS, and John only saw the negative actions of an explosive and short-fused temper. As a result, John is uncomfortable in any close relationship with someone who is EXPRESS because he associates people who express their emotions with his father.

The first step to help John is to point out his prejudice and identify where it came from. Next, you help him profile people with that trait and identify people who use their trait as a *positive*. Once he makes this connection, it's his first step toward living and working with a broader bandwidth of people. Respecting the *positive* differences in those with a different trait will increase his capacity to be more open and enhance his ability to develop long-lasting relationships.

I've worked with thousands of at-risk youth both for the books I've written and as a volunteer. Identifying trait prejudices and their roots is one of the first things I do when mentoring a youth, and it is just as important for helping adults. The *KPS* works to draw the "profiler" out of the "me" perspective while promoting insight and understanding of those who are different from us. Here is one example.

A military officer who was extremely NONASSERTIVE had difficulty working with other senior officers, and it was hurting his career. The stumbling block was that he stereotyped anyone who was ASSERTIVE as egotistical (a possible negative action) because it wasn't the way *he* communicated. When he learned to profile, he realized his error. He corrected it by deliberately looking for positive actions in those who were ASSERTIVE, and then worked on how to respect and interact with them to meet their needs. The result? His career fast-tracked, and he became a senior officer with significant responsibilities.

Personalize Your CONTROL–EXPRESS Wire/Gauge

You'll now personalize your CONTROL or EXPRESS wire/gauge. From the list of people in ILLUSTRATION 3, select examples who are easy to remember for the positive and negative extreme of each end of the gauge. Write them in the blanks provided in ILLUSTRATION 4. You can also select people you personally know, but their trait must be as extreme as the examples provided or your wire/gauge will be off. The key qualification is that you can quickly recall and visualize this person, even under pressure.

For example, pointed-eared Spock and his stoic manner is easy to visualize as extreme positive CONTROL. Queen Elizabeth II is also easy to recall as her emotions are always in check. For an EXPRESS person, Jim Carrey's outrageous portrayal in *The Mask* is easy to visualize as extreme EXPRESS.

The reason you'll identify a positive and negative example for each extreme is so you respect the fact that traits can be used both positively and negatively. (The purpose of acknowledging the negative extremes is to reduce trait prejudice and build a foundation that traits can be used positively and negatively.) When you profile someone, however, *you'll only use the positive examples*, as you just need one extreme on the end of each gauge to make a read.

Illustration 4

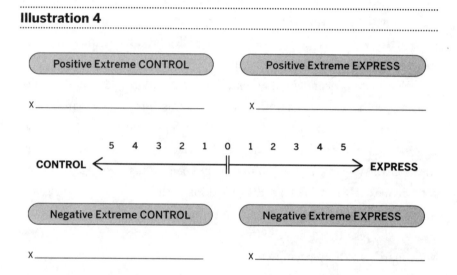

Plot yourself on the gauge

First, select whether you are CONTROL or EXPRESS. Then, try to approximate the strength of your trait by selecting a 1–5 plot point. Remember 5 is the strongest and 1 is the weakest.

If you think you are in the center (0), think carefully, as only 5–15% of any given population have a plot point of 1 or less, which will be addressed later in the chapter. While you may not always control or express your emotions in every situation, most people do tilt to one side or the other. Ask yourself: Am I more like the CONTROL or the EXPRESS actions on a typical day when I communicate? Resist what is called the "Barnum Effect." This is where people think that they possess more actions than they really do.

For example, horoscopes use the Barnum Effect to snag the unsuspecting, as observed by my colleague, Dr. Ray Hyman, an expert on the psychology of deception, who conducted the following test.

First, subjects completed a psychological test that identified their traits. Next, they were shown two lists of actions. The first list contains actions from their actual profile. The second list was a generalized "horoscope" list of actions that contain opposite traits. His study found that most people will select the generalized list over the list that is their actual profile. He said this is because we want to think of ourselves more expansively than accepting the specific traits we actually possess. Remember, it is extremely unlikely that you can be high CONTROL and high EXPRESS. If you do, you might need some assistance!

One humorous "aha" moment occurred where someone misread their own trait in a workshop. The gentlemen insisted, in an almost monotone voice, that he was EXPRESS. One person in the class whispered, "Not unless he's comparing himself to a land slug!" An important clarification is appropriate here: A person may or may not *feel* emotional, but this is isn't the same as *expressing* emotions, which is what we are trying to read.

At this point, all you are trying to determine is which side of the gauge you tilt toward on a typical day and the approximate strength of your trait. Anyone can express emotion on an atypical day, such as the day when your daughter gets married or when receiving recognition for an act of heroism. Or, one might be able to temporarily restrain any show of emotion during the signing of a long-sought-after contract. The key word is *typical*. How do you prefer to communicate on a typical day? Remember, assess yourself on *actual* traits and not what you *want* to be.

Helpful CONTROL–EXPRESS Questions

Here are some questions to help you identify your trait.

1. Is it natural for me to express my emotions? (EXPRESS)

2. Do I prefer to control or conceal my feelings? (CONTROL)

3. Is it easy for me to be sensitive about how others feel? (EXPRESS)

4. Am I more stoic about how others feel? (CONTROL)

If you're still uncertain about whether you are CONTROL or EXPRESS, or you can't select an approximate point, ask a trusted friend(s) for help. Ask for specific examples of actions they have seen from you. Their consensus should help resolve your uncertainty. Of course, ask for counsel wisely. Don't ask someone who may try to take advantage of your candid discussion or who lacks keen insight into others.

Work Versus Home

You may need to plot yourself based upon whether you're at work or home. Some people, who are CONTROL at work, may find it easier to express emotions at home or amongst their family and friends. The shift may not be significant, but it may help you develop a broader picture of your actual inventory of actions for your trait (more on this in Chapter 7). If you truly do operate on both sides of this gauge, or any other, this means you will have more than one COMPREHENSIVE profile: one that you exhibit at work and one at home. Before accepting this as fact, be sure to use the two safety checks explained in Chapters 6 and 12 to confirm that you truly do have these two profiles.

What Do You Do Under Pressure
Separate From Your Training?

Some people have difficulty identifying a trait because they've received formal or informal training that has forced them to operate on both sides of the line. In this case, you may have your actual core trait and then the trait which you have been trained to use.

For example, a hostage negotiator who may have a high ASSERTIVE trait has been trained to restrain his trait, which is important to calm a hostage taker. Or, teachers may have a NONASSERTIVE trait when they communicate, but have learned to "step it up" and be ASSERTIVE to keep that antsy fifth-period class in line.

If these examples sounds like you, identify your actual trait and your learned trait. You will need this later when you identify your type and COMPREHENSIVE profile as well as understanding how to work with others. And, if you've profiled someone who has learned how to operate on both sides of a trait, you will need to interact with them based upon their two profiles. This isn't common, but it is useful to know to avoid confusion.

The 10 Second Read: Increases Accuracy 20–30%

Now that you have personalized your CONTROL-EXPRESS wire/gauge, here's how to use it to profile someone. After you have observed or interacted someone for a minute or two, ask yourself:

Is he more like Queen Elizabeth or Jim Carrey?

People show emotion through the tone of the voice, choice of words, and non-verbals. Non-verbals are any physical action like the turn of the body, use of the hand, facial expression, and so on. (The popular term is "body language" but I don't recommend using it as there isn't a concrete "language.")

When you make your read, just take in the person's full persona.

Do not ask yourself: Is he CONTROL or EXPRESS? This is too subjective.

Just take in their full persona and compare the person to your two extremes. Also, don't make the comparison using the two negative extremes, as explained earlier.

Lastly, after you've observed someone, make your read in *ten seconds.* This will feel uncomfortable at first, but the longer you take to make your read, the lower will be your accuracy (which decreases every five seconds, as demonstrated by the thousands we've tested).[1] This is why this is called *rapid-fire* profiling. (Also, in the beginning, you might look at the list of actions for each trait to help orient yourself, but after several weeks of doing your assignments you'll typically only refer to them for a person who is difficult to profile.)

The data shows that if you take in a person's full persona, compare what you see to the extremes of your gauge, and then make your read within ten seconds, accuracy immediately increases 20–30%. Making reads in ten seconds based upon the two extremes helps take second-guessing and sub-jectivity out of the equation because you're simply making the read based upon a standard. Every group globally that has applied this technique has seen increases in accuracy without any additional instruction. This is even true when I simply give a speech on profiling and audience members have the interactive keypads. After they profile a couple of clips, they always increase accuracy a minimum of 20% in just minutes—even when shown clips of hard-to-read people.

Here is how one Dutch mental healthcare professional says he uses the wire/gauge. He said that he imagines a video game in his mind. There is a picture of the Queen on his right, Jim Carrey on his left. The person he is reading is in the middle and there is a slider underneath the person, as shown below. As he listens to someone, he mentally moves the slider so the Queen or Jim Carey is over the person's head and he quickly answers: Who is he/she more like? No more, no less.

You may ask, *What if I'm wrong? What if I miss?*

Queen Elizabeth II   Jim Carrey

First, most people start with 65–75% *inaccuracy*. Second, your accuracy will quantifiably increase using the *KPS*. And third, you will soon be given safety checks (Chapter 6) to know if your are incorrect and the ability to immediately correct your read.

Tips for beginners. When first learning to profile, it's usually best to start with those who aren't family or close friends. In the beginning, emotional attachments can cause confusion. It's common. That's why for the first few days, read people where there isn't a lot at stake. Then try those closest to you.

Caution about solely reading facial expressions. There are systems that teach you how to profile by observing facial expressions, but there's a problem. People don't only use facial expressions to show emotion. They can show express emotions through the tone of the voice, choice of words, and non-verbals. Facial expressions are just one type of non-verbal, and the use of hands is another. In fact, many of the photos used in facial read systems don't work cross-culturally or even within the same culture as the expressions can have multiple interpretations. That's why taking in a person's full persona and making a rapid-fire read is a more accurate and reliable method to rapid-fire profile (more on this in Chapter 7).

Extreme and NonExtreme Examples

Most people you profile won't be as extreme as Queen Elizabeth and Jim Carrey, and those who have extreme traits are easy to profile. The majority of the people you'll profile will be around 3 or less. To help you visualize examples of people who are extreme and nonextreme CONTROL or EXPRESS, please review the examples in TABLE 2. People who represent nonextreme examples are plotted around 2 or 3 on the CONTROL or EXPRESS side of the gauge, while extreme examples are plotted at 4–5.

Table 2

Extreme Examples

Positive CONTROL:	People who control their emotions during a volatile crisis and provide stability to a group.
Negative CONTROL:	The cold and suspicious recluse who refuses to help others for fear of having to express his feelings.
Positive EXPRESS:	Coach firing up his team in the locker room.
Negative EXPRESS:	People with short tempers who explode.

NonExtreme Examples

Positive CONTROL:	The usually quiet aunt or uncle who takes it all in and is full of wisdom.
Negative CONTROL:	Reserved corporate manager who, at times, is

indifferent to the feelings of others.

Positive EXPRESS: Genuinely warm salesperson who makes you
                          feel at home.

Negative EXPRESS: Some philanthropists who occasionally let their
                          emotions reject wise counsel.

The Concept of Range

Common sense tells us that no one uses his traits with the exact same
strength each day or in every situation. Most of us, however, operate within
a predictable range.

For example, let's assume that you plotted yourself at POINT A as in
ILLUSTRATION 5. The average person's range usually extends anywhere from
1/2 to 1 full point in each direction. So in the example below, we know that
your range is about 2–4 EXPRESS.

Illustration 5

In addition to predicting a possible range in which a trait will be used,
the idea of approximate points also helps us avoid stereotyping. It prevents
us from saying "She always does that," because people don't always act or
respond with the same degree of intensity.

A person who is plotted at POINT C, as noted in ILLUSTRATION 6 indicates
a person who can operate on both sides of the gauge. This is true for 5–15%
of most populations.

Illustration 6

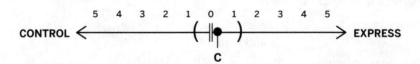

In fact, I've found that this can be as high as 25% in small towns and as little as 5% in big cities. I believe this is because it isn't as critical in small towns for a person's trait to be as well defined as in a big city where there are more pressures and knowing who you are is critical for self-protection as well as not getting lost in the masses. (Reminder: data quoted throughout the book is based upon responses from over 35,000 trained to use the *KPS* from many cultures, organizations, age demographics, professions, etc.)

Also, you'll find that there is usually a pattern regarding the side of the gauge on which you operate. In casual or brainstorming sessions, you will probably tilt toward EXPRESS, and when reviewing taxes or important critical reports, you will tilt toward CONTROL.

Before committing to a close-to-the-middle plot point, ask yourself this question: Am I a *little* CONTROL and a *little* EXPRESS?

If you and those close to you agree that you do, you probably have a close-to-the-middle plot point. (There is more on middle plot points in Chapter 6 when looking at combination types.)

If, however, you realize that only in very specific instances you are CONTROL and in most situations you are about 3 EXPRESS, then you are EXPRESS. Here's what is happening and how it relates to profiling others.

You can restrain what you have, but it's difficult to manufacture what you don't have. Consider this question: *Is it easier for a person who is* CONTROL *to be more* EXPRESS *or for an* EXPRESS *person to be more* CONTROL?

The answer is that it's easier for the EXPRESS to be more CONTROL.

To wit: It's easier for an EXPRESS person to restrain something they have (emotion), then for the CONTROL person to manufacture and show more emotion, something he doesn't have. This is one cause for a misread, but thankfully you can catch this using the two safety checks explained in Chapters 6 and 12.

Finally, if you profile yourself or someone else as having a plot point near the middle, this will mean that you will have more than one type and COMPREHENSIVE profile, which will be explained in greater detail in Chapter 6 when you learn about combination types.

Assignment 1

Goal: Learn to use the CONTROL–EXPRESS gauge.

Time Required: 30 minutes.

Aviation pilots are taught to trust their instrumentation. Not the horizon or anything else which can distract or deceive them, like heavy cloud cover or fog. In the same way, when profiling you're going to trust your wire/gauge and your process. To begin, review your personalized CONTROL–EXPRESS wire/gauge in ILLUSTRATION 4. Now imagine yourself in a situation where you have to instantly remember the extremes you chose. If you can't instantly visualize them, look for another example until you have two that for you are memorable. Just be sure the person you select is as extreme as the examples provided. Now you're ready to start profiling.

1. Write the names of six people you know in the spaces provided in ILLUSTRATION 7.

2. Compare each person's overall persona to the extremes of your gauge. Don't just focus on one isolated situation. Ask yourself: When he/she communicates, is he/she more like Queen Elizabeth or Jim Carrey (or the extreme examples you choose). You simply want to identify which side of the EXPRESS gauge that a person tilts toward. Write CONTROL or EXPRESS in the space provided.

3. If you are still unsure on which side of the gauge a person should be plotted, read the list of actions for CONTROL and EXPRESS in TABLE 1. You'll only use this list in the beginning until you are comfortable with your gauge. Ask yourself: When this person communicates, which set of actions seems to better fit this person—the CONTROL or EXPRESS actions? Like a pilot, trust that your gauges and your list of actions will direct you toward the right trait.

4. Assign a numerical plot point from 1–5 for each person, measuring the strength of each person's trait. Don't worry if some of your estimates are off or if you struggle with an exact numerical plot

point. This exercise is intended to help you become acquainted with comparing people to the two extremes of the gauge. With practice, your accuracy will steadily improve. Remember, it is not uncommon when first learning to profile to have some difficulty plotting someone to whom we are close, such as a spouse or best friend. The reason for this is that even though a person controls his emotions, we may remember those few instances when this person did express emotion, such as at a surprise party, at a daughter's wedding, and so on. Most everyone will express some emotion at some time in their life, even if they are high CONTROL. The key is to step back and ask yourself: *Does he express or control his emotions when he communicates with people on a typical day? What is his natural bent?* This should help you develop a more objective read.

5. Finally, put a plus or negative next to each name, indicating whether you think they typically use their trait positively or negatively. This will reinforce the idea that traits can be used positively and negatively, helping you avert unwanted biases against a particular trait.

Illustration 7

Name	CONTROL or EXPRESS	Plot Point
#1		
#2		
#3		
#4		
#5		
#6		

CHAPTER 5

WIRE #2: ASSERTIVE OR NONASSERTIVE?

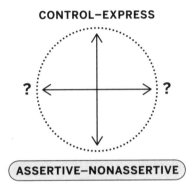

CONTROL–EXPRESS

ASSERTIVE–NONASSERTIVE

In this chapter, you will learn how to use the second point on your compass—the ASSERTIVE–NONASSERTIVE wire/gauge.

WIRE/QUESTION/GAUGE #2: ASSERTIVE OR NONASSERTIVE?

Does this person prefer to be assertive or nonassertive when he/she communicates?

This second wire identifies whether or not someone prefers to exert force or be more restrained when he *communicates*. The question you'll answer in your mind is: "Does this person prefer to be assertive or more nonassertive and laid back when they communicate?"

For example, someone who is polite and has an ASSERTIVE trait might ask a question as follows: "Tell me, what do you think of the situation?"

The tone is directive—*Tell* me...

A NONASSERTIVE person, though, might ask the same question as follows: "So John, can you share with me what you think of the situation?"

Note the softer, less assertive choice of words.

Like the CONTROL–EXPRESS gauge, people can use the tone of the voice, choice of words, and non-verbals to show their trait.

If Louis, an ASSERTIVE person, makes a statement, he might choose the following words: "I've reviewed the situation, and this is what I think we should do." He might also use the tone of his voice and his hand for emphasis.

If Alex, a NONASSERTIVE person, makes a similar statement, he might phrase his remark like this: "After reviewing the situation, it seems that we should take a different direction." Notice the less ASSERTIVE choice of words. He might also use a softer tone of voice than Louis.

For years, the notion in some psychology circles has persisted that people who are "assertive" want to dominate and get their own way. This is stereotyping. I have interviewed many people who are assertive, but who are thoughtful and selfless. When they communicate, there is simply more force behind how they communicate. Also, the term "assertive" is rarely used to specify *when* a person is ASSERTIVE : 1) Is he assertive when he communicates? 2) When he perform a task or makes decisions? 3) Or both? This lack of clarity causes confusion and doesn't work when profiling. Remember, the number one profiling misread is when a person's communication/talk trait is confused for a performance/walk trait. For this reason, the descriptor ASSERTIVE in the *KPS* only specifies a person who is assertive when he/she communicates.

The examples in ILLUSTRATION 1 list people representative of each extreme (5), and video clips of each, like the other examples provided for each gauge, are easily accessible online for comparison.

For those who remember Mr. Rogers, his famous line, softly delivered, "Won't you be my neighbor?" is easy to visualize as extremely NONASSERTIVE, as was Lady Diana's soft demure tone. While Martin Luther King's famous speech, "I Have a Dream," is easy to recall as extremely ASSERTIVE. Russell Crowe's portrayal of General Maximus in the film *Gladiator* is equally as memorable.

Illustration 1

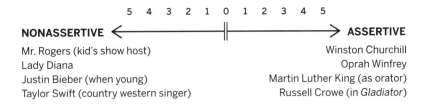

Other examples of people who are ASSERTIVE and NONASSERTIVE are Justin Bieber (NONASSERTIVE) and Oprah Winfrey (ASSERTIVE). Mother Theresa is another example who was world-renowned for her work with over 500 orphanages, homes for the poor, and other charity centers around the world. While she confidently made decisions, her manner of communicating with others was considerate, and not dominating. Margaret Thatcher, the former British Prime Minister, was also a much admired world leader for her direct and forceful way in which she consistently communicated her position.

Oprah Winfrey is an example of an extremely ASSERTIVE professional who sometimes appears NONASSERTIVE because of her ability to *restrain* her trait during interviews, a concept we reviewed in the last chapter. Remember, it is easier to restrain something you have than to manufacture something you don't have, and Oprah learned the art of restraining her trait as needed as an actress and a talk show host. However, like most of us, if she is under pressure, she'll use her actual trait which is extreme ASSERTIVE.

Common misconceptions about the gauge. A misconception about this gauge is that a person who is NONASSERTIVE doesn't like to talk and engage in conversation while a person who is ASSERTIVE always likes to talk. This is inaccurate, as the gauge doesn't identify whether or not a person likes to engage in conversation. Both ASSERTIVE and NONASSERTIVE people can enjoy a discussion. What we are looking for is *how* the person prefers to participate in a discussion or conversation. The NONASSERTIVE person's dialogue will have a more laid back and indirect flavor. The

ASSERTIVE person's dialogue will be more directive and forceful. Both Mother Theresa and Margaret Thatcher would no doubt enjoy a lengthy dialogue together, but Mother Theresa would probably be more altruistic and curious in her dialogue, while former Prime Minister Thatcher would be more directive and forceful. Two engaging, hospitable people. Two different communication styles.

Another misconception is that someone has to look you in the eye to be assertive. This is inaccurate. There are people who don't make significant eye contact, but show assertiveness through their choice of words, tone of voice, and even non-verbals. I knew a coach who rarely made lengthy eye contact with players, was high ASSERTIVE, and he added assertiveness by slapping his left hand with the back of his right and often started off with a forceful, *Hey dude.*

TABLE 3 provides both positive and negative actions for ASSERTIVE and NONASSERTIVE. Remember, these actions only identify how people typically prefer to communicate. For example, confident, a positive action for an ASSERTIVE person, doesn't mean this person is necessarily confident when making decisions. It only means that he is confident when he communicates—the talk part of his life.

And, to reemphasize, people express their traits many ways—through the tone of their voice (being forceful v. laid back), their words (Tell me what you think . . . v. May I ask you . . .), their actions (forcefully pointing a finger v. a placid expression), and so forth.

Table 3

People who are ASSERTIVE: Strong, confident, overbearing, unsympathetic, leads, egotistical, directive, blunt, and forceful

People who are NONASSERTIVE: Inquisitive, curious, appear uninformed or naive, agreeable, altruistic, weak, indirect, and laid-back

TABLE 4 provides positive and negative extreme examples of the ASSERTIVE–NONASSERTIVE gauge—people with a 5 plot point. While there are other famous people who are ASSERTIVE or NONASSERTIVE, such as General Colin Powell (about 4 ASSERTIVE), they are not included because their plot point is not a 5. (For those who are familiar with the first edition of this book, you will note the terms "tell" and "ask" have been replaced with ASSERTIVE and NONASSERTIVE for this gauge. This was done for added clarity, as explained in the Source Notes.)[1]

Table 4

Positive Extreme NONASSERTIVE

- **Dr. Ben Carson** (neurosurgeon)
- **Mr. Rogers** (the late, gentle children's educator)
- **Justin Bieber** (when young)
- **Taylor Swift** (female country singer when she was young)
- **Lady Diana** (the late British princess)

Positive Extreme ASSERTIVE

- **Russell Crowe** (in *Gladiator*)
- **Oprah Winfrey** (talk show host)
- **Chris Berman** (sportscaster)
- **Mel B** (*America's Got Talent*)
- **Martin Luther King** (inspiring orator)
- **Margaret Thatcher** (the late, British Prime Minister)

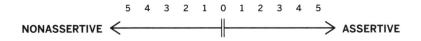

```
          5  4  3  2  1  0  1  2  3  4  5
NONASSERTIVE  <————————————||————————————>  ASSERTIVE
```

Negative Extreme NONASSERTIVE

- **Neville Chamberlain** (please see discussion of negative NONASSERTIVE)
- **Entrenched Bureaucrat** (never offers an opinion and appears weak and naive)

Negative Extreme ASSERTIVE

- **Adolph Hitler** (ruthless Nazi leader)
- **Brash Radio Talk Show Hosts**
- **Saddam Hussein** (arrogant Iraqi dictator)

Negative Extreme NONASSERTIVE

Most of the examples in TABLE 4 are self-explanatory, but try and think of a famous person who is extremely weak, naive, and uninformed. Not just a little weak, uninformed, and naive—but has the negative extreme of the NONASSERTIVE trait.

Don't be surprised if no one comes to mind.

Virtually few people since 1990 who possesses the negative actions of NONASSERTIVE to the extreme are easy to recall. Logically, who could distinguish himself on the world stage by being weak, uninformed, and naive to the extreme? Especially in a media-driven age, people who have NONASSERTIVE actions to the negative extreme are unlikely to rise to prominence on the world stage.

One candidate from recent history is Neville Chamberlain, the former British Prime Minister who preceded Churchill. When Chamberlain gave away Czechoslovakia to Hitler in his negotiations at the Munich Conference in 1938, his extreme negative NONASSERTIVE actions were displayed: extremely weak, uninformed, and naive.

A more common example of a person who is negative NONASSERTIVE to the extreme is an entrenched bureaucrat, but none are celebrities. Obviously, not all bureaucrats are NONASSERTIVE or possess the NONASSERTIVE trait to the negative extreme, but we all have dealt with those who are, especially at places such as the local drivers license bureau, a social security office, an institutional firm layered with unproductive managers, or a postal office.

Future Trend and Personalizing Your Gauge

There is an unhealthy global trend where it is difficult for anyone who is high NONASSERTIVE with *positive* actions to become recognized. The culprit is our brash crash-and-burn media. Media, which is an ASSERTIVE industry, has made it nearly impossible for those who are NONASSERTIVE and respectful to become public figures. Most news channels feature nonstop badgering with hosts constantly interrupting their guests. There are exceptions, but they are rare. Because you may not identify with the examples I've provided who are NONASSERTIVE, you may have to select a person you personally know to represent the extreme of NONASSERTIVE for your gauge. (As new examples appear, they will be posted on the "Live Addendum" for this book on the IFP website.)

Helpful ASSERTIVE–NONASSERTIVE Questions

Below are questions that will help you decide whether you or someone you are trying to profile is ASSERTIVE or NONASSERTIVE when making your comparison to the extremes of the gauge.

ASSERTIVE

1. Do I use mainly direct, forceful sentences and questions, such as:

- I think…
- I believe…
- Tell me…
- Tell me, what do you think…

NONASSERTIVE

2. Is my tone softer and more indirect, or do I use qualifying remarks when making statements or posing questions, such as:

- It seems…
- Perhaps this idea…
- It might be…
- May I ask you what you think about…

Extreme and NonExtreme Examples of ASSERTIVE–NONASSERTIVE

To help visualize the spectrum of people who are ASSERTIVE or NONASSERTIVE, here are positive and negative examples of those who have extreme and non-extreme ASSERTIVE and NONASSERTIVE traits.

Table 5

Extreme Examples

Positive NONASSERTIVE:	Doctor with refined bedside manner who always asks his patients how they feel.
Negative NONASSERTIVE:	The office "brown nose" who obsessively asks about everything to "score" points.
Positive ASSERTIVE:	General Norman Schwarzkopf who led US troops during Operation Desert Storm.

Negative ASSERTIVE:	A cult leader or dictator, such as David Koresh or Adolph Hitler, who tells and directs others with evil intent.

NonExtreme Examples

Positive NONASSERTIVE:	Truth-seeking reporter who asks questions but doesn't inject her opinion into the story.
Negative NONASSERTIVE:	Office subordinate who sometimes hesitates before offering an opinion when candor is needed.
Positive ASSERTIVE:	Salesperson who delivers a presentation that successfully matches his product or service with the client's needs and desires.
Negative ASSERTIVE:	The CEO who has occasional lapses of sensitivity when giving directives.

Assignment #2

Goal: Learn to use the ASSERTIVE–NONASSERTIVE gauge.

Time Required: 30 minutes.

Caution: Of the four gauges, the ASSERTIVE–NONASSERTIVE gauge is typically the most difficult to master. Please be patient. After using the gauge over a period of time, plotting people won't be difficult. Also, resist the temptation to skip this short assignment or any of the others throughout the book. Even if you think you understand a concept, work through each assignment as recommended, as this will accelerate your profiling comprehension and accuracy.

1. Personalize your ASSERTIVE–NONASSERTIVE gauge provided in ILLUSTRATION 2 on the next page with your choices for positive and negative extreme examples. You may select someone listed in TABLE 4

or you may select someone you personally know. If you choose people you know, be certain that they use their traits with the same intensity as the examples provided. Now plot yourself on the gauge. As before, if you are uncertain, seek the opinion of a friend or two for examples of specific actions they have seen from you.

Illustration 2

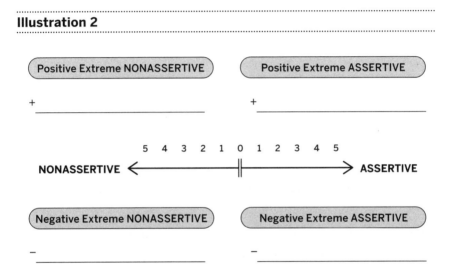

2. Select six people you know and write their names in the spaces provided in ILLUSTRATION 3. Now decide whether each person is ASSERTIVE or NONASSERTIVE by comparing the specific actions you have observed in their behavior with the list of actions in TABLE 3. Then estimate their 1–5 plot point and record. You may use the same six people you plotted from your first assignment, or you can select six others. And don't be shy about asking a friend you have plotted if he/she thinks you are correct. Most people will be more than willing to help.

Illustration 3

Name	ASSERTIVE or NONASSERTIVE	Plot Point
#1		
#2		
#3		
#4		
#5		
#6		

―――――――――――― **BRIEF RECAP** ――――――――――――

1. The first two questions/gauges used to profile someone are: CONTROL-EXPRESS and ASSERTIVE-NONASSERTIVE.

2. You have learned how to plot someone in relationship to the two ends of each gauge.

3. You have acknowledged the first part of Rule #1 for achieving systematic accuracy: People typically act in consistent, similar ways called traits.

4. We recognize that people can use their traits positively and negatively.

5. A plot point identifies a range in which people will use their trait.

Using the ASSERTIVE–NONASSERTIVE and CONTROL–EXPRESS Gauge in Everyday Situations

Here are some common sense strategies for using the first two gauges when communicating with others. For now, use them cautiously as your profiling skills are in the development stage, recognizing that you can make errors and no strategy works in every situation. Also, be sure to review additional examples in *Snapshot*.

When a person is NONASSERTIVE and . . .

1. You must be directive, use the ASSERTIVE side of your range if you are NONASSERTIVE, or find a person who is ASSERTIVE to assist, or find a NONASSERTIVE person whose plot point is closer to the ASSERTIVE side. (It will easier for them to assert themselves.)
2. You are asking an important question, use the NONASSERTIVE side your range.

When a person is ASSERTIVE and . . .

1. You must be directive, use an ASSERTIVE person whose ASSERTIVE trait is stronger, or risk the possibility of a confrontation.
2. You must make an inquiry, use direct, concrete language such as, "Tell me what you think about..." rather than being indirect. (NONASSERTIVE people can use assertive words, even though their tone of voice and non-verbals may not be ASSERTIVE.)

When a person is CONTROL and . . .

1. You must be directive, use the CONTROL side of your range or they may discount your perspective because of your emotions.
2. You're inquiring about facts, use the CONTROL part of your range to be taken seriously. When inquiring about a subjective issue, use the EXPRESS side of your range to help stimulate someone's subjective thought process.

When a person is EXPRESS and . . .

1. You must be directive, use the CONTROL side of your range or they may discount your perspective because of the use of emotions.
2. You're inquiring about facts, use the CONTROL side of your range. When inquiring about a subjective issue, use the EXPRESS side of your range to help stimulate someone's subjective thought process. (Note: You use the same strategies when addressing those who are CONTROL or EXPRESS.)

Assignment #3

Goal: Learn to plot people on *both* gauges at the same time.
Time Required: One hour over a one-week period.

You've learned how to plot people on each gauge. Now you'll practice plotting people on both gauges simultaneously.

1. Take a week and plot thirty people, six people from each of the groups listed on both the CONTROL–EXPRESS and ASSERTIVE–NONASSERTIVE gauges.

   • Family
   • Close friends
   • Social acquaintances
   • Work—people you work with in your organization
   • Work—people outside of your organization

   First identify on which side of the gauges each person should be plotted and estimate their 1–5 plot point. Right now your focus is to identify on which side of the gauge a person should be plotted. Refinement of your plot point will come with practice.

   Be sure that your selections include people you like and get along with as well as those who are not "favorites." This will prevent stereotyping that one trait is better than another. Then ask two or three people whom you trust and respect for their insight to help assess your accuracy. As recommended in Chapter 2, when possible, work with another person who is also learning to profile so that you can sharpen one another.

   Don't rush practicing your new skill. Time is required to absorb the idea of plotting people against the extremes of more than one gauge at a time. Remember, like a pilot, to trust your instrumentation—the extreme ends of each gauge (and the list of actions for each trait if needed). If a person's actions don't seem to fit with the side of the gauge you selected, reevaluate the person's daily actions against the list of actions for each trait.

2. Commit to memory the four rules for promoting systematic accuracy noted in Chapter 3. They are the anchors that will enable you to thoroughly trust your gauges as you read others.

Cautionary note: The theatrical examples that are provided throughout the text, such as Spock and Jim Carrey, refer to a character or actor's public persona. Some actors or public figures, however, display one trait on television or in the cinema, but are actually another trait in their private lives. Therefore, exercise caution when profiling them. Also, be careful if you practice your profiling skills by reading the personalities of fictional characters in a favorite TV series. Good writers maintain trait continuity in their characters. Poor writers, however, can place their characters all over the trait landscape to add artificial dimensions to their characters. So if you practice profiling on TV characters, be sure and pick those that don't seem to change much in how they approach daily situations.

After you complete your current assignment, the shaded areas in ILLUSTRATION 4 show the steps you have learned in order to identify someone's profile. In the next chapter you'll now learn how to combine the CONTROL–EXPRESS and ASSERTIVE–NONASSERTIVE gauges together to identify someone's COMMUNICATION type—the talk.

Illustration 4

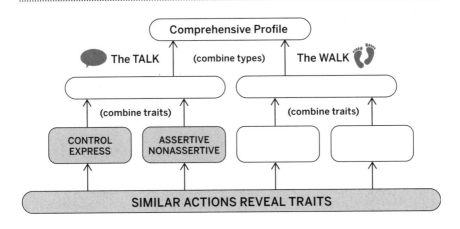

CHAPTER 6

IDENTIFYING COMMUNICATION TYPES

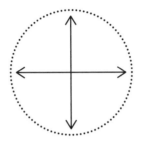

As you will recall, Rule #1 to achieve systematic accuracy (Chapter 3) states:

People typically act in consistent, similar ways called traits. When two or more traits are combined together, we have what are called types. *Combine two or more types together and you identify a profile.*

Rule #1 also states the three steps for profiling. First, identify a person's traits. Second, combine two traits together to identify a person's type. Third, combine two types together to reveal a COMMUNICATION profile.

In Chapters 4 and 5 you used two questions/gauges to identify the first two traits: CONTROL–EXPRESS and ASSERTIVE–NONASSERTIVE. In effect, once you've plotted someone on these two gauges, you've actually completed half of the work necessary to develop someone's COMMUNICATION profile. The next step, combining these two traits together to reveal a person's COMMUNICATION type has already been done for you, as detailed in this chapter.

You'll learn how to combine the CONTROL–EXPRESS and ASSERTIVE–NONASSERTIVE traits together to assess how a person prefers to communicate. We call this a person's COMMUNICATION type because it identifies the *talk* part of a person's life. You'll also learn the first of two "safety checks" that you'll use to evaluate the accuracy of your reads. It's one of the most valuable tools you'll use when profiling.

Communication Types

Types provide a more complete description of a person than a single trait because they summarize how different traits work together. Types also show us how people differ who have a trait in common. For example, let's assume that Bob is CONTROL and NONASSERTIVE while Sherry is CONTROL and ASSERTIVE. While both CONTROL their emotions, Sherry will tend to be more forceful then Bob when they communicate because she is ASSERTIVE.

Identifying COMMUNICATION types help us:

- Predict with greater accuracy the likely actions we'll see in a person when he/she interacts with others.
- Interact more efficiently and sensitively with people based upon their unique communication style.

To get an idea of how much information we can access about a person when we combine the CONTROL–EXPRESS and ASSERTIVE–NONASSERTIVE gauges together, look at the list of possible actions for the SERGEANT type on page 80. Like traits, there are potential positive and negative actions for a SERGEANT, as well as "other tendencies" which can be used either in a positive or negative manner.

Combining the Gauges

To combine the CONTROL–EXPRESS and ASSERTIVE–NONASSERTIVE wires/gauges, we turn one gauge on its end as shown in ILLUSTRATION 1. Instead of reading both gauges as horizontal lines, the CONTROL–EXPRESS gauge is turned vertically, like a thermometer. Nothing else has changed. You still use the same process to plot people on each gauge.

When we combine the two gauges together, four quadrants are created. Each quadrant represents the combination of two traits, and each of these combinations is called a type. So the quadrants are easy to remember and visualize, each is given a descriptor as shown. (If the four-quadrant illustration looks similar to other two-gauge schematics, it should, as the *KPS* is based upon established principles for behavioral profiling, like combining traits to produce a richer inventory of actions.

Illustration 1

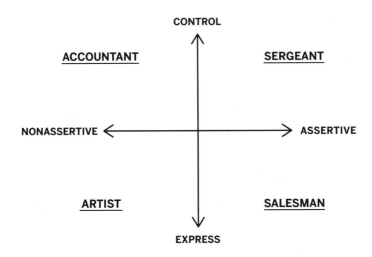

A brief summary of the traits associated with each type are:

Sergeant	CONTROL and ASSERTIVE
Salesman	EXPRESS and ASSERTIVE
Accountant	CONTROL and NONASSERTIVE
Artist	EXPRESS and NONASSERTIVE

Four Helpful Descriptors

The four descriptors, SERGEANT—SALESMAN—ACCOUNTANT—ARTIST, were carefully selected so that people from any cultural background can quickly visualize each type and its associated traits. Additional descriptor options for each type are also provided if you can't relate to those suggested.

SERGEANT—The SERGEANT identifier provides a visual picture of a person who is CONTROL–ASSERTIVE, like a sergeant in the military controlling emotions while forcefully giving orders. This doesn't mean that all sergeants in the army have these traits, but it's easier to visualize a "sergeant" possessing these traits than a clerk. Other suitable descriptors for a SERGEANT might be a LEADER or COMMANDER.

SALESMAN—The SALESMAN identifier provides a visual picture of a person who is EXPRESS–ASSERTIVE because it visually conveys the image of a salesman assertively telling you about his product as he conveys enthusiasm through his emotions. Another possible descriptor is COMMUNICATOR or PRESENTER. (The SALESMAN identifier is used instead of SALESPERSON because in some countries there isn't an equivalent non-gender-specific descriptor, thus SALESMAN is easier to translate for cross-cultural use.)

ACCOUNTANT—The ACCOUNTANT CONTROL–NONASSERTIVE provides a visual picture of a person who is an ACCOUNTANT because it conveys the image of an accountant maintaining emotional composure as he nonassertively, but thoroughly, makes inquiries. Other suitable descriptors are INVESTIGATOR or DETAILER.

ARTIST—The ARTIST identifier provides a visual picture of a person who is EXPRESS–NONASSERTIVE person because it conveys a person who communicates nonassertively with emotion. Other possible identifiers are COUNSELOR or SENSOR.

How to Plot a Type

ILLUSTRATION 2 shows how to plot someone who is a SERGEANT—CONTROL and ASSERTIVE. POINT A is the CONTROL–EXPRESS plot point, and POINT B is the ASSERTIVE–NONASSERTIVE plot point. If you draw a perpendicular line out from each point, they will intersect at POINT C, identifying a SERGEANT type. You use the same process to plot any of the other types. Remember, this only identifies how a person *communicates*.

Illustration 2

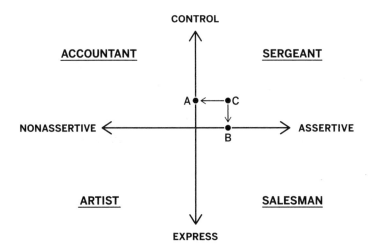

Not All Sergeants Are Alike

Now let's compare two people who are both SERGEANTS, but who differ in how they communicate. Compare SERGEANT A and SERGEANT B, shown in ILLUSTRATION 3.

Illustration 3

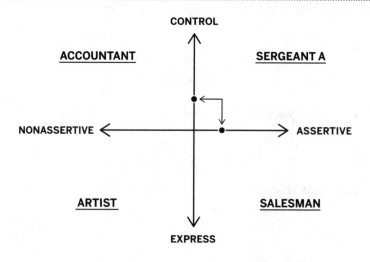

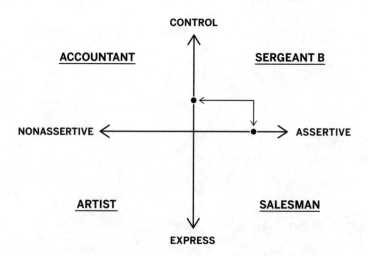

Notice that SERGEANT B is more ASSERTIVE more than SERGEANT A. Not only does this mean that the two SERGEANTS are different, but we can also make some predictions about their differences.

First, we can predict that SERGEANT B is more likely to take charge, be directive, or be forceful than SERGEANT A when he communicates. Why? Because SERGEANT B has a stronger ASSERTIVE trait than SERGEANT A. Thus, SERGEANT B is more likely to be directive or firmer in the way he gives orders.

However, since SERGEANT B's ASSERTIVE trait is stronger than SERGEANT A, we can also make another prediction. Let's imagine that both SERGEANTS have a tendency to be insensitive. We can then predict SERGEANT B is more likely to be more insensitive than SERGEANT A. Why? Because his ASSERTIVE trait is stronger.

Some people who are ASSERTIVE need to work on listening habits as they are likely to be more concerned about getting their point across than listening. Also, when ASSERTIVE is combined with controlling one's emotions (CONTROL), this can translate into being insensitive. Therefore, since SERGEANT B's ASSERTIVE trait is stronger, we can predict he'll likely struggle more with being insensitive than SERGEANT A.

To claim that all SERGEANTS are insensitive is to needlessly stereotype SERGEANTS. Recognizing the differences between people who are the *same type* not only helps us avoid stereotyping, but also increases our predictive accuracy when trying to estimate how someone will act in the future.

Identifying Your Own Type

In Chapters 4 and 5 you plotted yourself on the CONTROL–EXPRESS and ASSERTIVE–NONASSERTIVE gauges. Now plot yourself again on the gauges in ILLUSTRATION 4 on the next page. Don't let the fact that the CONTROL–EXPRESS gauge has been turned to the vertical confuse you. Just plot yourself on the two gauges like you did in the last chapter. You may want to look at your original plot points. Now draw a line out from each plot point until they intersect.

You have now identified your COMMUNICATION type, and you didn't have to answer any more questions! Please record your type in the space provided, and we'll now look at the actions associated with each type, including yours.

Illustration 4

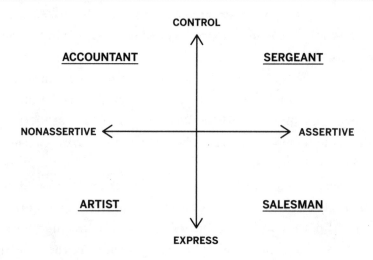

Your Type: _____

Communication Types and Actions

TABLE 6 lists the possible positive and negative actions for the four COMMUNICATION types. Also listed are "Other Tendencies," which are actions that are neutral or can be used in a positive or negative way.

As already noted, each of us will display a unique set of actions as well as how we use/display each action. ARTIST A, for example, might only display two-thirds of the positive actions listed for an ARTIST, while ARTIST B might display three-fourths of the listed actions. If both display the positive action of "supportive," one may do so through written correspondence while another through face-to-face dialogue. What we'll find, though, is that an ARTIST will possess more of the actions listed in the ARTIST list than those actions in the SALESMAN list.

It is possible that an ARTIST might learn to cultivate an action(s) from the SALESMAN or ACCOUNTANT types because an ARTIST shares at least one trait with them. For example, he might learn to be a bit more "outgoing" when teaching a class, which is a positive SALESMAN action, or a little more "analytical" when reviewing a report with a team, which is a positive ACCOUNTANT action. The majority of his actions, though, will be from the ARTIST pool. (We'll look at the concept of learned actions outside of one's type in more detail in Chapter 7.)

Types are also a guideline for predicting the possible actions that a person may display over time, rather than pinpointing how a person will specifically act or respond in every situation. An ARTIST, for example, may not display all of his actual actions at one time, or even during a short period of time. He may experience an entire month at work without using his natural tendency to avoid conflict, a common ARTIST action. (Some people would call this a holiday!) But, because we have identified his type, we know that avoiding conflict is a possible action that might appear.

Table 6

SERGEANT: CONTROL–ASSERTIVE

Positive Actions	Negative Actions	Other Tendencies
Takes charge/Strong	Overbearing	Strong-willed
Directive/Forceful	Myopic	Self-sufficient
Confident	Egotistical	Forceful
Influential	Insensitive/Indifferent	To the point
Assertive	Relentless	Stubborn
Determined	Hot-tempered	Private
Pragmatic	Won't accept direction	Controlled
Action-oriented	Impatient	Introspective
Persistent	Unsympathetic	Blunt
Objective		
Cool under pressure		
Poised		

SALESMAN: EXPRESS–ASSERTIVE

Positive Actions	Negative Actions	Other Tendencies
Outgoing	Impulsive	Talkative
Optimistic	Oversells	Dreamer
Passionate	Undisciplined	Emotional
Politically attuned	Unfocused	Desires to please
Excitable	Easily discouraged	Reactive
Happy-go-lucky	Short-fused	Dramatic
Confident	Egotistical	Open
Trusting	Gullible	Expressive
"Joiner"	Overly influenced	Sensitive
Forceful/Directive	by emotion	Fiery
Friendly	Overbearing	Idealistic

ACCOUNTANT: CONTROL–NONASSERTIVE

Positive Actions	Negative Actions	Other Tendencies
Easy-going	Uninvolved	Introspective
Poised	Weak	Indifferent/Aloof
Analytical	Suspicious	Stubborn
Detailed	Pessimistic	Proper
Moralistic	Unexcitable	Introverted
Calm and cool	Slow	Tranquil
Orderly	Critical	Private
Efficient	Appears uninformed	Perfectionist
Objective	Resists interaction	Indirect
Thoughtful	Focuses on history	Laid back
Curious/Inquisitive	Stuffy	
Agreeable	Naive	
Altruistic		
Discreet		

ARTIST: EXPRESS–NONASSERTIVE

Positive Actions	Negative Actions	Other Tendencies
Creative	Critical	Idiosyncratic
Sympathetic	Moody	Respectful
Agreeable	Appears weak	Tolerant
Curious/Inquisitive	"Spineless"	Enduring
Supportive	Emotionally rash	Retiring
Compassionate	Weak	Focuses on feelings
Deep-feeling	Unsure	Naïve
Self-sacrificing	Resists interaction	Dramatic
Loyal	Appears uninformed	Avoids conflict
Amiable	Naïve	Sensitive
Thoughtful		Indirect
Self-effacing		Passionate
Altruistic		

Remember, these are actions people display when they communicate—their talk. A negative SALESMAN action, *oversells*, only applies when he communicates, not when he takes action—his walk. How he performs tasks and makes decisions are a function of two other traits, which are covered in Chapter 8.

Your First Safety Check

In addition to identifying a richer inventory of actions about a person, one of the most powerful ways to use types is as a check on the accuracy of your reads. It's especially helpful in the beginning if you're a little unsure of your profile. Here is how it works.

Step 1: Compare the actions in the type you identified to those actions you observed. Let's assume that you profiled Leta as ASSERTIVE and EXPRESS, which is a SALESMAN type. To be sure you've read the two traits accurately, review the list of the SALESMAN actions. If Leta's COMMUNICATION actions that you've observed are in the SALESMAN type, you have a match. You can use the same strategy if you're unsure about your own profile.

Type actions are an effective check because when you combine two traits together, you get another set of actions—the type actions. If your reads are accurate, you'll find the actions you observed in that type. If, however, you don't find the actions you observe, you've probably misread one or both of the traits, and you go to Step #2.

Step 2: If the actions don't match, review which type is a better match. In most cases, we miss one trait and not both. To correct your misread of someone you misprofiled as a SALESMAN type, first review the list of actions for the types that share one of the SALESMAN traits (ASSERTIVE and EXPRESS), which are the ARTIST and SERGEANT types. If you eliminate the ARTIST actions, you'll most likely find Leta's actions in the SERGEANT list, which means you misread Leta as EXPRESS. This means her actual trait was CONTROL.

While it's possible to misread both traits, it's not common. If you do miss both traits, it means you profiled someone as the exact *opposite* type from her actual type. In the case of Leta, if you first profiled her as a SALESMAN, it's statistically less likely that her actual type is an ACCOUNTANT. Look as the list of ACCOUNTANT and SALESMAN actions, and you'll see that they have nothing in common. To visualize this difference, look at one of the type illustrations in this chapter, and you'll see that the ACCOUNTANT and SALESMAN types are in diagonally opposite quadrants. This is why ACCOUNTANTS and SERGEANTS are what we call "opposite types." For this reason, it's quicker to correct a misread by first looking at types that *share* a trait with the type you first profiled.

Step 3: Review which trait you misread and why. Once you've corrected your misread and identified the correct type, think back to what you might have misread and why. In the case of Leta, let's assume you misread her as EXPRESS when she was actually CONTROL. Then, think back to the action that you thought was EXPRESS, which in this case was when she expressed frustration about a missed deadline. Moderately forceful and directive, you now realize that you misread Leta's ASSERTIVE frustration as EXPRESS. Thankfully, though, you have a check to correct your misread.

While there are major patterns why we misprofile people, which is explained in greater detail in Chapter 11, there are an infinite number of specific reasons for misreads. This is because we are all unique, and even people with the same traits use their traits differently. This means we will always have some measure of inaccuracy. And this is good! Why? Because it reminds us that we are not organic machines that can be stereotyped.

No matter how many reads you make, you'll always find new twists when you misread someone, as well as your unique tendencies of who you misread and why. As you identify your tendencies and the unique nuances you encounter, you'll learn when you should take another read or find someone to help who is better when reading a specific trait.

In Chapter 12 you'll be provided a second safety check. You'll use this when you have identified all four traits and you can review a person's COMPREHENSIVE profile. Together, these two safety checks will significantly decrease your inaccuracy and the time required to correct a misread.

When we flesh out the nuances of our own profile first,
we are better able to understand the profiles of others.

Assignment 4

Goal: Scan the possible actions for your own type.
Time Required: 30 minutes.

Find your type, read over the list of actions, and check off the actions that you believe are a part of your personal inventory. As recommended in previous exercises, find a trusted friend to assist you, as sometimes we are unaware of a specific positive or negative action that we possess.

As noted, you may find that some of the actions from the types adjacent to your type match who you are. For example, if you are a SERGEANT, you may possess an action or two of a SALESMAN. This is because both types share the ASSERTIVE trait. It is unlikely, however, that you will have many common actions with an ARTIST, who is NONASSERTIVE–EXPRESS, because ARTISTS and SERGEANTS don't share any common traits.

If you find you have a large number of actions from two adjacent types, such as ACCOUNTANT and ARTIST types, which both share the NONASSERTIVE trait, you may be a combination type which is explained in the next section.

Combination Types

There are two reasons why someone may be a combination type. The first is that one of his plot points is near the middle. As explained in Chapter 3, we use our traits within a *range*—usually a point or so in each direction. Therefore, because he operates within a range he shares actions from *both* sides of the gauge, as shown in ILLUSTRATION 5.

Illustration 5

CONTROL ⟵ 5 4 3 2 1 0 1 2 3 4 5 ⟶ EXPRESS

The second reason why someone is a combination type is that he has a bigger range than most of us, and one of his plot points is closer to the middle, ILLUSTRATION 6. Notice that this person's plot range (POINT A1 to POINT A2) is almost three full points.

Illustration 6

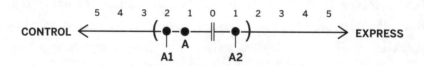

CONTROL ⟵ 5 4 3 2 1 0 1 2 3 4 5 ⟶ EXPRESS

A1   A   A2

ILLUSTRATION 7 shows an example of someone who is a combination type who operates on both sides of the CONTROL–EXPRESS gauge. His plot point is POINT A but his range extends to POINT A1 and POINT A2. Because he operates on both sides of the CONTROL–EXPRESS gauge, he is both a SERGEANT and a SALESMAN—a combination type.

As noted in Chapter 3, only about 5–15% of a given population have a close-to-the-middle plot point on one of the four traits. Once you've identified the two types, there is usually a pattern when a person uses each type. For example, a SERGEANT–SALESMAN will more likely use the SERGEANT actions when giving directives and SALESMAN actions when giving presentations. Identifying the pattern of when they will use each type takes a bit more work, but it's better than being confused by a gallery of actions which may seem contradictory.

In the rarest cases, less than 1%, are people who have a middle plot point on *both* gauges. This means that they operate out of all four types, but their actions in each type are typically low to moderate and not extreme (because of the low plot points). For these people, you need to think through how they might operate and in which situation based upon all four types.

Illustration 7

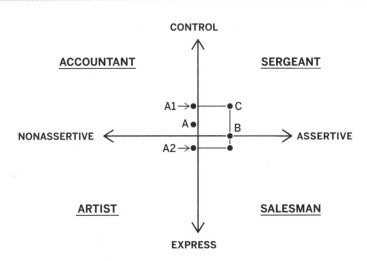

Entrepreneurs and combination types. Combination types are common in multi-role environments, such as entrepreneurial companies in which a person must wear multiple hats to perform varied responsibilities. It's my experience that most entrepreneurs are combination types.

Leaders, who are combination types, should take time to review this with their team and which type is likely to surface in which situation. For clients I've coached, it's paid big dividends. Clarification provides stability for management teams, eliminating uncertainty about "who is showing up and in which situation," and it allows people to understand the hats someone wears and why it works.

Leading people who are combination types. If people work for you who are combination types, it's imperative to give them a variety of responsibilities that allows them to use both of their types. Otherwise, over time they'll feel boxed in and often resign in frustration. I've observed organizations lose good people who didn't follow this advice. Today, when everything changes so quickly, people who are combination types are an invaluable asset because they don't mind wearing more than one hat or being put into varied situations and roles.

An Enigma Wrapped in the Walls of a Castle Library

A number of years ago, I was asked to pay a visit to a prominent restauranteur, whom we will call Ned. His peers often referred to him as the "Walt Disney" of the restaurant industry. He possessed the uncommon combination of a knack for managerial details and artistic fire-power, allowing him to develop one of the most successful restaurants in America. Unquestionably, he was one of the most interesting people I have ever met.

An art graduate of a West Texas university, one of his first jobs was running the family dry-cleaning business—a huge jump from one end of the thought process to the other.

When I arrived at his office, I noticed that his office was also a lesson in contradictions, reflective that he was a combination type.

The corporate offices were in a Fortune 500 defense contractor's plain concrete building, complete with metal curtains shading the windows from sunlight and industrial listening devices. From the outside, you'd expect a fairly conservative office interior. The lobby was fairly traditional, but the lobby door was made from handsome leaded cut-glass panels, showing an artistic flair. Nothing in the lobby, though, prepared me for Ned's office.

He had dismantled a richly wooded library that resided in an European castle, sent it to the US by ship in containers, and reassembled it down the corridor from the lobby. Behind his desk, dimly lit, was a painting by one of my favorite American maritime master painters, worth millions.

Attired in a conservative but richly tailored suit, I didn't hear a word of what Ned said to me during the first few minutes of my visit. I was overwhelmed.

Ned was an ARTIST–ACCOUNTANT, and, understandably, a genuine enigma to his senior management staff. If he were not a thoughtful and considerate CEO, he would have been a terror to try and please. On one side he was an expressive artist, and on the other side he was a controlled and detailed CEO with a bottom-line corporate mission.

I made a conscious decision, after our meeting, to understand how this type of person was wonderfully put together. About ten years later, when I started to develop the profiling system in this book, I got my wish.

Helpful Hints When Reading Types

Respect each person's natural traits and positive actions—Everyone has a contribution to make. We must respect the fact that we are all different. Imagine an organization in which everyone is a SERGEANT: the president is a SERGEANT; the receptionist is a SERGEANT; the personnel manager is a SERGEANT. It would be miserable to work where everyone tried to direct everyone else. Be thankful for diversity of types. Even if you feel uncomfortable with another person's style of communicating and interacting with others, learn to respect the positive aspects of his type.

If you are biased against a particular trait or type, it is often the result of one of three reasons:

- This person is your opposite type and you feel uncomfortable because you don't understand them and his/her unique needs.
- This person is the same as your trait or type and reminds you of your shortcomings. (You probably share some of the same negative actions.)
- This person's trait or type reminds you of someone whom you justifiably or unjustifiably don't like.

Persisting in your bias will only diminish your ability to profile with clarity and will limit the types of people with whom you can successfully interact. To counteract the above, focus on finding the *positive* actions in people who have the types or traits toward which you have a bias. Better yet, practice the next tip.

Learn from your opposite type—Often, if you try to emulate the positive qualities of your opposite type, your negative qualities will begin to diminish. For example, SERGEANTS and SALESMEN, who are both ASSERTIVE, can be poor listeners—a common negative action they both possess. They can improve their listening skills by learning from and associating with those who are NONASSERTIVE—ARTISTS and ACCOUNTANTS. In fact, this type of learning is the basis of many "management development" programs.

Learning from and associating with those whose traits are the opposite of ours is something we should practice both professionally and socially. In successful marriages, when spouses, who are opposites, value and work to emulate their spouse's positive actions, their own negative actions often begin to diminish with the passage of time. (This was a priceless lesson for me, when I realized this after twenty-five years of marriage.)

For example, let's imagine that Trent has a strong ASSERTIVE trait, and he isn't a good listener. His wife, Lynne, is medium NONASSERTIVE, and she has excellent listening skills. If Trent works at emulating Lynne listening skills, his inattentiveness will begin to diminish. This doesn't mean Trent will adopt, to the same degree, Lynne's exceptional listening skills. But he can move from being a poor listener to a moderate listener in most situations and an excellent listener in specific short-term situations.

By making a conscious effort to learn from those who have different traits, we can also reduce biases, and we can appreciate the benefit of another person's strengths which we don't possess.

Learn to modify how you communicate with each type—Successful interaction with others demands that we respect the positive actions associated with each type and try to accommodate another's shortcomings. Here are some examples:

If you're a SALESMAN or an ARTIST, learn to reign in your emotions when interacting with SERGEANTS and ACCOUNTANTS, who may have difficulty expressing emotion or responding to your emotions.

If you're a SALESMAN or a SERGEANT, practice listening more when with ACCOUNTANTS and ARTISTS, who aren't ASSERTIVE.

If you're an ACCOUNTANT or ARTIST, practice voicing your opinion a little more when around SERGEANTS and SALESMEN. You are less likely to be discredited because of a lack of input or a low-key manner when delivering your point.

Modify, don't mimick—When modifying how we communicate, we're not talking about *mimicking* another person's style of interaction. Instead, we try to meet people halfway to promote better interaction and understanding.

There are some misguided notions that if we are communicating with Trent, that we should "mirror" or copy Trent's communication style to become like Trent (also called "modeling"). The rationale is: If you act like them, they will like you. The end result, however, is usually a phony, surface-based relationship. (One of the key proponents of this type of modeling himself was paranoid. Afraid to be himself, he mimicked the actions of others and sold it as an effective communication tool. The reality is that when you video-record people who try to appear like others, their behavior looks affected, off, and even foolish, especially when they don't share a trait with the person they are mimicking.)

As noted in Chapter 1, the foundational attitude of this book is rooted in the idea of treating others right the first time, which is how we would like to be treated. No one wants to be artificially mimicked. People want to be treated uniquely, based upon their unique combination of traits, actions, skills, knowledge, likes, and dislikes. Let this perspective reinforce your philosophy toward how you will use profiling: *I know who you are. Good for me, better for you. It's the art of treating people right the first time.*

BRIEF RECAP

1. Actions reveal traits.
2. Combine two traits together to identify a type.
3. Each trait has a list of potential positive and negative actions as well as "other tendencies."
4. Types are a guideline for predicting possible actions over time, rather than pinpointing a person's actions in every situation.
5. Types are not stereotypes:
   - Not every ACCOUNTANT, for example, will display every action listed in the ACCOUNTANT list.
   - Similar types, such as two ACCOUNTANTS, won't necessarily display the same actions with the same degree of intensity because their plot points may vary on each gauge, nor will they use their actions in exactly the same way.
6. Familiarity with the list of possible actions will:
   - Increase predictive accuracy.
   - Help you better interact with others.
7. Combination types are people who can operate on both sides of a gauge because of their plot point and range. An example is an ARTIST–ACCOUNTANT, who is both EXPRESS and CONTROL.

Assignment 5

Goal: Learn to identify the different COMMUNICATION types.

Time Required: Two hours over a one-week period.

At the end of Chapter 4 you practiced plotting people on both the CONTROL–EXPRESS and NONASSERTIVE–ASSERTIVE gauges. During the next week, you will do the same thing, but you'll also identify each person's COMMUNICATION type and review the actions associated with his/her type.

1. Over the next week, plot twenty people from each of the five categories listed below. Don't rush. It takes time to absorb the concept of types. Reflection is needed when we compare ourselves to others.

- Family
- Close friends
- Social acquaintances
- Work—People you work with in your organization
- Work—People you interface with outside your organization

2. Identify each person's COMMUNICATION type.

3. Check off the actions associated with each person's type that you observe. If one person doesn't seem to fit the list of actions, scan the other types and see which type seems to fit better. Perhaps you didn't accurately plot someone on the ASSERTIVE–NONASSERTIVE or CONTROL–EXPRESS gauge. If you did misread someone, consider what you missed. Were you operating out of a bias? Did you fail to read someone based upon the extreme ends of each gauge? If someone's actions appear to be a solid mix of two types, this person may be a combination type, and you will need to combine the actions found in each of the two types.

After you have completed the assignments in this chapter, you'll have learned how to use two of the points on your profiling compass—ASSERTIVE–NONASSERTIVE or CONTROL–EXPRESS gauges—and how to combine them together to identify a person's COMMUNICATION type. In effect, you have learned half of the *KPS*.

The shaded area in ILLUSTRATION 8 depicts the first two steps you have learned to develop a COMPREHENSIVE PROFILE: (Step 1) Identify whether someone is ASSERTIVE–NONASSERTIVE and CONTROL–EXPRESS, and (Step 2) How to combine these traits to identify someone's COMMUNICATION type— the talk part of our persona. Two icons, a cartoon dialogue ballon and a pair of feet, will appear throughout the rest of the book to remind you that we have to read talk and walk traits and types separately.

In Chapters 7 and 8, you'll learn how to identify the last two traits and combine them to reveal a person's PERFORMANCE type—the walk part of our persona. First, though, we look at some helpful tips that will improve the accuracy of your reads.

Illustration 8

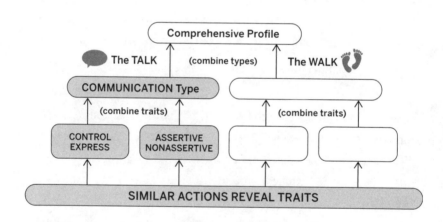

Easy-to-use tool available—For ease of use and to reduce memory work, a laminated "gauge/type" sheet is available that has all four gauges and all nine types and type actions on one page. Please see the back of the book for details.

CHAPTER 7

TIPS FOR
SUCCESSFUL READS

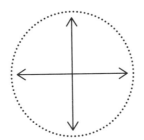

Before you learn the last two gauges, here are tips that will help you increase the accuracy of your reads. Be sure to review them periodically until they are instinctive. Then, after completing the chapter, go back to the exercises in the previous chapters and see if you can't sharpen or correct reads you made of others. Later chapters will provide additional guidance for improving the accuracy of your reads. Chapter 11 reviews the nine key reasons why people misread others and the antidote for each, and Chapters 16 and 17 provide additional suggestions for successful reads and the five clue categories from which to make your reads.

1. Read Overall Persona While Looking for "Leakage"

When trying to read a specific trait, like ASSERTIVE–NONASSERTIVE, there isn't one specific action you can look for because there are many actions that can express the same trait.

For example, Keith may display his ASSERTIVE trait by sharply pointing his hand at you when he speaks. It's his non-verbal way of being directive. Linda, however, may simply keep a strong, firm gaze on you while speaking to you and not use her hands at all. For Linda, a firm gaze is her way of being directive. And Cheryl may point with her hand, have a firm gaze, and use an assertive tone of voice.

Because there is an infinite number of ways of expressing the same trait, the quickest way to develop and sustain accuracy when making rapid-fire reads is to:

- Observe a person's overall persona—the sum total of a person's actions, speech, posture, attire, and so on—as you first learned in Chapter 4.

- Watch for any *leakage*—any breaks that appear in the consistency of a person's actions.

Overall persona—When we observe a person's overall persona, we don't look for one specific action over another, rather we absorb the combined effect of a person's actions, speech, attire, etc. If using the NONASSERTIVE-ASSERTIVE gauge, we then ask: Is his overall persona more like Mr. Rogers/Lady Diana or Oprah Winfrey/Winston Churchill? Then, if stumped, there are several options. (1) Have someone else you trust check your read. (2) Review the list of actions associated with NONASSERTIVE and ASSERTIVE, and see which set of actions is a better match. (3) Identify the person's CONTROL–EXPRESS trait. Then look at the two types that have that trait and see which type looks most like the person you are profiling.

For example, if you think Jacob has the EXPRESS trait, look at the list of actions for the SALESMAN and ARTIST types. If it's clear Jacob has the ARTIST actions, then you know that he is NONASSERTIVE.

Most beginners don't take in the full persona when making reads and instead attempt to profile by trying to spot something specific, like a certain look, phrase of speech, or facial expression. Then, when that action doesn't appear, they misread someone, and their success is limited. When the same group of beginners is instructed to take in a person's whole persona—and make their read in comparison to the extremes within 10 seconds of having made their few minutes of observations—accuracy immediately increases.

When beginners make reads from the sum total of the person, they'll often make correct reads and won't know exactly what they observed that was the deciding factor. They just allow the sum of a person's actions to speak for themselves when compared to extremes like Lady Diana and Churchill. While specific actions, such as speech, can tip you in the right direction when first learning, taking in someone's overall persona is more efficient.

A simple practice exercise is to record several of the better quality television news interview programs, such as *60 Minutes*. As you watch a clip, plot the subjects of each interview segment on the NONASSERTIVE-ASSERTIVE and CONTROL-EXPRESS gauges. Compare their personas to the extremes on your gauges, and record your reads. Now watch the interviews again and see if you can see what specific action tipped you off on your accurate reads.

With experience you'll eventually pinpoint and even direct your attention to look for specific actions. Like when veteran athletes describe that the "game seems to slow down," the same happens when you continue to make and apply your rapid-fire reads.

Look for "leakage"—There are times when people deliberately or unknowingly conceal their actual traits, which can cause misreads. To overcome this common stumbling block, we look for breaks in consistency or what is called *leakage.*

Leakage is when there is a break in the consistency of a person's actions that leaks out. A person's actions seem to be consistent, and then there is that one action that doesn't fit. Someone appears reserved in a meeting (CONTROL), but when pressured, a clear EXPRESS trait suddenly erupts. Or a person who seems to be in the background during a dialogue (NONASSERTIVE) suddenly becomes forceful and directive (ASSERTIVE).

The following is an example of a man who wasn't trying to fool anyone, but who often fooled those trying to profile him. By looking for leakage, however, his actual trait was spotted.

Leaking Eyes and Smiles

Bill was a salesman I interviewed who had been deceived by a "psychic surgeon." Bill related how a fraudulent healer from the Philippines seemingly reached into his body, without making an incision, removed damaged tissue, and repaired his hernia—all without the trace of a scar or a scratch. The charlatan had fooled hundreds using sleight of hand to create the illusion that his hand entered a "patient's" body. The tumor, which he "removed" from Bill, was actually a small animal organ that he concealed in his hand.

When I ask people to rapid-fire profile Bill by watching an unedited video clip from his interview, most profile him as CONTROL. They don't observe Bill expressing any emotion as he recalls what he observed. Bill's facial expression doesn't change much, his voice is steady, and his speech content is void of anything dramatic, but leakage did occur during—a break in his consistent actions.

Bill told me the healer cured him of his hernia.

I politely asked: "Would your doctor say that you are healed?"

Bill's eyes sparkled, and smiling pleasantly for the first time, he said that he didn't know what his doctor would say but he felt better. Specifically, expressive warmth could be seen in the area around his eyes that matched his warm smile. His eyes twinkled, and the crows feet on the sides of his eyes lit up. It was Bill's way of expressing emotion when I politely asked him an important question.

Up until my question, Bill's face remained steady—almost placid. This is common when people know what they are sharing is being recorded and will be seen on television. They try to appear calm and in control of the facts.

Most people when asked to profile Bill, easily identify that he is low ASSERTIVE, by the moderately directive tone of his voice. But, if one didn't observe Bill for a couple of minutes, one might think he was a SERGEANT (ASSERTIVE and CONTROL). But, Bill, a salesman by profession, leaked a little bit of inconsistency through his eyes and smile that revealed he was a SALESMAN type (ASSERTIVE and EXPRESS).

There isn't one pat way that leakage occurs. To spot a break, you must simply be observant. With experience, spotting breaks in consistency becomes second nature. While not all breaks in the consistency of a person's actions will indicate a specific trait, they should be noted. So if a person's persona seems to indicate that a person is NONASSERTIVE, and then a demonstrative ASSERTIVE action surfaces, it is wise to test your first read and reexamine the NONASSERTIVE and ASSERTIVE actions you observe in that person.

As explained in Chapter 4, a principle to remember when observing leakage is that people can restrain something they have, but usually can't manufacture something they don't have. In the case of Bill, he *restrained* his EXPRESS trait to be believed—just the facts, please. Usually when leakage occurs it's when someone has restrained their actual trait.

Lastly, as suggested in Chapter 6, you can make a second read of the other COMMUNICATION type trait, identify Bill's type, and then compare type actions. In Bill's case, we would read his ASSERTIVE–NONASSERTIVE trait, and when we see he is low ASSERTIVE, we compare the SERGEANT (CONTROL) and SALESMAN (EXPRESS) actions. It helps us confirm that Bill is EXPRESS when we see his SALESMAN type actions are a match.

2. Two Quick Strategies to Test Reads

Opposite assumptions. Let's assume you think someone is EXPRESS. Quickly form opposite assumptions about your read, such as: If my read is accurate, he will probably show some emotion when we talk about the new project, but if he's CONTROL, he may be restrained as he thinks through the strategic elements.

Here's an example if you profiled someone as ASSERTIVE: If my read is accurate, he may be forceful when presenting his ideas to win me over, but if he's NONASSERTIVE, he will be more reserved to give me space to consider the options.

Creating opposite assumptions gives you another way to quickly test your reads, in addition to using the type safety check (Chapter 6).

Would your extreme examples for your gauges do *that*? Another quick strategy is to simply ask yourself: Can I see Jim Carrey doing that? Can I see Queen Elizabeth doing that, or whoever you use for the extremes of your gauges. Often, it makes the trait jump out, and can be used instantly without distracting you from the task at hand or the person in front of you.

3. Past Behavior: Best Predictor of Future Behavior

Most of us are creatures of habit. We prefer to operate in the same way we have in the past because it's comfortable. People don't usually jump from extreme EXPRESS one day and then extreme CONTROL the next, unless they are confronted with a potentially life-changing experience as per Rule #1 for systematic accuracy: *People typically act in consistent, similar ways called traits.* This common sense idea, which has been quantified through psychological testing, can be put to immediate use when reading people.

We can make rapid-fire reads by looking at how someone dealt with a situation in the past, especially if there was some stress involved. This is one way it's possible to profile people before we meet them, a concept we'll look at in detail in Chapters 16 and 17. This is especially useful if you have to negotiate, lead, present, or sell to people you've never met. This principle is also a key to conducting successful behavioral interviews when hiring staff (Chapter 16).

4. Under Pressure, Our Actual Traits are Typically Revealed

Similar to what we just covered in Tip #3, under pressure our actual traits typically come out. Yes, we may mature, become wiser, and so forth, but the style of how we communicate and perform will typically remain the same. For most of us, when change does occur it usually manifests itself in whether we use the positive or negative actions associated with our traits.

In the example of Bill, who thought he was healed by the psychic surgeon, when pressure was injected into the situation by asking, *would your doctor say that you were healed?*, Bill expressed emotion, which he had tried to restrain in order to be believed.

Now let's link two concepts together: (1) people typically show their actual traits under pressure. (2) past actions are the best predictor of future actions.

One of the most reliable reads we can make is to identify how someone dealt with a *stressful* situation in the *past*. Here are some practical reads to identify how someone dealt with a stressful situation in the past:

- During a downsizing, merger, or acquisition.
- How criticism was received (both justifiable and unjustifiable); how criticism was presented to another person.
- How someone adapted to stressful change; how someone initiated stressful change.
- How someone reacted when confronted; how someone reacted when he had to initiate confrontation.
- How someone worked under a deadline; how someone reacted to others when he was the initiator or presenter of a deadline.
- Response to a negative report; how he presented a negative report.

An exception to how people respond to pressure are past or present life-changing or life-threatening pressure/stress. Anyone can step out of character when their existence or daily life is in jeopardy. Death threats, for example, can elicit very strong EXPRESS actions even from someone who is strong CONTROL. Or, challenging a person's moral fiber can temporarily elicit strong ASSERTIVE actions from someone who is NONASSERTIVE. Examples of positive and negative sources of stress that can elicit uncharacteristic actions include: divorce, unexpected promotion or recognition, moving, public humiliation, loss of job, death of a family member or friend, and so on.

In a team environment, it's possible to use this principle and pool reads by team members to develop profiles, explained in more detail in Chapter 16 to achieve objectives swiftly, efficiently, and sensitively.

5. First Reads Can Be Productive

When we first meet people, there is often a little bit of pressure and discomfort because it is the first time we have interacted with them. In other words, there may be some pressure or awkwardness due to uncertainty. That's why reads we make of people within the first few minutes of interaction often reveal their traits.

For example, let's assume Eric's first independent comment when you meet is a question about your *feelings* on an issue. Because he asked about your feelings, rather than about your *perspective* (which is how a CONTROL person is more likely to ask the same question), your first hunch might be that Eric is EXPRESS. Then, if you asked Eric a question about *his feelings* on the same issue, and he provides a descriptive, personal response, you are closer to concluding that he is EXPRESS.

Your first read might be very different if Eric asks you a question to control the interaction. Then your hunch might be he is ASSERTIVE—that he tried to assert himself and direct the conversation. In either case, the initial observation can produce hunches that can be quickly tested, providing a more reliable read of Eric's traits.

6. People Can Learn Actions Outside Actual Trait or Type

A famous journalist, noted for her strong ASSERTIVE trait, once quipped about herself, "I got wide hips by learning to ask a question and not stepping on a person's answer. I learned not to intrude on a person's thoughts. When I was less experienced, I wanted to finish their statements for them."

Related to her traits, this journalist was saying: I learned an action that isn't naturally a part of who I am. In this case, a reporter with a strong ASSERTIVE trait, learned three NONASSERTIVE actions: to be agreeable and genuinely inquisitive when asking people about their opinions and thoughts, and to use restraint so they could answer the question.

Many of us can learn and master an action or two that is outside of our trait and type inventory of actions. It may not come naturally, but with practice we can do something that is uncomfortable for us. Some can acquire their actions through formalized training, while others do so through practice and sheer will.

One remarkable example is the story of a friend who, as a young entertainer, possessed a strong NONASSERTIVE trait. He also stuttered. Yet, he had a strong desire to become an effective communicator, and he knew that he had to overcome his stuttering and his natural desire to resist being directive. So what did he do? He took a job as a disc jockey for a low watt radio station! He reasoned that if he put himself under enough pressure, he could find a way to develop some directive actions and overcome his stuttering. He succeeded, and today he is an effective communicator for a national prison ministry speaking to and encouraging tens of thousands of inmates each year.

It's good to know that people can learn an action or two that isn't in their type when we're puzzled by actions that don't fit their profile. This is one reason why we take more than one read and test our reads, which reinforces Rule #3 for systematic accuracy: *Anything worth measuring once is worth measuring at least twice.* While it's unlikely you'll daily be confronted with the learned action factor, it's wise to make a second read so you aren't needlessly baffled or confused.

For the astute profiler, this raises the question: How can I tell the difference between leakage of a trait and a learned action? That is, how can I know the difference between a break in consistency that reveals a person's actual trait versus a learned action? The answer is experience. Taking more than one read, and testing your reads. Here's an example of two famous people who each learned a specific action.

Will the Real ASSERTIVE and NONASSERTIVE Please Step Forward?

Mike Wallace, the noted journalist for TV's *60 Minutes*, conducted a fascinating interview in 1995 with Radovan Karadzic, then the Serbian leader in Bosnia who later was captured as a war criminal. Both men are high ASSERTIVE, yet both displayed NONASSERTIVE actions by mastering specific actions to restrain their actual trait. By taking more than one read, however, the necessary leakage appeared that would enable you to profile each man with precision.

Mike Wallace, to the casual observer, was moderately NONASSERTIVE because of his ability to ask questions in an inquiring style. However, at one point, Karadzic asked Wallace: "Who did more damage during WWII? Hitler or the Allies?"

In response, Wallace responded: "Damage to property. No doubt. The Allies. Of human life. No doubt. Hitler."

Wallace's language and tone in response to Karadzic's question were clearly ASSERTIVE. When he said, no doubt, he sharply snapped his chin down and a strong forceful gaze emanated from his eyes at Karadzic.

Karadzic, a psychiatrist before the Bosnian-Serb war, clearly showed his ability to portray someone who was NONASSERTIVE, which he probably cultivated as a psychiatrist. Before he posed his question to Wallace, he softly asked the following question with his head slightly tilted and without the least whisper of the ASSERTIVE trait: "May I ask you a question?"

Clearly, he had mastered the agreeable and inquisitive action of a NONASSERTIVE person, although the rest of the interview indicated a strong ASSERTIVE person.

If you only made one read of each man when their learned NONASSERTIVE actions were employed, your reads would have been inaccurate.

As already discussed, while people can restrain their ASSERTIVE or EXPRESS traits, it's not common for people who are NONASSERTIVE or CONTROL to learn ASSERTIVE or EXPRESS actions. Learned actions, however, are more likely the *lower* their actual trait or when there is an imperative that affects them daily, like Mike Wallace asking questions with a NONASSERTIVE tone to improve the quality of his interviews. When they do use an action *outside* their trait (or type), though, is it usually for *short spans of time* or in very specific contexts as it is still disquieting and even irritating for them. Why?

Because *people typically act in consistent, similar ways called traits*— Rule #1.

7. Unobtrusive Reads to Increase Accuracy

One way to increase the accuracy of your reads is to use unobtrusive reads. Unobtrusive reads are made in the background or indirectly, like when parents want to know more about their child's friends. Rather than directly asking the child, wise parents find opportunities to observe their child's friends inconspicuously, like at a party or a school event.

If you walk up to someone and ask, "Do you control or express your emotions when you communicate?" you're not likely to receive a transparent answer. In fact, the person himself might not be able to articulate an answer because he has never thought about his profile.

Or, if you ask someone, "Did you express or control your emotions during the last merger?" it's risky whether you'll get a reliable answer. The person might respond with the answer he thinks will best serve himself, or an answer you want to hear, or he may not remember at all. Here are some suggestions for making unobtrusive reads.

Past history—A simple unobtrusive read is to find out how a person responded to a past situation. This can be done by making inquiries of others, or even dialoguing with that person about a past situation. More is provided on making background information reads in Chapters 16 and 17.

Observing someone in the background—A common hiring practice is for a potential candidate to travel for several days with a few of his future colleagues. Rather than solely relying upon an interview process, management can make unobtrusive reads by observing how the candidate responds when he is on the street with those who carry out the same responsibilities. During interviews, people can put on a "game-face," but in the field with potential peers, this usually gets stripped away. This unobtrusive process is beneficial to both management and the candidate so that he isn't hired for a position that isn't a fit.

Nonthreatening, open-ended questions or request—There are many courses which teach how to use questions or requests that allow people to be themselves more naturally when they respond. For those not familiar with open-ended questions and requests, here are some examples counter-pointed with closed-ended examples.

- Do you remember what happened last night?
  Closed: What happened at 6:00 p.m.?
- How do you feel about it?
  Closed: Tell me what you think about the merger.
- How about helping us?
  Closed: Please review that stack of reports.

The following is an example of how to adapt open-ended questions and requests to profiling.

This is your first meeting with Don, who just emerged from battling rush-hour traffic. Not only was he nearly hit by two rude drivers, one of whom drove a red truck, but he is also late for your meeting. He apologizes to you while simultaneously expressing quite a bit of emotion with what appears to be a strong EXPRESS trait. Then, two of his colleagues, Rick and Mary, enter your office.

Here's a simple, nonthreatening and open-ended question/request you could toss to Don: *Don, tell Rick and Mary what all you had to do just to get here this morning.*

This allows Don the freedom to retell his morning traffic story to his colleagues, and you can see if he uses an EXPRESS trait, which allows you to test your first read. If he uses the same trait with a similar degree of intensity, you will know that Don is probably EXPRESS.

Notice your request is indirect. You ask Don to recall his experience for his colleagues, which allows you to observe Don more unobtrusively than if you simply asked him a question directly or made a direct request.

Also, notice the language used is open-ended. The request isn't: *Tell them about the guy in the red truck who pulled in front of you.* Rather, *Tell Rick and Mary what all you had to do just to get here this morning.*

The words *what all* are open-ended. (This conversational phrase, while not the Queen's English, is one of the most effective phrases I've encountered. It was taught to me by Dr. Margaret Singer, one of my mentors.) The phrase gives Don space to choose how to retell his morning drive experience and allows him to be himself. He can talk about the guy in the red pickup, or he might recall a similar incident the week before and how he reacted.

Indirect questions and requests that use open-ended language allow people to more naturally and unobtrusively be themselves. The dialogue doesn't force Don to respond with specific facts or subjective observations in a specific manner. He can express himself as he chooses, which allows his traits to emerge.

Reading people up and down the "corporate ladder"—When making unobtrusive reads, it's important to recognize the "position" of the person you are profiling. Logically, if Joy is addressing a superior in her organization or most any setting she uses the NONASSERTIVE side of her range as a sign of respect. And if Joy is addressing subordinates, she will use the ASSERTIVE side of her range. This is an important factor to take into consideration when identifying the strength of someone's trait.

8. Environment and Time: Does It Affect Actions?

As explained in Chapter 4, people operate within a range, and not at a specific plot on a gauge. People can move from one end of their range to the other, depending upon whether they are at the office or at home, or if they are talking to management or those down the corporate ladder.

Let's assume Ted is an executive who is a SERGEANT type. He is also moderately ASSERTIVE—about a 2. At work because of the high-stress demands of his job, he often operates at about 3, but at home he is comfortable at about 1—where he doesn't feel compelled to use his ASSERTIVE trait. He may even appear NONASSERTIVE if he's tired or in a social environment where he is restraining his trait.

If you first meet Ted and his wife for dinner at their house, and later you unexpectedly do business with Ted, it's wise to reassess your read of Ted based upon his professional environment. At home, for example, you may find his SERGEANT actions, such as assertive, takes charge, and influential, are less pronounced than when you meet him at his office.

Because environment can affect the end of the range where a person prefers to operate, it's common to take job candidates to lunch or play a round of tennis—a completely different setting—so their full range can be observed.

Actions changing over time—The plot point for most people remains consistent. If, however, someone takes on a new responsibility or is placed in an environment that requires them to operate at one side of his range, over time, they can move their plot point, but this usually requires a few years to occur. For example, if Angela's plot point is 2 NONASSERTIVE and she is in a work environment that forces her to operate at 1 to be effective, over time she may actually move to low ASSERTIVE.

Another common sense reason why a person may shift is if they experience a life-changing situation. Some experts estimate that as many as 20% of US adults are currently going through some kind of plot-point change. A 2003 study by researchers at the University of Berkeley, California, for example, of over 130,000 people, ages 21–60, clearly demonstrated that our traits do change over time as we get older.[1]

What I can share from a practical perspective is that people tend to become *less* ASSERTIVE and EXPRESS the older they get because it requires energy to use these traits! In other words, an ASSERTIVE person will become less ASSERTIVE and a NONASSERTIVE person will become even more NONASSERTIVE. Or, an EXPRESS person will become less EXPRESS and those who are CONTROL become more CONTROL. I have also observed that as people age, the healthier they are physically and the happier they are in life generally, the *less likely* this shift will occur. And, if the shift does occur, it will be less pronounced.

Regarding the other two traits, which are explained in the next chapter, people tend to be more CONVENTIONAL the older they get because doing and adapting to things that are different, more UNCONVENTIONAL, also requires more energy. Regarding the CONFIDENT-CAUTIOUS/FEARFUL, age doesn't seem to have an impact, unless a person becomes infirm, and then people tend to move toward CAUTIOUS/FEARFUL.

Over the next decade or so, I believe that the number of people whose plot points will change will increase in the US (and in many other countries) as the deteriorating social pressures of the past thirty years persist, causing sustained upheaval in individual lives, as well as the constant changes in the workplace and technology. For this reason, I recommend that those in leadership positions semi-annually review the profiles of those in their organizations.

9. Learn to Read Your Opposite Traits and Types

Most people have difficulty reading people who are the *opposite* of their trait or type. For example, ARTISTS have trouble reading SERGEANTS. Those who are EXPRESS struggle reading those who are CONTROL, as shown below in ILLUSTRATION 1. The obvious reason for this is that we don't understand as clearly what we are not. We don't live in the other person's shoes. How often do we hear spouses or those in opposite work groups, such as sales and audit, voice the complaint: *They're just different. I don't understand them.*

Illustration 1

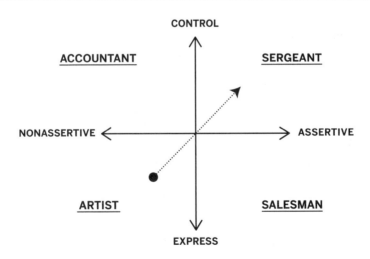

Logically, if reading our opposites is where we're most likely to struggle, we should consciously focus on reading those who have our opposite traits and types.

Have someone who is your opposite help you read your opposite traits or types—When first learning to profile, be sure to find someone who is your opposite *type* to assist you. For example, if you are an ARTIST type, find a friend who you are iron-clad certain is a SERGEANT type—who doesn't share your NONASSERTIVE or EXPRESS trait. Ask him to tell you about his thought process. How he reacts to situations. Ask him to describe how other colleagues and friends, who are also SERGEANTS types, think and deal with people and situations. Ask for both positive and negative examples. Have him point out other people who are SERGEANTS types, and see if you can spot their specific SERGEANT traits and actions.

If you only struggle with one of the traits, find someone who you are absolutely certain is that trait and ask him to assist you as you read others.

Have someone who is your opposite help you on a team—One of the quickest ways to develop competency in an organization is to have your opposite type work with you on projects, review presentations, counseling a client, teaching a student, or assisting in your local fund raiser.

Learn how your opposite responds to you—Have the person assisting you explain how various people who are your opposites respond to you. Have them point out a variety of situations. It's amazing how quickly they will help you understand the impact you have on others.

One of the wisest tips in this book—Dave Sullivan worked for several of the finest American companies during his career. He was the first sales manager to have his entire sales team and their technical counterparts trained how to use the *KPS* to improve customer service as well as sales. He shared an insight that I personally use often, and it goes like this:

If you're having difficulty reading a particular person,
start with the assumption that he or she is your *opposite*.

There are other reasons for misreads, explained in Chapter 11, but failure to profile one's opposite is one of the most common, and strangely, by following Dave's advice, one of the easiest to correct.

While asking for assistance from those who are your opposite type is a must, you can also ask someone who *shares* one of your traits what they like about someone who is your opposite type. For example, if you are a SERGEANT you might ask Ashley, a SALESMAN, what she likes about Pete, an ARTIST, and why she can connect with Pete. Since you and Ashley both have the ASSERTIVE trait, it might be easier for her to explain to you in a way you can understand how to navigate Pete's EXPRESS trait.

Applying the Profiling Tips

The following story illustrates how the tips in this chapter can be practically applied. It is based upon an actual case in which Jack, a sales consultant, was able to profile that Diane, the president of a prominent company, was a SERGEANT. Each tip that was applied is noted in brackets as well as the trait that was revealed or suspected.

Jack was first introduced to Diane at a benefit-sponsored tennis match. Jack couldn't initially tell if Diane was NONASSERTIVE or ASSERTIVE, as Diane seemed pleasantly at ease. [Tip #8 Environment affects actions]

During the match, Jack and Diane agree to discuss a new equipment line her company might be interested in purchasing. A follow-up meeting was set.

A week before the meeting, Jack received a letter from Diane in which she wrote, "As you prepare for our meeting, be sure to focus on how your equipment can help us meet our bottom line productivity issues." [ASSERTIVE; directive language]

Jack is also informed by a noncompetitive vendor that Diane is forceful when negotiating contracts. [ASSERTIVE; Tip #3 Past behavior best predictor of future behavior]

Upon entering Diane's office, she firmly meets Jack's eye, and, without fanfare, invites him to sit down. [ASSERTIVE/CONTROL; Tip #5 First reads productive]

Still standing, Diane warmly asks, "Can I fix you a cup of coffee?" pointing to her personal coffee maker on the back corner of her credenza. [Tip #6 Learned action]

Jack politely refuses and they get down to business.

A few minutes later, they are interrupted by an intercom request from Diane's assistant. Diane must take a time-sensitive call.

"Look, I told you we'll not back off from opening the Central European market. Now follow through," she tells her caller. [ASSERTIVE/CONTROL; Tip #4 Under pressure traits are revealed, and Tip #7 Unobtrusive reads—Jack indirectly observed Diane, confirming his initial reads]

As you can see, it's wise to make these tips a permanent part of your understanding when you profile. Be sure to review the tips in this chapter as you learn the last two traits, PERFORMANCE types, and the COMPREHENSIVE profiles. And, as suggested at the beginning of the chapter, review the exercises you completed in the previous chapters and see if you can sharpen or even correct reads you made of others by applying the concepts you have just learned.

Now let's learn the last two points on your profiling compass—the CONFIDENT-CAUTIOUS/FEARFUL and CONVENTIONAL-UNCONVENTIONAL gauges.

A TWIST ON CEMENTING RELATIONSHIPS

During a book signing, a gregarious chap, whose extended family were members of a notorious crime family, told me his relatives had a different take on *treating people right the first time.*

"I told my family that I like to get to know people I sell to, so I show clients pictures of my family. But, they told me, 'Johnny, if you really want the big deals, show your clients pictures of *their* family. Capiche?"

CHAPTER 8

WIRES #3 & #4
CONFIDENT-CAUTIOUS/FEARFUL
CONVENTIONAL-UNCONVENTIONAL

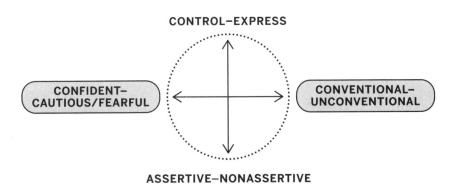

CONTROL–EXPRESS

CONFIDENT–CAUTIOUS/FEARFUL

CONVENTIONAL–UNCONVENTIONAL

ASSERTIVE–NONASSERTIVE

You've learned the first two wires/questions/gauges which identify how a person prefers to communicate. In this chapter, you'll learn the two PERFORMANCE wires/gauges which identify a person's walk. They are:

1. Is this person confident or cautious/fearful when making decisions?
2. Does a person prefer to be conventional or unconventional when performing tasks?

Practical applications include:

• Identify who should be presented more or fewer options (sales, negotiations, instruction).
• Identify who is and isn't resistant to change (leading teams or individuals).
• Reduce cancellation of appointments (sales, appointment secretaries).
• Identify who needs more or less structured follow-up (medicine, instructors, team leaders).

• Increase accuracy for detecting truthfulness (just about anyone, including investigators and mothers!).

Once you've learned how to use these gauges, you'll have almost all the tools necessary to identify someone's COMPREHENSIVE profile (Chapter 12). In the next chapter you'll learn how to combine the PERFORMANCE gauges to identify PERFORMANCE types.

WIRE/QUESTION/GAUGE #3
CONFIDENT OR CAUTIOUS/FEARFUL?
Is this person typically confident or cautious/fearful when making decisions?

Wire/question/gauge #3, shown in ILLUSTRATION 1, is the "confidence" gauge, and it's the only wire that has three plot points that must be considered—from confident to cautious to extreme fearful. The reason one side of the wire is called CAUTIOUS/FEARFUL is because cautious is just a "little fearful."

Illustration 1

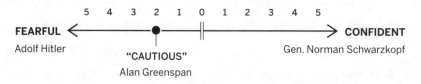

This wire helps identify how confident people are when they typically make decisions, including: Who needs more or less time to process a decision. Who needs more support, coaching, and training before making decisions. Who is decisive and who is most likely to second-guess decisions. Who should lead and who should follow. And, to the extreme, 5 FEARFUL, who displays paranoia. At a plot point of 4–5 FEARFUL people typically don't feel in control of their lives and generally act on the assumption that most events in their lives are outside of their control or are heavily influenced by external factors that dictate their personal success or failure.

They often take little responsibility or ownership for events in their work, family, or social settings.

Before you learn how to use the gauge, there are four important concepts you must first recognize.

1. Why three points?—This gauge has more complexity than the other three you've learned because it has three spots on the wire to identify someone's traits. They are: confident, cautious, and extreme fearful (paranoia).

This wire has three key points so we can accurately read the degree of fear people have on the CAUTIOUS/FEARFUL side. Those who are at 0–3 are cautious, over 3 are fearful, and 5 is full-blown fear or paranoia. The paranoia may be just extreme fear or a diagnosable condition, such as paranoid schizophrenia. Also, a person who is about 4 fearful might spike out to 5 due to a stressor.

2. Decisions *separate* from competency—What we are looking for is how people make day-to-day decisions *separate* from their area of competency. This is their core decision-making trait.

Someone may be gifted in the arts or well trained in engineering, but we want to know how people make decisions separate from their giftedness or area in which they've been trained. We want to identify how people make everyday decisions, like buying a car, ordering off a menu, tackling a new project, or choosing which class to take.

A common misread is to assume because a person is confident "on the job" he'll be just as confident when a new project is presented. If his core trait is cautious, though, that's what will pop out—cautious decision making. That's why we need to read the core trait separate from competency. Conversely, if someone is cautious, but trained to develop expertise, he can perform confidently.

3. The moral and protective factor—Another consideration is how people make moral decisions may or may not to be reflective of how they make daily decisions. Moral decisions are a reflection of character. People who are on either side of the wire can refuse to drink excessively, ingest illegal drugs, honestly report their taxes, or decide to tell the truth.

Some people drink excessively to numb their emotional pain. It's a common indicator they may be a fearful decision maker. Others, though, who are confident decision makers, may also drink to excess.

Related to protective factors, we have to be careful we aren't making a read based upon a protective survival decision, like the fear of being burned or shot, or losing one's family. Any profile may take protective action and make a quick decision or be paralyzed by fear. Other examples are: fear before major surgery; fear of an uncertain future after the loss of one's spouse; fear of rejection while waiting for a letter of acceptance to a university.

4. No positive actions when 5 FEARFUL—The only point on any of the four wires where there aren't any positive actions is 5 FEARFUL—it's an inherently negative plot point. For the other three gauges, any point on the wire can be used positively or negatively. It is different, however, when a person is plotted about 4 or higher on the FEARFUL side of the gauge.

There are no positive actions associated with making decisions out of extreme fear, which is paranoia. Think about it. What positive action is possible when making decisions based out of extreme fear? Adolf Hitler, Saddam Hussein, the Columbine killers, and others possessed this trait.

Although Hitler had a strong ASSERTIVE trait and could whip mass rallies into a frenzy with his forceful and ASSERTIVE communication actions, he typically made decisions out of extreme paranoia. Some examples: He perceived all ethnic groups and minorities to be a threat and sought to exterminate them; he rarely trusted the wisdom of his generals and often dismissed them, replacing their war plans with his own irrational strategies.

David Koresh, the Waco, Texas cult leader, is another example of someone who operated at the extreme end of FEARFUL. He built a tightly controlled cult compound, fanning extreme paranoia of the world amongst his followers as he molested children of cult followers. In 1993, when law enforcement closed in on the Branch Davidian cult, he directed his followers to burn down the compound, killing over eighty cult members—many were children. In the 1978, another cult leader, Jim Jones, took similar action when he directed over nine hundred and nine followers to drink Kool-Aid laced with cyanide.

Most people who have this trait, though, obviously don't kill, but they do lead troubled lives. The late Steve Jobs, the brilliant founder of Apple, is a one example. Like others who are extremely talented, they are often described as "gifted but troubled." Presently in our schools, approximately 6% of all youth have this trait.[1]

When someone is 3 or higher on the FEARFUL wire, it is possible some actions associated with paranoia will become evident. The further one moves to the end of the FEARFUL side of the gauge, the more likely negative actions will become full-blown. This raises the question: Can these people change? The answer is yes, and this issue is addressed in Chapters 9 and 15.

The CAUTIOUS plot point—People with a plot point of about 3 or less on the FEARFUL end of the gauge are cautious decision makers, which can be a positive or a negative, like the other traits.

Alan Greenspan, for example, who steered the interest rate for the Federal Reserve bank for many years, is about 1 or 2 on the FEARFUL side. He cautiously and with a little fear and trepidation carefully weighed detailed decisions before making even the smallest of moves. Air traffic controllers are another example of those who as a group operate with caution when making decisions. You don't hear directives from the tower like, "Yea, no problem flight 208, just bring that puppy in here." The tone is always careful and measured: altitude, position.

Some dentists would also qualify as they exhibit caution before drilling for oil in our teeth! ILLUSTRATION 2 shows an example of a person who is CAUTIOUS in comparison to the extreme ends of the CONFIDENT–CAUTIOUS/FEARFUL gauge.

Illustration 2

This doesn't mean all administrators in the Fed, air traffic controllers,

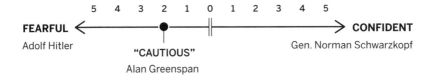

or dentists will be plotted at 3 or less on the CAUTIOUS/FEARFUL end of the gauge, rather, these are examples that can help us visualize those who have the CAUTIOUS trait. The key is to focus on how people make day-to-day decisions in nonlife-threatening or life-changing situations.

As noted in Chapter 2, when people go through life-changing or life-threatening experiences, they may or may not operate the same as they have in the past. We've all heard stories of people who are at about 2 on the CAUTIOUS/FEARFUL side of the gauge, but who act heroically to save someone's life. And we have also seen people who are usually extremely CONFIDENT, freeze up when confronted with life-changing pressure.

CONFIDENT–CAUTIOUS/FEARFUL Actions

CONFIDENT or FEARFUL actions are provided in TABLE 7 below. Note that some of the CAUTIOUS/FEARFUL actions have an asterisk. These are actions that can be used both positively or negatively and are typically present only when a person is CAUTIOUS (3 or lower FEARFUL). As was true for the COMMUNICATION traits, each of us has our own unique blend of positive and negative actions and how we use them.

Table 7

CONFIDENT Actions:	Poised, self-reliant, candid, conceited, independent, callous, durable/stable, arrogant, self-assured, determined, and action-oriented, bold, decisive
CAUTIOUS/FEARFUL Actions:	Guarded,* reserved*, measured*, restrained*, insecure, anxious, timid, unstable, envious, gullible, cowardly, passive, self-pitying, and defensive

Positive and Negative Extremes

ILLUSTRATION 3 shows positive and negative examples of the extreme ends of the CONFIDENT–CAUTIOUS/FEARFUL gauge. As already stated, there are no positive examples of people who are extremely FEARFUL (which is paranoia). If it helps, look up video and profile article examples of each on the web to assure you have a clear understanding of each extreme.

Illustration 3

Positive Extreme FEARFUL

• No Examples

Positive CAUTIOUS

• **Alan Greenspan**
(Fed who set interest rates)
• **Prince Charles**
(cautious and measured in most of his actions)
• **Air traffic controllers**
(trained to be)
• **Dentists** (some)

Positive Extreme CONFIDENT

• **Russell Crowe** (in *Gladiator*)
• **Oprah Winfrey**
• **General Norman Schwarzkopf**
• **Winston Churchill**
• **Martin Luther King**

Negative Extreme FEARFUL

• **Adolf Hitler**
(paranoid dictator)
• **David Koresh**
(cult leader)
• **Columbine killers**
• **Some people who have extreme phobias**

Negative Extreme CONFIDENT

• **Brash radio talk show hosts**
• **Arrogant athletes**

Personalizing Your CONFIDENT–FEARFUL Gauge

After studying the positive and negative examples, personalize the CONFIDENT–CAUTIOUS/FEARFUL gauge in ILLUSTRATION 4 with your choices for the positive and negative extremes as well as the CAUTIOUS plot point (remember, there isn't an example of a person who is *positive* extreme FEARFUL). As you did with the first two gauges, if there is someone that you personally know that you would like to use as an example, be sure this person expresses his/her trait with the same degree of intensity as the examples provided. Then plot yourself on the gauge.

Illustration 4

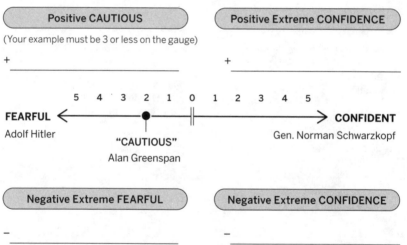

Helpful CONFIDENT–FEARFUL Questions

If you have difficulty selecting which end of the gauge you tilt toward, ask yourself the following questions:

1. Do I prefer to initiate actions? (CONFIDENT)
2. Do I prefer to let others take the lead? (CAUTIOUS/FEARFUL)
3. Do I prefer to act to take control of my circumstances? (CONFIDENT)
4. Do most things just happen to me as a result of events that are outside of my own control? (CAUTIOUS/FEARFUL)

5. Do I make decisions confidently? (CONFIDENT)

6. Am I usually hesitant and somewhat fearful when making decisions and taking action—and second-guess my decisions? (CAUTIOUS/FEARFUL)

If you are tempted to plot yourself in the center, remember: most people can be plotted on one of the two sides of the gauge. If necessary, ask a trusted friend for insight. Together, review the CONFIDENT and CAUTIOUS/FEARFUL actions and discuss the specific actions you have displayed.

Extreme and Nonextreme Examples of CONFIDENT–CAUTIOUS/FEARFUL

Most people aren't the extreme of CONFIDENT–FEARFUL, but fall between the center and one of the extremes. To help you visualize the difference between extreme and non-extreme examples, some positive and negative examples of each are provided in TABLE 8.

Table 8

Extreme Examples

Positive CONFIDENT: Hard-charging coach.

Negative CONFIDENT: Arrogant tycoon.

Positive FEARFUL: None.

Negative FEARFUL: Manager who is unjustifiably paranoid of those around him.

Nonextreme Examples

Positive CONFIDENT: Leader who exudes quiet confidence.

Negative CONFIDENT: Slightly cocky athlete.

Positive CAUTIOUS: Operator of a "fail-safe" system for a nuclear warhead or barge operator who navigates channels cautiously.

Negative FEARFUL: Bureaucrat who avoids making a decision when a decision is necessary.

Assignment 6

Goal: Learn to use the CONFIDENT–CAUTIOUS/FEARFUL gauge.
Time Required: 30 minutes.

On the spaces provided in ILLUSTRATION 5, plot six people you know. Think of people who can be plotted on the CONFIDENT side of the wire, those who can be plotted at 4 or higher on the FEARFUL side of the gauge, and those who are 3 or lower on the CAUTIOUS/FEARFUL side. Consider the positive and negative actions for each in TABLE 7.

Illustration 5

Name	CONFIDENT–CAUTIOUS/FEARFUL	Plot Point

#1 _____

#2 _____

#3 _____

#4 _____

#5 _____

#6 _____

You're now ready to learn the last wire: CONVENTIONAL–UNCONVENTIONAL.

WIRE/QUESTION/GAUGE #4
CONVENTIONAL OR UNCONVENTIONAL?
Does a person prefer to be conventional or unconventional
when performing tasks?

Wire #4 shown in ILLUSTRATION 6 helps us to determine if a person's actions are generally conventional or unconventional. It helps us identify how people prefer to use their assets and skills.

Illustration 6

Queen Elizabeth II exemplifies the CONVENTIONAL side of the gauge as she conducts her office bound by traditions with consistency and uniformity. In movies, John Wayne portrayed the dependable and reliable sheriff. The UNCONVENTIONAL side of the gauge is characterized by actions that are spontaneous, random, novel, and unconventional. People on this end of the gauge can range from unconventionally creative to rebellious and reckless. This side of the gauge also gives us a measure of a person's tendency to act outside the norms of a given situation.

The brilliant scientist, Albert Einstein, often displayed this trait, even forgetting to wear socks at awards ceremonies in which he was attired in a tuxedo. Comics Jim Carrey and Bill Cosby are examples of those who operate "way out of the box." Hitler, Saddam Hussein, and David Koresh, however, exemplified the extreme negative of this trait, displayed through their vacillating, violent, and explosive actions.

(For those who are familiar with the first edition of this book, you will note that the terms "predictable" and "unpredictable" have been replaced with CONVENTIONAL and UNCONVENTIONAL for this gauge. This was done for added clarity, as explained in the Source Notes.)[2]

TABLE 9 lists common positive and negative actions associated with the CONVENTIONAL–UNCONVENTIONAL gauge. You'll notice that people who are UNCONVENTIONAL find it a little bit easier to "get themselves into trouble" because of their freewheeling nature while also filling our lives with wonder and amazement.

Table 9

CONVENTIONAL Actions:	Organized, staid, reliable, rigid, dependable, precise, stuffy, persistent, formal, punctual, consistent, predictable, logical, industrious, orderly, self-disciplined, and bureaucratic
UNCONVENTIONAL Actions:	Spontaneous,* impulsive,* random, creative, aimless, reckless, negligent, imaginative, unpredictable, inconsistent, frivolous, surprising, novel, forgetful, nonconforming, undisciplined, rebellious, irreverent, intemperate, quirky, freewheeling, and anarchistic

*Note: Spontaneous and impulsive often are used by psychologists as both a positive and negative action. I recommend using *spontaneous* when there is some reasoning or logic behind one's actions while *impulsive* is when there is no rational thought process to back-up one's actions.

Positive and Negative Extremes of the CONVENTIONAL–UNCONVENTIONAL Gauge

ILLUSTRATION 7 provides negative and positive examples of the extreme ends of the CONVENTIONAL–UNCONVENTIONAL gauge. You'll notice, though, there aren't any specific examples of notable people who are negative extreme CONVENTIONAL. These people typically have the same notoriety as those who are negative extreme NONASSERTIVE: they rarely distinguish themselves. The "entrenched bureaucrat" is an example of this person whom we all have engaged that most people can immediately visualize.

As you review the examples provided, consider the specific positive and negative actions each person uniquely possesses from those listed in TABLE 7. For example, while John Wayne's persona in the movies could best be described as one of dependability, Queen Elizabeth might best be characterized by punctual and conventional. As previously suggested, find video and profile article examples of each to ensure you have a clear understanding of each extreme.

Illustration 7

Positive Extreme CONVENTIONAL

- John Wayne
- Queen Elizabeth II
- Jeb Bush
  (Governor of Florida)
- President Dwight Eisenhower
- Condaleeza Rice
  (Sec. of State—public persona)

Positive Extreme UNCONVENTIONAL

- Albert Einstein
  (often forgot to wear his socks)
- Whoopi Goldberg
  (comedienne and actress)
- Jim Carrey
  (zany comic/actor)
- Howie Mandel
  (comedian and TV host)

5 4 3 2 1 0 1 2 3 4 5

CONVENTIONAL ⟵————————⟶ UNCONVENTIONAL

Negative Extreme CONVENTIONAL

- Entrenched Bureaucrat

Negative Extreme UNCONVENTIONAL

- Adolf Hitler
  (moody and always vacillating)
- Saddam Hussein
  (Iraqi dictator)
- Howard Stern
  (as irreverant radio talk show host)
- Dennis Rodman
  (professional basketball player)

Personalizing the CONVENTIONAL–UNCONVENTIONAL Gauge

After studying the extreme examples in ILLUSTRATION 7, personalize the extreme ends of the CONVENTIONAL–UNCONVENTIONAL gauge in ILLUSTRATION 8 with your choices. Then plot yourself on the gauge. If you have ambiguity regarding on which side of the gauge you should be plotted, review the questions that below.

Illustration 8

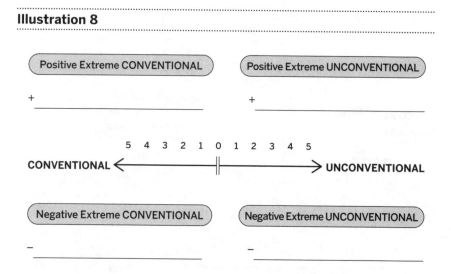

Helpful CONVENTIONAL–UNCONVENTIONAL Questions

1. Would most of my friends describe me as fairly conventional? (CONVENTIONAL)

2. Would most of my friends describe me as fairly unconventional? (UNCONVENTIONAL)

3. Am I usually consistent in how I handle situations and tasks? (CONVENTIONAL)

4. Am I typically imaginative and/or creative in how I handle situations and tasks? (UNCONVENTIONAL)

5. Do I resist change, even when it is needed? (CONVENTIONAL)

6. Do I welcome needed change? (UNCONVENTIONAL)

7. Do I resist spontaneity? (CONVENTIONAL)

8. Do I enjoy being spontaneous? (UNCONVENTIONAL)

9. Do I prefer to operate out of the box? Is it more comfortable to *be* outside the box? (UNCONVENTIONAL)

Extreme and Nonextreme Examples of CONVENTIONAL–UNCONVENTIONAL

TABLE 10 provides both extreme and non-extreme examples of the CONVENTIONAL-UNCONVENTIONAL traits.

Table 10

Extreme Examples

Positive CONVENTIONAL:	Winston Churchill in his defense of England during the Battle of Britain.
Negative CONVENTIONAL:	Bureaucrat who adamantly resists positive change.
Positive UNCONVENTIONAL:	Unconventional inventor.
Negative UNCONVENTIONAL:	Reckless leaders and cult figures, such as Adolf Hitler and David Koresh.

Nonextreme Examples

Positive CONVENTIONAL:	Dependable support personnel in a company.
Negative CONVENTIONAL:	A stuffy and staid banker.
Positive UNCONVENTIONAL:	Ad executive who adapts well to changing trends and forecasts.
Negative UNCONVENTIONAL:	Absentminded and undisciplined employee whose mind constantly wanders.

Assignment 7

Goal: Learn to use the CONVENTIONAL–UNCONVENTIONAL gauge.
Time Required: 30 minutes.

Plot six people that you know on the CONVENTIONAL–UNCONVENTIONAL gauge and write their names in the spaces provided in ILLUSTRATION 9. Be sure to include your estimate of their 1–5 plot points.

Illustration 9

Name	CONVENTIONAL or UNCONVENTIONAL	Plot Point
#1		
#2		
#3		
#4		
#5		
#6		

Using Performance Gauges in Everyday Situations

Below are some practical ways/principles for how you can use the two PERFORMANCE gauges (for additional applications see *Snapshot*) followed by cases of how people have applied them. Like other suggestions in this book, they've demonstrated consistent effectiveness, but won't necessarily apply to everyone with these traits in every situation.

When a person is FEARFUL and . . .

1. You need to be directive, use a person who is low CAUTIOUS/ FEARFUL.
2. You are providing choices, provide fewer choices.

When a person is CONFIDENT and . . .

1. You need to be directive, use a person who is more CONFIDENT.

2. You are providing choices, you can provide more choices.

When a person is CONVENTIONAL and . . .

1. You are suggesting change, be prepared for more resistance.

2. You are providing choices, can provide more as he will usually know what he wants (like banker who always wears black or gray).

When a person is UNCONVENTIONAL and . . .

1. You are suggesting change, will likely be more receptive.

2. You are providing choices, can provide more, but be prepared to spend more time as options are considered.

Here are case examples of how these concepts have been applied.

Sales—The owner of an exclusive jewelry store adapted a couple of the above suggestions in his sales process. He found it was more efficient to offer more choices to people who are CONFIDENT and fewer choices to those who are FEARFUL. He observed that customers who are FEARFUL often have a more difficult time making up their mind, shifting from one option to another. He also realized he could present more choices to people who are CONFIDENT because they are confident and they tend to expeditiously eliminate options that do not meet their needs. (He also used this strategy to determine who might take longer to service if he chose to let his customers evaluate all possible options, thus enabling him to prioritize his time more efficiently.)

The jeweler also discovered a fine nuance.

Typically, if a buyer was 3 or higher on the CONVENTIONAL gauge, he presented more choices because the buyer usually possessed a more predefined idea of what he wanted. This person's CONVENTIONAL trait could sometimes even override a FEARFUL trait and cause decision-making to be slightly more predictable. (In the next chapter you will learn that this combination of traits is called a CONFORMIST type.)

Similarly, when a buyer was UNCONVENTIONAL and CONFIDENT, he sometimes presented fewer choices because the buyer often wanted to see and consider everything—because they liked variety—before making a decision.

Keeping Appointments—Appointment secretaries in a physician's office came up with a clever plan to decrease cancellations. They focused their attention on identifying whether or not a new patient who phoned in was CONVENTIONAL or UNCONVENTIONAL. They found that those who were CONVENTIONAL were more likely to keep appointments and appear on time. Those who were UNCONVENTIONAL, however, tended to be more erratic when keeping appointments. So what did they do to reduce cancellations? They double-scheduled appointments for people who had a plot point of at least 3 UNCONVENTIONAL.

The secretaries fleshed out this trait by listening for UNCONVENTIONAL dialogue and by asking a new patient questions like: Where do you record your appointments? If the new patient airily replied, "Oh, I don't write it down, I'll just remember," then this person, who is more likely UNCONVENTIONAL, might receive a double-booking.

If, however, the patient replied with a firm response, "Oh, I always put them in my appointment book," then this person, who is more likely CONVENTIONAL, wouldn't be double-booked.

Effective Follow-up—Some Swiss doctors developed a strategy for deciding which patients should and shouldn't receive a regimented follow-up for physical therapy, taking medications, and so on. Like the secretaries in the above example, the physicians, nurses, and aides noted whether a patient was CONVENTIONAL or UNCONVENTIONAL. For patients who were observed to be UNCONVENTIONAL, their trait was noted on their charts and they were provided with a stricter and more carefully monitored regimen. Another example of: *I know who you are. Good for me, better for you.*

Acceptance of Change—A group of auditors for an international organization faced a different kind of challenge. They had to make recommendations for change in several different countries where there was typically resistance to change. So they looked for those in each organization who had the UNCONVENTIONAL trait: those who were less likely to be resistant to change. Then, they sought opportunities in which these individuals could facilitate the needed recommendations, thus increasing the chances for a successful transition.

Identifying the Truth—If you are an auditor, detective, or investigator, the ability to read a person's PERFORMANCE traits can help diminish inaccurate reads of a person's truthfulness. For example, people who are CONFIDENT can appear more convincing—when compared to those who are FEARFUL—regardless of whether or not they are telling the truth. So if you perceive someone to be CONFIDENT, be alert that the trait may fool you.

People who are FEARFUL, however, sometimes send signals which make them appear they are concealing the truth, when in fact they are simply less convincing because they are afraid. Their eyes may avoid contact. They may clear their throats. They may directly or indirectly plead with you to believe them. Additionally, a person who is FEARFUL, but who also possesses a strong ASSERTIVE trait, can be convincing in some situations.

For example, Hitler, who was FEARFUL when making decisions, utilized his strong ASSERTIVE trait to persuade Chamberlain to turn over the keys of Europe. This example illustrates the need to evaluate a person's complete trait inventory, especially in critical situations, before taking action.

Please use these suggestions cautiously, as they are only intended to point out common patterns. We must respect that people are unique and we can make mistakes, especially when first learning how to profile.

Shift in the Earth's Profile

For the first time in history, the majority of people in North America and Europe have the UNCONVENTIONAL trait. This shift is also occurring in the rest of the world, but at a slower pace.

Up until the 20th century, most people lived on farms—up to 90%—and most were CONVENTIONAL. With the injection of technology and our ability to do what we want, wherever, when, and with whomever we want, the profile has shifted to the UNCONVENTIONAL trait.

In the typical school in 1990, approximately 75% of all students were CONVENTIONAL. Almost overnight, that number has reversed with the injection of computers, cell phones, and all kinds of technologies. Today, approximately 75% of all students have the UNCONVENTIONAL trait. This has wreaked havoc in classrooms as teachers, who are CONVENTIONAL as a group, struggle to relate to and lead students. This trend has now extended into the workplace and requires completely different approaches to leading organizations.

I've written extensively about this trend and how to navigate this trend in *Snapshot*, but one of the most important guiding principles is to learn to *innovate with discipline, between the lines.* It is a value that must be heralded and taught, beginning with kids at home and at school. If this is disregarded, all you have to do is look at the negative UNCONVENTIONAL actions to be able to predict the outcome.

To navigate the shift to the UNCONVENTIONAL trait . . .
Innovate with discipline between the lines.

Assignment 8

Goal: Practice plotting people on the CONFIDENT–CAUTIOUS/FEARFUL and CONVENTIONAL–UNCONVENTIONAL gauges.

Time Required: One hour over a one-week period.

As you did with the first two gauges, plot six people from each of the groups listed on the two UNCONVENTIONAL gauges and record your observations in the spaces provided in ILLUSTRATION 10.

- Family
- Close friends
- Social acquaintances
- Work—people you work with in your organization
- Work—people outside of your organization

Now ask two insightful people whom you trust to help assess your accuracy. As with the previous major assignments, take a week to complete this assignment, as time is needed for reflection.

Illustration 10

	CONFIDENT or CAUTIOUS/FEARFUL	
Name	CONVENTIONAL or UNCONVENTIONAL	Plot Point
#1	_____	
#2	_____	
#3	_____	
#4	_____	
#5	_____	
#6	_____	

BRIEF RECAP

1. You've learned how to use the four profiling wires/gauges:
   - CONTROL–EXPRESS
   - ASSERTIVE–NONASSERTIVE
   - CONFIDENT–CAUTIOUS/FEARFUL
   - CONVENTIONAL–UNCONVENTIONAL
2. And, you've learned how to identify someone's COMMUNICATION type by combining the CONTROL–EXPRESS and ASSERTIVE–NONASSERTIVE gauges.

The shaded area in ILLUSTRATION 11 on the next page represents the steps you've have learned to develop someone's profile.

Illustration 11

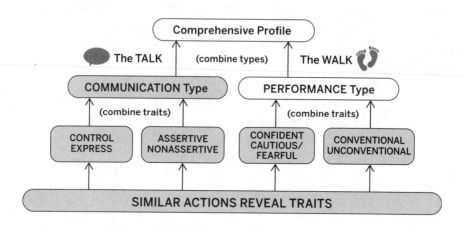

There are just two steps left, and the next is to learn how to identify PERFORMANCE types.

PROFILING ANIMALS . . .

If you aren't satisfied with an extreme example you've selected for a specific gauge, try using one of the animals I've selected below. Just be discreet if you do! Don't let on that your read is: *Is Joe more like a hippo or a gibbon?*

Elephants and Giraffes—CONTROL
Chimpanzees and the Superb Bird of Paradise—EXPRESS

Lions and Tigers—ASSERTIVE
Panda Bears and Lambs—NONASSERTIVE

Hippopotamus and Cows—CONVENTIONAL
Acrobatic Gibbon Monkeys—UNCONVENTIONAL

Lions and Orcas—CONFIDENT
Turtles and baby Monkeys—CAUTIOUS
Hyenas and wild Mustangs (when first approached)—FEARFUL

CHAPTER 9

IDENTIFYING
PERFORMANCE TYPES

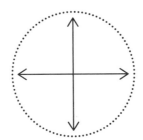

In this chapter you'll learn the next building block of the *KPS*: combining the CONFIDENT–CAUTIOUS/FEARFUL and CONVENTIONAL-UNCONVENTIONAL traits to identify a person's PERFORMANCE type, which enables us to better predict how a person is likely to perform in a given situation, tackle responsibilities, and make decisions.

You'll also notice there are *five*, not four PERFORMANCE types. The fifth type is a new addition to the *KPS*—the CAUTIOUS INNOVATOR. It's the fastest growing profile in industrialized countries and has caused much confusion in the workplace and personal encounters.

As we did with the COMMUNICATION types, the PERFORMANCE traits are placed over each other to create four quadrants and one "mini" quadrant for the CAUTIOUS INNOVATOR. Each "quadrant" is indicated by an easy to visualize identifier.

Illustration 1

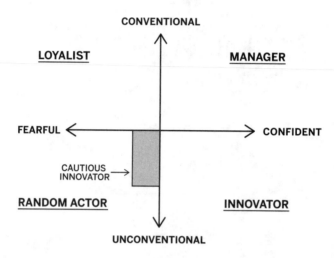

A brief summary of the traits associated with each type are:

Manager	CONFIDENT and CONVENTIONAL
Innovator	CONFIDENT and UNCONVENTIONAL
Cautious Innovator	CAUTIOUS and UNCONVENTIONAL
Loyalist	CAUTIOUS/FEARFUL and CONVENTIONAL
Random Actor	FEARFUL and UNCONVENTIONAL

You'll use the same process to identify PERFORMANCE types as you used to identify COMMUNICATION types except you'll use the PERFORMANCE traits. ILLUSTRATION 2 shows how two different MANAGER types are plotted. As we learned with the COMMUNICATION types, one of the differences between MANAGERS is the specific plot points on each gauge. This also reminds us that not all MANAGERS are alike, which retards stereotyping.

At the end of the chapter, a simple but powerful principle is explained for using types to expand the inventory of your available positive actions as well as for leadership development.

Illustration 2

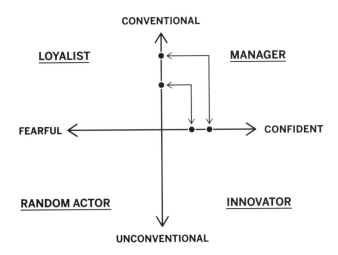

The Five Performance Types

A brief summary of each PERFORMANCE type follows and alternative identifiers are provided. Before changing identifiers, please remember that those selected have proven their mettle cross-culturally. Those familiar with *KPS* from the first edition will note that CONFORMIST has been replaced with LOYALIST as "conformist" has subtly taken on a negative connotation over the last few years.

> MANAGER—The MANAGER identifier provides a visual picture of a person who is CONFIDENT–CONVENTIONAL, like those who guide organizations. MANAGERS prefer to make decisions in methodical and standardized ways and are most comfortable in steady, predictable environments and prefer to "live within the system," which is why they're often suited to lead in an organization. Alternative identifiers are ORGANIZER, DECISION-MAKER, or LEADER. (Note: I prefer LEADER as I believe emphasis should be directed at leading, empowering, and helping people grow rather than on managing people, but at the present most still prefer MANAGER.)

INNOVATOR—The INNOVATOR identifier provides a visual picture of a person who is CONFIDENT-UNCONVENTIONAL; the idea-generator in a group or organization who will usually "try anything once." They are motivated by change and variety. The higher CONFIDENT the more likely they'll challenge situations and take risks. The higher their UNCONVENTIONAL trait, the more likely they will be viewed as "absentminded" professor types if unrestrained and undisciplined. When extreme negative actions are dominant, they can be anarchists, negligent of responsibilities, rebellious, and destructively antagonistic. Alternative identifiers are IMAGINATOR and CREATIVE SPARK PLUG.

CAUTIOUS INNOVATOR—CAUTIOUS INNOVATORS (CAUTIOUS/FEARFUL–UNCONVENTIONAL) are similar to INNOVATORS except they aren't risk takers and usually need more time to process decisions and accept change. The fastest growing profile in our culture, they are often found in creative environments that require careful application of creative skills, like graphics, design, and software development; they like change, variety, and creativity, but need more time to move ahead in an area outside of their expertise when compared to INNOVATORS. Regarding their UNCONVENTIONAL trait, it can be anywhere on the gauge, but their CAUTIOUS/FEARFUL trait is 3 or lower. An alternative identifier is CAUTIOUS IMAGINATOR.

LOYALIST—The LOYALIST identifier is a visual picture of those who are CAUTIOUS/FEARFUL–CONVENTIONAL and are typically compliant, dutiful, reliable, and obedient. LOYALISTS are usually precise and easy to direct and are team players. The down side is their sense of insecurity and fear when making decisions can instill in them an aversion to taking risks. While LOYALISTS can fit into most environments, the higher their CAUTIOUS/FEARFUL trait, the more likely they are to be viewed as somewhat nervous or uninteresting because they're motivated by a fear of failure. Alternative identifiers are SUPPORTER or SUSTAINER.

RANDOM ACTOR—The RANDOM ACTOR identifier is a visual picture of those who are FEARFUL–UNCONVENTIONAL and are typically severely troubled people. Of the COMMUNICATION and PERFORMANCE types, this is the only one that is inherently negative and has a plot point of 4 or higher on each gauge. While people with the RANDOM ACTOR traits may be imaginative/creative, they are typically troubled, unsettled, suspicious, and even volatile/destructive. This is true even if someone has various positive UNCONVENTIONAL actions, such as imaginative, because of their high fear/paranoia, which creates a combustible combination. As noted with those who have the high FEARFUL trait (4 or higher), a person might display paranoia that isn't a diagnosable condition or is a diagnosable condition like paranoid schizophrenia.

Identifying Your Performance Type

To identify your PERFORMANCE type, take your plot points from Chapter 8, plot yourself on the CONFIDENT–CAUTIOUS/FEARFUL and CONVENTIONAL–UNCONVENTIONAL gauges in ILLUSTRATION 3. Now extend a line from each plot point until the two lines intersect, and write your type in the space provided.

Illustration 3

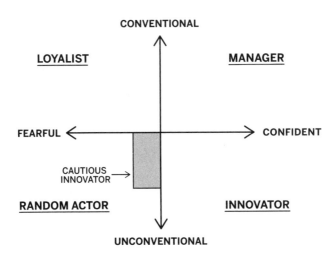

Your Type: _____

Performance Types and Associated Actions

TABLE 11 lists the possible positive and negative actions as well as "other tendencies" for each of the five PERFORMANCE types. Remember, the key word is "possible" since not every MANAGER, for example, is going to display every action or use their actions in the exact same way. Take a few minutes to familiarize yourself with this handy reference list.

Table 11

MANAGER: CONFIDENT–CONVENTIONAL

Positive Actions	Negative Actions	Other Tendencies
Organized	Bureaucratic	Predictable
Persistent	Arrogant	Logic oriented
Thrifty	Conceited	Can operate
Goal-oriented	Unyielding	independently
Decisive/Determined	Entrenched	Adapts to a system
Efficient	Compulsive	Candid
Practical/Pragmatic	"Nitpicker"/Fault-finder	Prefers to operate
Precise	Staid	within boundaries
Action oriented	Will unnecessarily	Resists change,
Stable/Dependable	defend status quo	disruption of
Logical	Micro-manages	schedules
Assumes responsibility	Conceited	Relies upon experience
Poised	Self-centered	vs. creativity to solve
Self-assured	Dismissive	problems
		Prefers challenge with
		predictable outcome
		Will initiate within
		boundaries

INNOVATOR: CONFIDENT–UNCONVENTIONAL

Positive Actions	Negative Actions	Other Tendencies
Risk-taker	Reckless	Nonconformist
Free-thinking	Anarchist	Impulsive
Creative	Frivolous	Idea driven
Self-assured	Egocentric	Needs freedom
Initiates action	Rebellious	Uninhibited
Isn't afraid of change	Aimless/Inconsistent	Motivated by change
Decisive	Antisocial	Spontaneous
Likes/Seeks challenges	Irresponsible	Operates without
Innovative	Disorganized	structure
Problem-solver	Flippant	Relies upon creativity
Independent	Forgetful	to solve problems vs.
Flexible	Undisciplined	experience
Adapts to change	Negligent	Quirky
Imaginative	Self-centered	
	Not thorough	
	Unreliable	

CAUTIOUS INNOVATOR: CAUTIOUS–UNCONVENTIONAL

Positive Actions	Negative Actions	Other Tendencies
Loyal	Aimless	Nonconformist
Manageable	Irresponsible	Uninhibited
Adapts to change[1]	Flippant	Impulsive[4]
Free-thinking	Negligent[3]	Dislikes repetitive
Dutiful[2]	Indecisive	actions
Supportive	Gullible	Guarded
Innovative	Insecure	Spontaneous[5]
Problem-solver	Fear of failure	Needs freedom
Flexible	Rebellious	Idea driven
Imaginative	Unwilling to assume	Avoids risks, ownership
Creative	blame	of problems
		Follower
		Quirky

[1] More time required to process outside area of expertise/competency

[2] More likely the lower UNCONVENTIONAL (2 or less)

[3] More likely the higher UNCONVENTIONAL (3 or higher)

[4] The higher UNCONVENTIONAL (3 or higher)

[5] More common for higher UNCONVENTIONAL and lower CAUTIOUS

Reminder: The key distinguishing characteristic differences between INNOVATORS and CAUTIOUS INNOVATORS is the latter requires more time to process decisions, accept change, and less likely to take on risk outside their area of competency.

LOYALIST: CAUTIOUS/FEARFUL–CONVENTIONAL

Positive Actions	Negative Actions	Other Tendencies
Loyal	Unquestioning	Obedient
Manageable	Subservient	Compliant
Precise	Uninteresting	Analytical
Reliable	Uncreative	Repetitive actions
Cautious	Indecisive	Guarded
Supportive	Mindless	Rule-oriented
Dutiful	Insecure	Doesn't require
Industrious	Fear of failure	challenge
Organized	Unwilling to assume	Avoids risks, ownership
Orderly	blame	of problems
	Gullible	Follower
	Neurotic (high FEARFUL)	Compulsive

RANDOM ACTOR: FEARFUL–UNCONVENTIONAL

Positive Actions	Negative Actions	Other Tendencies
Imaginative	Dangerous	Impulsive
Creative	Deceptive	Hard to read
	Anxious	Rigid/Unbending [2]
	Insecure	Dependent
	Blindly loyal [1]	Seeks protection
	Indecisive	through control
	Moody	Surprising
	Egocentric	Unpredictable
	Lack of conscience	Quirky
	Lack of empathy	Spontaneous
	Irresponsible	
	Vacillating	
	Unwilling to accept	
	responsibility	
	Self-absorbed	
	Manipulative	*(cont'd next page)*

Hot-tempered
Volatile
Antisocial
Distrusting
Undisciplined
Unreliable
Not thorough
Secretive

[1] More likely if person has NONASSERTIVE trait
[2] More likely if person has CONTROL trait

Type Reminders—As noted with the COMMUNICATION types, each PERFORMANCE type will have some of the same actions as other types that share a common trait. For example, MANAGERS and LOYALISTS both share the positive action of precise. This is because they are both CONVENTIONAL. Those who are CONVENTIONAL often prefer a semblance of order, which can translate into a desire for precision—things that predictably fit together.

Be certain to periodically review the list of descriptors for each type and how it applies to your personal or professional needs. Remember, types show the various actions people can show over time. Thus, we may not show specific type actions at a specific point in time. Also, specific action descriptors may need to be updated over time because the meaning, value, and weight of how we use specific words can change or have a different meaning in a specific culture. For example, it was necessary to replace the type identifier CONFORMIST with LOYALIST because in our high UNCONVENTIONAL world CONFORMIST had taken on a negative ring in many cultures. Similarly, the trait identifier NONASSERTIVE in some communities in Ohio is used to designate someone who is weak, rather than who is pleasingly agreeable. If you're working with a group of people who are considering the type actions and one action causes confusion, replace it with a similar word.

Assignment 9

Goal: Identify the possible actions for your own type.
Time Required: 30 minutes.

Find your type and read over the list of actions. Then, check off the actions you believe are a part of your personal inventory. Seek the counsel of a wise and trusted friend if needed as previously suggested.

Brief Observations About RANDOM ACTORS

Because of the significance of the RANDOM ACTOR and the significant growth of people who have this profile, a short introduction is provided here and expanded in Chapter 15. Consider this. Virtually all of the following have the RANDOM ACTOR profile: postal and mass company shooters (where the term "going postal" was drived), suicide terrorists (including the 9–11 attackers), mass school shooters/bombers (the Columbine High School and Virginia Tech massacres), and serial killers. I have spent over twenty years identifying strategies that have prevented many attacks, including a predictive grid of where incidents are likely to occur and not occur. Oddly, as explained in Chapter 15, the *safest locales are the most likely to experience an incident.* For in-depth insight and analysis, please see my book *Rage of the Random Actor—Disarming Catastrophic Acts and Restoring Lives.* It is based on over twenty-five years of research and includes proven intervention and prevention strategies for just about every kind of situation and environment.

May or may not be a threat—Thankfully most people who have this profile don't pose a threat, although many lead troubled lives. I've also encountered people with the RANDOM ACTOR traits who have strong moral and spiritual convictions which help them resist destructive acts.

RANDOM ACTORS **with positive qualities**—The RANDOM ACTOR PERFORMANCE type only identifies how a person is likely to *perform* in a given situation and make decisions—his walk. A person's COMMUNICATION type, however, identifies how he prefers to communicate—the talk.

Because RANDOM ACTORS also have a COMMUNICATION type, this is where they usually show positive actions. This means that while RANDOM ACTORS can be troublesome when called upon to perform, when they communicate, they can display any of the positive actions associated with each of the four COMMUNICATION types, such as:

Sergeant	Determined, takes charge, or self-confident
Salesman	Passionate, outgoing, or friendly
Accountant	Easygoing, orderly, poised, or thoughtful
Artist	Creative, gentle, or sensitive

This is one reason people who are confused or deceived by the actions of a RANDOM ACTOR and will often say: *But he seemed like such a nice guy.* What confused them were the positive actions in the RANDOM ACTOR's COMMUNICATION type.

Because RANDOM ACTORS can draw upon positive actions from their COMMUNICATION type, it is best to interact with them on a communication level and don't ask them to "perform" outside their area of competency. If you do, this is when potential negative actions can surface, such as: manipulative, moody, dangerous, and insecure. When the COMPREHENSIVE PROFILES are covered in Chapter 12, which is the combination of a person's COMMUNICATION and PERFORMANCE types, we'll review suggestions for interacting with each of the four different RANDOM ACTORS, such as the SALESMAN–RANDOM ACTOR.

Another source of positive actions for those with the RANDOM ACTORS traits is if they have competencies or are gifted with abilities. This is why they may do well on a team if led by a competent leader. Additionally, they may have positive UNCONVENTIONAL actions, such as creative, imaginative, and spontaneous.

How many?—Today, approximately 6% of all students in schools have the RANDOM ACTOR profile. In the young adult population, it's approximately 3–6%, which was probably only 1% in the 1950s. There is more on this data in Chapter 15, but the sheer increase is why there have been unprecedented violent acts like the homicidal-suicidal massacres at Columbine

High School in 1999 and Virginia Tech University in 2007. Today, approximately 100 times a day, students are found with guns, bombs, and plots to take out their schools. This is the most extreme end of the behavior, followed by tens of millions who are severely troubled, and the numbers have been steadily rising for over 20 years. Similarly, the number who are over 35 has steadily increased, approximately 2–4%.

Can RANDOM ACTORS change?—As discussed in Chapter 7, people can change their traits when they undergo a life-changing experience. RANDOM ACTORS are no exception. The key for a RANDOM ACTOR is to move from FEARFUL to CAUTIOUS (3 or lower) or even CONFIDENT. This means they must learn to trust, and for some, without selfish motives. For many, this effort in itself is life-changing, and for others the desire to change is triggered by a significant event.

Chapter 15 details a three-step process for guiding someone out of the profile. It has been successfully used to prevent catastrophic attacks here and abroad, and help troubled adults, as well as hundreds if not thousands of students as applied by over 15,000 educators. Also explained are the three powerful themes for successful interactions. When I identified these themes, it enabled me to solve the riddle of why there are RANDOM ACTOR mass shootings at the post office but not FedEx, even though both are in the delivery business. Or, why there are RANDOM ACTOR massacres in accounting departments and on assembly lines, but not in the art department! Unknowingly, very specific companies and areas in companies were applying the three themes. Unfortunately, this isn't always the case. The following story illustrates one RANDOM ACTOR's tragic response when trust was violated.

Love Is a Trick

In 1981, I obtained what was believed to be at the time the only video-recorded confession of a cult-like leader. James Hydrick, a twenty-two-year-old martial arts instructor with a criminal record, had developed what he described as a cult-like following in Salt Lake City. Hydrick used sleight-of-hand tricks to convince his "followers" that he possessed powers and that he could teach them to develop the same powers. After a lengthy undercover investigation, which included filming the modus operandi behind each trick, I confronted Hydrick (using a strategy described later in this chapter). After he was confronted, he agreed to explain on camera: (1) How he fooled millions of people on US television into believing he had powers; (2) How he built his group; and (3) His thought process and motivations for developing a cult-like group.

At one point during our taping, we did a word association sequence with Hydrick. My colleague, Hugh Aynesworth, assisted me. The most revealing moment was when he was given the word "love."

He replied: *To me, love is a trick.*

Severely abused as a child and placed in an institution for the "mentally retarded" when he was nine—and he wasn't—Hydrick's reply illuminated his lack of trust for any adult in a position of authority.

Sadly, he never made the conscious character decision to learn to trust others. His half-sister did, and she had experienced similar abuse. Because she chose a different path through an act of character, she now leads a healthy and fulfilled life.

One day Hydrick called her, lamenting his childhood. He listed all the reasons why he couldn't assume responsibility for his actions, which had oft landed him in prison. She rebuked him. She pointed out that he did have a choice. He did not have to be a slave to his past. She endured the same kinds of abuse, and she chose to redeem her suffering by using her experiences for the benefit of others. He could do the same, she encouraged. Yes, even today, if he chose to trust, her brother could change.

The lesson to be learned from their exchange is that even those whose trust has been severely maligned can learn to trust.

Trust is a choice, not a fate.

Brief Introduction to the CAUTIOUS INNOVATOR profile

When developing the *KPS*, psychologists I consulted in the early 1990s, who were industry leaders, held the view that the combination of UNCONVENTIONAL and low FEARFUL (less than 3 on the FEARFUL side of the CONFIDENT–CAUTIOUS/FEARFUL gauge) was inherently destructive. I was skeptical, but didn't have evidence to the contrary. My subsequent research and on-camera interviews with adults and students with these two traits confirmed what I suspected: the combination of low FEARFUL and low UNCONVENTIONAL is *not* inherently destructive. That's why I added the CAUTIOUS INNOVATOR as a fifth type to distinguish people who are low FEARFUL (CAUTIOUS) and UNCONVENTIONAL from those who are FEARFUL and UNCONVENTIONAL—the RANDOM ACTOR profile.

Significantly, the CAUTIOUS INNOVATOR profile is the fastest growing in North America and many other industrialized countries. It is a profile that is now common in almost any environment where creative detail is required. The reason it can be a confusing profile to lead is because while they like change and innovation, their caution causes them to put on the brakes at inopportune moments. If you're leading a team, this is a problem because change is needed quickly, forced by markets and demands that change and mutate with lightning speed. So how do you lead these people and help them to make decisions quicker and more decisively? Insights on this issue and why this profile has ballooned almost overnight are discussed in Chapter 14 and an entire chapter in *Snapshot*.

A Powerful Concept: Leadership Development and Learning Actions Outside of Your Type

Have you ever wanted to improve who you are for a new responsibility but didn't know exactly where to begin? Or, perhaps you are coaching someone else to take on new responsibilities. Or, you or someone you know needs help broadening your profile so you can lead.

What follows is one of the most useful tools to help people develop actions outside of their type, especially for leadership development where someone will take on responsibilities that don't match their profile. And best of all, what and how it should be done is clear to everyone.

Imagine Taylor is an executive for a manufacturing company and she is a MANAGER type. In charge of logistics for several years, most of her responsibilities have been directed at CONVENTIONAL objectives that have required her to be organized, reliable, precise, logical, and orderly.

A selfless person, Taylor also has an uncommon gift for mentoring which she learned from her parents who were teachers. While most MANAGERS aren't natural mentors, the owner of the company, Preston, recognizes Taylor's gift and thinks she would be a good choice to oversee the new research and development unit. He wants a creative team that is disciplined and has a healthy respect for compliance, budget constraints, etc.

To accomplish this, Preston wants Taylor, who is a MANAGER, to learn two INNOVATOR actions: flexible and adapts to change. He thinks that if she can add these two actions to her tool kit, combined with her natural discipline and mentoring abilities, she would be an excellent fit. The reason Preston thinks Taylor can do it is because mentors must be adaptable and flexible when helping someone else.

As you've already learned, we can learn an action or two from a "neighboring" type that shares a similar action. In this case, Taylor is a MANAGER, INNOVATOR is a neighboring type, and *both* are CONFIDENT. To help Taylor add these two actions, she is given tasks related to her current responsibilities that require her over a period of several months to be a little more flexible and adaptable. She is also provided a mentor who is low CONVENTIONAL, who has also learned these two actions and shows Taylor ways she can be more flexible and adaptable in the context of their company culture.

The key is to select only one or two actions from a neighboring type and engage in on-the-job or situational guidance. This principle can be used for either PERFORMANCE or COMMUNICATION types.

Here's another example.

Austin is an ACCOUNTANT and a valuable volunteer in a service organization. While Austin is thoughtful and agreeable, the leader of the organization would like him to show just a little more emotion like an ARTIST with certain people to more quickly establish trust. All Austin needs is a little bit of guidance on how to add appropriate phrases, a thoughtful note, and so on to show a little more emotion.

The reason this approach to using type actions is effective is that everyone can grasp the goal with clarity. They can see on paper why it will work. You're not asking for a change of personality, just a small positive addition over time with mentoring by someone who has that action.

Here is what you should almost always avoid, however. *Don't ask someone to learn an action that is the opposite of his or her type—the diagonal opposite.* For example, resist asking a LOYALIST to learn the actions of an INNOVATOR or for a SERGEANT to learn the actions of an ARTIST. While possible, successful results aren't common or may require years to perfect.

A graphic representation of this action-leadership principle is provided in ILLUSTRATION 4, which shows that INNOVATORS and MANAGERS can learn an action from each other (each has the CONFIDENT trait), but not INNOVATORS and LOYALISTS (don't share any traits) unless one is willing to work hard over a sustained period of time.

Illustration 4

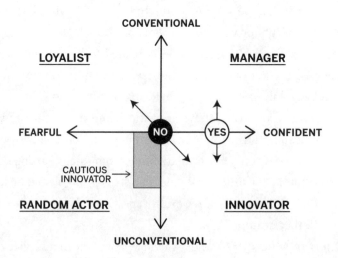

Assignment 10

Goal: Learn to identify each of the PERFORMANCE types.

Time: Two to three hours over a one-week period.

1. Review the specific actions associated with your type. Check the actions in your type that you and others observe, and confirm with a couple of insightful friends or relatives.

2. As you did with the COMMUNICATION types, identify the PERFORMANCE types of thirty people, six from each of the five categories listed below. Be sure to select people whom you get along with as well as those you don't. Also, note the specific COMMUNICATION type actions you observe in each person.

- Family
- Close friends
- Social acquaintances
- Work—people you work with in your organization
- Work—people outside of your organization

Reminder: An easy-to-use tool—As noted in Chapter 6, to reduce memory work, a laminated "gauge/type" sheet is available that has all four gauges and all nine types and type actions on one page. (Please see the back of the book for details.)

You have now learned all the steps necessary, except for one, to identify someone's COMPREHENSIVE PROFILE. The shaded area in ILLUSTRATION 5 on the next page represents the steps you have learned.

Illustration 5

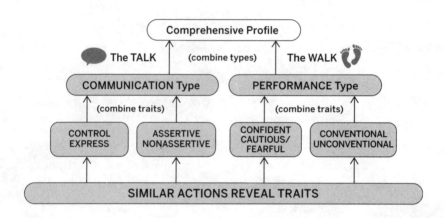

In the next two chapters you will learn how to use what you've learned to make and use SNAPSHOT and FINE-TUNED reads as well as the most common reasons for misreads.

CHAPTER 10

SNAPSHOT AND FINE-TUNED READS

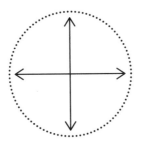

As noted in Chapter 2, the *KPS* provides access to three amounts of information using the same four gauges. In some situations you will need the full data sheet of information provided in a COMPREHENSIVE PROFILE (Chapter 12). There will be other instances, however, when a smaller amount of information will be adequate. That's when a SNAPSHOT or a FINE-TUNED read can be useful. Since you know how to identify COMMUNICATION and PERFORMANCE types, you can use both kinds of reads.

In this chapter you will learn how to assess and apply each type of read in a variety of situations, including:

- How sales personnel can remember the unique attributes of clients.
- Technicians on service calls smoothly servicing individual needs.
- How to write job advertisements to attract people with a specific type.
- New plant managers quickly interacting with a multitude of workers.
- Entrepreneurs establishing ground rules for partners in a new venture.
- Teachers and parents uniquely nurturing children with the same type.

The difference between a SNAPSHOT read and a FINE-TUNED read is the SNAPSHOT read provides a brief, short-list general descriptor of someone's type. It is primarily useful in first-time or noncritical interactions.

A FINE-TUNED read, however, identifies most of the specific actions in a person's COMMUNICATION or PERFORMANCE type. Tracking someone's specific actions using a FINE-TUNED read provides two distinct advantages over a SNAPSHOT read. FINE-TUNED reads can help you:

- Interact with people based upon their unique strengths and weaknesses.
- Remember the unique characteristics about a person.

You have already learned two of the three steps necessary to develop each type of read, so your learning curve will be short.

We will begin with the simplest of the two reads, the SNAPSHOT read.

Developing a SNAPSHOT Read

A SNAPSHOT read is a brief summary statement of a person's type. It helps you quickly size up people, shortening the time necessary for effective interaction. SNAPSHOT reads are useful because they:

- Provide general information about a person.
- Are helpful when interaction is brief or short-term, and detailed information isn't required.
- Are helpful when first interacting with someone.
- Require little time to assess.

When you use a SNAPSHOT read of someone's COMMUNICATION type, you are trying to determine how to communicate with that person.

When you use a SNAPSHOT read of someone's PERFORMANCE type, your focus is on how someone is likely to perform a task or make a decision.

You will use the following three steps to assess a SNAPSHOT read:

1. Plot a person on each gauge.
2. Identify the person's type.
3. Apply the brief summary statement to that person's type.

You already know steps #1 and #2. In order to complete step #3, you will use one of the nine summary statements provided.

The Nine Summary Statements

The SNAPSHOT reads in TABLE 12 are summary statements comprised of common positive and negative actions from each type. SNAPSHOT COMMUNICATION reads *only* relate to how someone *communicates*. For example, "weak" in the ACCOUNTANT SNAPSHOT read and "discouraged easily" in the SALESMAN SNAPSHOT only identifies how someone may *communicate*, as this person may be a strong performer when taking action.

Table 12

SNAPSHOT Reads for Communication Types

SERGEANT (CONTROL/ASSERTIVE)—Prefer to control emotions and be assertive when they communicate. They often like to be directive and take charge of a conversation/dialogue, but this doesn't necessarily mean they can lead during tasks. Their downside is they can be overbearing and insensitive to others.

SALESMAN (EXPRESS/ASSERTIVE)—Prefer to express emotions and be assertive when they communicate. They initially appear outgoing and open and are suited for sales and communication roles. Their downside is they can get discouraged easily and have idealistic expectations.

ACCOUNTANTS (CONTROL/NONASSERTIVE)—Prefer to control emotions and be nonassertive when they communicate. They typically wear well under pressure and are suited as support, sustainer roles. Their downside is they can be weak and critical.

ARTIST (EXPRESS/NONASSERTIVE)—Prefer to express their emotions and ask others what they think or what to do. They typically are creative and are sensitive to the needs of others. Their downside is they can become moody and resist interactions.

SNAPSHOT Reads For Performance Types

MANAGER (CONFIDENT–CONVENTIONAL)—They are typically confident when making decisions, and their actions are conventional. They are suited for managing others because they are usually organized and efficient. Their downside is that they can be self-centered and bureaucratic.

INNOVATOR (CONFIDENT–UNCONVENTIONAL)—They are typically confident when making decisions, and their actions tend to be unconventional. Because they are unconventional and willing to take risks, they can be the creative spark plug in an organization. Their downside is that they might not be suitable for a structured environment, and they can be rebellious.

LOYALIST (CAUTIOUS/FEARFUL–CONVENTIONAL)—They are typically cautious when making decisions, and their actions are conventional. They are often easy to manage because they are loyal and dutiful. Their downside is that they can be unquestioning and become immobilized due to a fear of failure.

CAUTIOUS INNOVATOR (CAUTIOUS–UNCONVENTIONAL)—They are typically cautious when making decisions, and their actions are unconventional. They like change and new ideas if given time to consider and adapt. Their downside is that they can get stuck weighing the options and be indecisive.

RANDOM ACTOR (FEARFUL–UNCONVENTIONAL)—They are extremely fearful when making decisions, and their actions are unconventional. They are often troubled individuals, and to the extreme they can be volatile, manipulative, self-absorbed, and sometimes even dangerous.

As you can see, a SNAPSHOT read is a summary statement that identifies a person's traits together with a couple of positive and negative actions from their type. It is intended to condense a SERGEANT's action list, for example, into a short summary that allows us to quickly remember the kind of arena in which most SERGEANTS prefer to operate (as not every SERGEANT will have the exact actions you choose for a SNAPSHOT read). This, in turn, helps us to recall how to interact with someone who is a SERGEANT.

The SNAPSHOT read is not designed to be detailed or equally precise and reliable in all situations. You will use the FINE-TUNED read or a COMPREHENSIVE PROFILE when you need more reliable and durable reads that includes more details.

If someone that you read is a combination type, as described in Chapter 6, you will need to apply two descriptive statements to this person. If, for example, someone is an ARTIST/ACCOUNTANT combination type, then you would apply the summary statements for both an ARTIST and an ACCOUNTANT. SNAPSHOT reads of combination types should be used sparingly, however. FINE-TUNED reads or COMPREHENSIVE PROFILES are preferred as they provide a more complete base of information to understand these often difficult-to-understand individuals.

Writing Your Own Summary Statements

While you can use the summary statements that are provided for each SNAPSHOT read, you can also personalize each for your specific needs. For example, you might work in an idea-driven office environment, such as an advertising firm. Here, the potency of one's ideas and being persistent in conveying one's idea may be more important than being a leader. In this situation, it may be helpful to replace the "takes charge" descriptor with "influential" or "persistent" in the SERGEANT SNAPSHOT read.

To write your own SNAPSHOT reads, follow the steps below. Start with the COMMUNICATION or PERFORMANCE type that is of the greatest importance for you to remember in your professional and private life. For example, related to a specific COMMUNICATION type, ask yourself: What are the most important actions I personally need to remember about this type so I can immediately recall how this person prefers to communicate? Then complete the following three steps:

1. Review the possible actions for that type.
2. Select two positive and two negative actions that will help you immediately recall how this person prefers to communicate. (Later, you can add as many actions as you would like to memorize.)
3. Create a brief two-sentence summary statement using the actions

you have selected. First, state the traits associated with that type, then follow with the positive and negative actions.

The key to constructing useful summaries is to focus on actions that are typically the most important for you to recall when interacting with others. Here is a sample of a customized SNAPSHOT read for SERGEANTS using alternative actions.

SERGEANT (CONTROL/ASSERTIVE)—Prefer to control emotions and be assertive when they communicate. They can be influential and persistent. Their downside is they can be aloof and unwilling to accept direction.

You may also want to create different SNAPSHOT summaries for different kinds of professional and social situations. For example, certain actions may be more important to you when interviewing versus leading those who work for you. In your private life, you may want to use one summary statement when socializing and another version around the house with your family and friends.

Using SNAPSHOT Reads

TABLE 13 provides a list of some noncritical and critical situations when a SNAPSHOT read can improve your interactions with others. Remember, because SNAPSHOT reads are based on limited observations, they will usually be less reliable and more vulnerable to change over time than a FINE-TUNED read or a COMPREHENSIVE PROFILE.

Table 13

Noncritical or brief one-time only interactions

- Sales with non-repeat customers that require a short period of interaction, such as over-the-counter retail.
- Brief, noncritical interactions, such as: auditors conducting a low-key fact-finding interview; casual acquaintances in one's company; providing instructions to temporary personnel.
- Social gatherings.
- Many first-time exchanges.

Critical interaction that is short, but is over a sustained period of time

- Manager of a large plant interacting with staff.
- Repeat sales where interactions are short, such as industrial sales.
- Pressure situations for medical personnel, social workers, or law enforcement officers when one must quickly assess how to interact with someone.
- Technician who is dealing with people where the human face on the service is important.
- Screening applicants over the telephone.
- At the beginning of a hiring interview.
- A reporter conducting an interview during a fast-breaking story.

The following are suggested applications for using SNAPSHOT reads.

Hiring—You are running an ad in a local newspaper for an administrative assistant who will work with a SERGEANT type. You believe an ACCOUNTANT type (NONASSERTIVE–CONTROL) is best suited for the job. To attract people who are ACCOUNTANT types to your ad, use words in your ad from the list of positive actions ACCOUNTANT that will appeal to this person—or similar words that fit the ad. Some examples: "Executive seeks detailed and efficient assistant . . ." or "Can you restore order to the office of an executive?" or "Amiable, friendly environment seeks dependable . . ." If you are uncertain about specific wording, find someone that possesses the type to whom you are trying to appeal and ask for their input.

Sales—You own a retail jewelry business. As noted in Chapter 8, you can typically provide more choices to people who are CONFIDENT (MANAGERS and INNOVATORS) than those who are CAUTIOUS/FEARFUL (LOYALISTS and RANDOM ACTORS). This is because people who are CONFIDENT tend to eliminate undesirable options more quickly than those who are CAUTIOUS/FEARFUL and often less decisive. Therefore, to improve your sales process, it might be wise to train sales personnel to quickly identify PERFORMANCE types and include the descriptors of "indecisive" for CAUTIOUS INNOVATORS and LOYALISTS and "decisive decision-maker" for MANAGERS and INNOVATORS. Or, the SNAPSHOT read can focus on who might require more time to service.

Leading Teams—Your company has just acquired a new plant. SNAPSHOT reads can help you quickly size up the situation when first visiting the facility. By reading the COMMUNICATION types of key employees, you can quickly decide where and how to seek critical information. For example, ACCOUNTANTS and ARTISTS will often be evaluative/critical of the situation. SALESMEN, however, are more likely to provide the positives of a new situation. SERGEANTS will typically paint a picture that allows them to maintain as much control as possible.

Confrontational Settings—You are an investigator. You suspect fraud and must ask questions. When pressured SERGEANTS and SALESMEN are more likely to use their directive/forceful skills to defend themselves—the *stronger* their ASSERTIVE trait. ARTISTS and ACCOUNTANTS, however, often become less forceful, more silent, the *higher* their NONASSERTIVE trait. Recognizing these natural tendencies can help one avoid false positives about truthfulness simply because one person is more or less forceful/convincing than another.

Assignment 11

Goal: Customizing SNAPSHOT reads.
Time Required: 30 minutes.

Use the format to create a SNAPSHOT read and write a customized synopsis for one COMMUNICATION type and one PERFORMANCE type. Make certain that one summary can be used in your professional career and the second summary in your personal life.

Developing a FINE-TUNED Read

The FINE-TUNED read is more detailed than a SNAPSHOT read. FINE-TUNED reads use the *entire action list for a specific type*, and you identify the specific actions you have observed in someone's profile. FINE-TUNED reads require more time to create than SNAPSHOT reads and are useful because they:

- Provide more detailed information about a person's positive and negative actions and other tendencies.
- Are vital when interaction must be precise.
- Are useful for long-term interaction.

The three steps for assessing a FINE-TUNED read are as follows:

1. Plot a person on the two gauges for the type that you want to identify. For example, if you want to assess a FINE-TUNED read for a COMMUNICATION type, plot that person on the NONASSERTIVE–ASSERTIVE and CONTROL–EXPRESS gauges.
2. Identify the type.
3. Over a period of time, check off the specific actions that you observe in that person on the appropriate type action list—TABLE 6 in Chapter 6 for COMMUNICATION types and TABLE 11 in Chapter 9 for PERFORMANCE types. The ability to observe as many actions as possible will be driven by the number of situations in which you can observe people and how much information you can obtain about their past history.

As with the SNAPSHOT read, you've already learned the first two steps to create a FINE-TUNED. Step #3 is simply observing a person's specific actions associated with his type and then checking off those actions on the action list for that type. This provides a way to track specific actions. On the next page is an example of a FINE-TUNED read of Jeremy, who is an ARTIST.

FINE-TUNED Read of "Jeremy" Who Is an ARTIST

Positive Actions	Negative Actions	Other Tendencies
✓Creative	✓Critical	Idiosyncratic
✓Sympathetic	✓Moody	✓Respectful
✓Agreeable	Appear weak	✓Tolerant
Curious/inquisitive	"Spineless"	Endearing
✓Supportive	Emotionally rash	Focus on how they feel
✓Compassionate	Weak	Naive
Deep-feeling	✓Unsure	Dramatic
Self-sacrificing	Resists interaction	Avoids conflict
✓Loyal	Uninformed	Sensitive
✓Amiable		Indirect
Thoughtful		Passionate
Self-effacing		
Altruistic		

Updating FINE-TUNED Reads

For important professional and personal relationships, make a copy of the action list for each person's type and check off the actions that you observe. Keep this list filed, and periodically review and update it. Over time, you will typically see more specific actions. People's specific actions can change due to maturity, change of environments, and so on.

When you have a critical interaction, review that person's list and review it so you can take into consideration all of the specific actions you have observed.

Assignment 12

Goal: Identify your personal FINE-TUNED read.
Time Required: 30 minutes.

1. Check off the specific actions that you know you possess in both your COMMUNICATION and PERFORMANCE types.
2. Ask a trusted friend or relative to review your list with you to be sure that it is complete. When identifying negative actions, candid

honesty is the best policy. When people deny that they have a specific negative action, they usually put on mental blinders so they don't see the same action in others. Another common response is over-reacting when someone else displays the same action as it reminds them of themselves. In either case, anything less than transparent honesty about one's actions only impedes profiling accuracy skills and derails effective interactions with others.

Using FINE-TUNED Reads

Identifying specific actions is a quick way to see the difference in two people with the same type. For example, if you are selecting someone to lead a specific team, you may want a SERGEANT who specifically takes charge rather than just influences. However, if you want someone to work in an environment that might be frustrating, a SERGEANT who is persistent might be a better choice as they can push through the frustration. Even better, a SERGEANT who has both actions!

TABLE 14 lists situations in which you might use a FINE-TUNED read.

Table 14

Critical one-time interaction that may or may not be short in duration

- When you must pinpoint one or two specific actions.
- Coaching a specific person on a team.
- Teacher meeting with a troublesome parent.
- Crucial negotiations.
- High-powered sales environment.
- Counselors in a clinic.
- Volunteering on a project.
- Investigators conducting interviews.
- Critical ongoing interaction that may or may not be short in duration.
- When you must pinpoint one or two specific actions.
- Sales in which individualized personal rapport is crucial.

- Medical doctors on rounds or seeing a cancer patient during office visits.
- Manager making final hiring or promotion decisions.
- Leaders working with teams.
- Any relationship with a family member or friend.

Here are some specific applications in which FINE-TUNED reads can be beneficial.

Promotions—You have three candidates in your organization who are all ACCOUNTANT types. You have a slot open for a new controller, and you anticipate stress in this department for a year or two due to a recent merger. Therefore, you want an ACCOUNTANT type who specifically wears well under pressure. By identifying which of the three candidates possesses this action, you will be able to make a better selection. This not only benefits the organization, it benefits the person you will promote, as it gives them a greater chance to succeed in the new post.

Sales—Virtually any on-going consultant or strategic selling relationship requires FINE-TUNED reads to avoid relying on shoot-from-the-hip interactions. Competitors are always looking for ways to capture your clients. FINE-TUNED reads can help retain business by directly respond to your client's unique personality.

One successful financial broker and consultant maintains a FINE-TUNED read for each of his clients in his contact database. Before each critical consultation, he reviews his client's unique actions and adjusts his written proposals and presentations accordingly. Through this one simple action, several difficult-to-please clients told him that his presentations were the best structured and the easiest to digest of any of his competitors.

Working with a partner—In entrepreneurial environments, talented people often come together because they are driven by a vision. But how often do you hear the story: They started off with a flurry, but their differences eventually destroyed their venture. Fine-tuned reads at the front end of a relationship can do the following:

- Pinpoint potential weaknesses in a relationship so that ground rules, buffers, and other relationship-saving devices can be explored and put into place before trouble erupts.

- Encourage a respect for the fact that partners often have—and should have—different types and actions that can complement one another to get a bigger job done.
- Help forecast the types and specific actions desired in senior personnel to complement the strengths and weaknesses of the partners.

Instructing and disciplining children—Speaking from experience, fine-tuned reads are invaluable when nurturing, instructing, and disciplining kids. For example, let's assume there are two siblings, William and Sarah. Both are ACCOUNTANT types, but the weaknesses of each child are different. One of William's weaknesses is that he tends to be slow. Sarah, however, tends to be pessimistic.

One way to help William is to give him responsibility accompanied by appropriate discipline if he doesn't carry out his responsibility on time. He should also be encouraged to pursue a friendship with a classmate who is energetic.

Sarah, however, struggles with pessimism. She needs to develop a more positive bent on life. To help her move past her pessimism, her parents can encourage Sarah, an avid reader, to read books about people who have overcome great obstacles to achieve their goals. Also, Sarah may need more personal praise than William, who will likely need more disciplining because of his laziness.

A fundamental principle for using FINE-TUNED reads is to interact with a person based upon his *positive* actions and not activate his *negative* actions.

Additional Thoughts on FINE-TUNED Reads

FINE-TUNED reads are not complete—Don't assume that a FINE-TUNED profile will provide all you need to know about a person. A FINE-TUNED read of a person's COMMUNICATION type, for example, is not a complete profile of the person. It is only a detailed description of his COMMUNICATION type.

Actions outside the target type—Let's assume you have identified that Bob is a SERGEANT type. Then, as you develop his FINE-TUNED read, you notice he also has a couple of SALESMAN actions, such as outgoing and optimistic. As discussed in previous chapters, this is probably due to one of three factors.

First, Bob may share actions with the SALESMAN type because both share the ASSERTIVE trait. Second, he may have learned a specific action, like a reporter with an ASSERTIVE trait who learns to ask questions like a NONASSERTIVE person. Or third, he may have a plot point near the middle, and thus he is a combination type, described in detail in Chapter 6. If Bob is a SERGEANT–SALESMAN combination type, then you will have to review the actions for both the SERGEANT and the SALESMAN.

Assignment 13

Goal: Learn to assess a FINE-TUNED read.
Time Required: 1 hour.

1. Identify the COMMUNICATION and PERFORMANCE types of ten people whom you have known for a period of time. Be sure they are evenly distributed amongst professional and personal acquaintances.
2. Check off the specific actions you have observed in each. If you have difficulty, seek assistance from someone who knows the same people.

Summary of When to Use SNAPSHOT and FINE-TUNED Reads

Selecting when to use a SNAPSHOT or a FINE-TUNED read will be dictated by your interaction needs. TABLE 15 provides an easy-to-use comparative summary of when to use each type of read.

Table 15

SNAPSHOT **Read**

- Need general information.
- Interaction is brief and short-term.
- When first interacting with someone.
- Have little time to assess.
- Noncritical, one-time only interactions.
- Critical, short interaction over a sustained period of time.

FINE-TUNED **Read**

- Need information about specific actions.
- When interaction must be precise.
- Critical long-term interactions.
- Critical one-time or ongoing interaction that may or may not be short in duration.

A typical situation in which it is desirable to use both reads is when you are interviewing someone for a job. When beginning the interview, make a SNAPSHOT read to:

- Determine if the person's COMMUNICATION type is the one you are seeking.
- Help you communicate and pose questions during the interview.

As the interview progresses, you can then begin to develop a FINE-TUNED read, based upon what you observe, the resumé, references, previous work history, and so forth.

Assignment 14

Goal: Practice using both SNAPSHOT and FINE-TUNED reads.
Time Required: 4 hours over a 2-week period.

1. Memorize SNAPSHOT reads for both the COMMUNICATION and
   PERFORMANCE types. You can use the summaries in this chapter or
   create your own.
2. Plot ten different people on all four gauges and identify both their
   COMMUNICATION and PERFORMANCE types. As you identify each
   person's type, recite from memory each person's SNAPSHOT read.
   Reminder: Be sure to include people from each of the five categories
   below—those whom you like as well as people you dislike—to avoid
   stereotyping.

   • Family
   • Close friends
   • Social acquaintances
   • Work—people you work with in your organization
   • Work—people outside of your organization

3. Use the same group of ten people in #2 and assess a FINE-TUNED
   read of each person. If you haven't had sufficient contact with some
   individuals, replace them with another person from the same category.

CHAPTER 11

NINE KEY REASONS FOR MISREADS

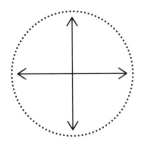

Alexis was frustrated. She thought Mason was interested in her proposal, based on her first one-hour phone consult, but now she wasn't sure.

"Dan, he didn't show any emotion on the phone on our follow-up call. I don't know if he's interested or not."

"What's his profile?" I asked. I knew Mason's profile, and I recommended Alexis as a consultant for his next major project. Alexis was not only the leading expert in her field, but she always over-delivers for her clients. I though she'd be a great match.

"He's a SERGEANT–INNOVATOR," she said, and she was spot on.

"And, what do SERGEANTS usually do with their emotions?" I asked.

"Control their emotions," she popped back.

"And, is he high or low CONTROL?," I probed.

"High CONTROL," she said confidently.

"Right. So why are you trying to decide if he is going to take action based on his communication trait?" I reminded her.

Alexis was one of my coaching clients, she learned how to profile, but like all of us, she fell prey to one of the most common misreads. She misread Mason's *talk* for his *walk*. When Mason is considering taking action, he reverts to the CONTROL side of his range. In other words, Mason is about 2 CONTROL but when weighing a decision based upon facts, he moves to 3 CONTROL. Alexis sensed this shift, forgot about Mason's CONTROL trait, and assumed that when he didn't show any emotion, his natural trait, it signaled disinterest. Yet, the *content* of what he said signaled commitment towards making a decision.

Misreads like these affect everyone from the novice to seasoned expert. Once you've learned the *KPS*, you should be able to read most people accurately, but there are common reasons why we misread that smaller percent. In this chapter you'll learn how to avoid the potholes in the road that cause the nine most common misreads and their antidotes.

Misreading people is just a part of life. People can act uniquely on a given day because they choose to do so or because of a unique situation. The concepts in this chapter, though, will help you reduce your inaccuracy when you were the cause of the misread. Now, when you do misread someone, in most situations you'll be better equipped to pinpoint the reason for your misread. This will give you another layer of protection to add to the types "safety check" explained in Chapter 6. As a quick reminder, here are the "safety check" steps.

1. Make your reads of two traits, like ASSERTIVE–NONASSERTIVE and CONTROL–EXPRESS.
2. Identify the type (such as ARTIST).
3. Review the ARTIST actions and see if they match what you observe.
4. If they match, great.
5. If they don't match, find which set of type actions do and make your correction.

As you learn the misread concepts and antidotes, think back to people you've misread and how the antidotes may have helped you. With a little reflection, you'll uncover patterns of those you are most likely to misread and why as well as how to avoid those mistakes in the future.

Reason #1: Someone Restrains a Trait

As explained in Chapter 4, some people may *restrain* a trait knowingly or unknowingly. The principle is: You can restrain what you have, but it's difficult to manufacture what you don't have.

Here is the pattern of which traits can be restrained: EXPRESS, ASSERTIVE, UNCONVENTIONAL, and CONFIDENT.

- A person who is EXPRESS can be less expressive.
- A person who is ASSERTIVE can be less assertive.
- A person who is UNCONVENTIONAL can be less unconventional.
- A person who is CONFIDENT can be a little more cautious.

Regarding the last two traits, it's difficult for the CONVENTIONAL person to be more UNCONVENTIONAL, but it's easier for most UNCONVENTIONAL people to be more CONVENTIONAL for short periods of time.

Regarding CONFIDENT, it's easier to be more cautious than for a CONFIDENT/FEARFUL person to be more confident.

> △ **Antidote:** First, be sure you take more than one read to check your reads. Second, check the type actions to see if they fit. Third, check the COMPREHENSIVE PROFILE, which can also be used as another safety check (explained in the next chapter).

Reason #2: Confuse One Trait for Another

The most common misstep that causes misreads, even for experts, is when one trait is mistaken for another. An example from history is when people are asked to identify whether or not Adolf Hitler was CONFIDENT or FEARFUL when making decisions. Many people will say CONFIDENT, because they recall his fiery oratory staged in front of his mass rallies. We know for a fact, however, that he was extreme FEARFUL when making decisions, exemplified by his displays of paranoia. The reason people misread Hitler is that he possessed a strong ASSERTIVE trait. He could talk a powerful game, but when called upon to perform when Russian troops captured Berlin, he operated out of fear and took his life.

Hitler's negative actions can also cause some confusion.

Some might assume, for example, that Hitler was arrogant and conceited when he made decisions, two negative CONFIDENT actions. Actually, when called upon to make important decisions, Hitler was unstable, anxious, and defensive—negative FEARFUL actions. What created the illusion of arrogance and conceit when making decisions was that he was egotistical (a negative ASSERTIVE trait) in the talk part of his life. That is, when Hitler spoke, he was often egotistical. This is different from being arrogant or conceited when called upon to make a decision, which may or may not require him to communicate with others. In fact, it was this seeming contradiction that caused him to be an enigma to those around him. While appearing pompous and egotistical when he communicated, his paranoia fueled his decisions.

This may seem like splitting hairs, but if one doesn't carefully identify from which trait his negative actions originated, one might type Hitler as an INNOVATOR (which has a CONFIDENT trait) instead of a dangerous RANDOM ACTOR (which has a FEARFUL trait).

> △ **Antidote**: With some awareness this cause for misreads can be minimized by:
>
> 1. Recognizing which traits are the easiest to confuse for another.
>
> 2. Faithfully follow Rule #3 for systematic accuracy: Anything worth measuring once is worth measuring at least twice.
>
> 3. When profiling, always read each trait separately, and when necessary, review the list of actions for the type you've identified. Don't look at someone and think: He looks like an ACCOUNTANT type. Be disciplined to read each trait individually, because unique combinations of traits can fool you if not read separately. Don't take shortcuts. One day you will pay the price for a lack of discipline.

The most common traits which are mistaken for another and who is most likely to make each misread are as follows:

ASSERTIVE misread for CONFIDENT—This is common when SALESMAN or SERGEANT types who are CAUTIOUS/FEARFUL present a strong and/

or powerful image when they communicate. The more pronounced the ASSERTIVE trait, the greater the chance for misreading their ASSERTIVE trait for CONFIDENT. Also, those who are NONASSERTIVE, CAUTIOUS/FEARFUL, or low CONFIDENT are the most susceptible to making this misread because they aren't as instinctively familiar with the ASSERTIVE and CONFIDENT trait. Thus, they are more prone to misinterpret ASSERTIVE for CONFIDENT.

NONASSERTIVE misread for CAUTIOUS/FEARFUL—It is common for people to misread ARTIST or ACCOUNTANT types who are also CONFIDENT as being CAUTIOUS/FEARFUL. Their NONASSERTIVE trait is misread for CAUTIOUS/FEARFUL, and specifically indirect or laid-back style of communicating is misread as CAUTIOUS/FEARFUL. This is especially true the stronger the NONASSERTIVE trait or if someone has negative communication actions that are weak, naive, or appear uninformed. People who are CONFIDENT or ASSERTIVE are usually more susceptible to making this misread, because they are not as familiar with the nuances of a person who is NONASSERTIVE.

CAUTIOUS/FEARFUL misread for UNCONVENTIONAL—This is a common misread when people who are CAUTIOUS/FEARFUL act to protect themselves, such as reversing a previous commitment. This can create the illusion of unpredictability, even though someone is CONVENTIONAL. People who are CONFIDENT are typically the most susceptible for making this misread, particularly the stronger their CONFIDENT trait.

CONVENTIONAL misread for CAUTIOUS/FEARFUL—People who are CONVENTIONAL are often misread as being CAUTIOUS/FEARFUL—even if they are CONFIDENT. Imagine a situation where someone says, "Jessica, you always eat at the same sushi bar. Why don't you try another one around the corner that's even better. What are you afraid of?" The point is Jessica isn't *afraid*, she just likes to stick with what is familiar to her.

Or imagine a high school language arts teacher who says, "Stephen, why do you only read action books? Why don't you try a little poetry? What are you afraid of?" If Stephen is CONFIDENT, she's going to create hostility. He's not afraid, he just doesn't like all the UNCONVENTIONAL poetry filled with airy-fairy ambiguity.

These are the kinds of daily misreads that cause arguments and push people to be defensive. Some people just like to do the same things. They don't like changes in the appearance of reports, they like to eat at the same familiar haunts and not venture out, they don't like change in their circle of colleagues and friends, and they may prefer that their attire is consistent. People who are UNCONVENTIONAL or low CONVENTIONAL are the most vulnerable to making this misread. They mistakenly interpret predictability as CAUTIOUS/FEARFUL—that someone is afraid to try something new. The fact is they are not CAUTIOUS/FEARFUL, rather they just prefer things remain consistent and predictable.

To summarize, to avoid confusing one trait for another, read each trait separately based upon observable actions, take more than one read, and be aware of which trait(s) you are more likely to confuse for another.

Reason #3: Difficulty Reading Our Opposite Trait/Type

The following reason for misreading people is closely associated with the one just covered.

As noted in Chapter 7, we usually have trouble reading people who possess our opposite trait or type. This is because we aren't familiar with the nuances of our opposites. Some suggestions were provided in Chapter 7, but the antidote is worth repeating here.

> △ **Antidote:** Recruit someone who is the opposite of both your COMMUNICATION and PERFORMANCE types to help you navigate and deepen the understanding of your reads. Be sure that whoever you select has keen insight. Additionally, you may need to find two people—one for each of your types if one person can't be found who matches both your COMMUNICATION and PERFORMANCE types.

Although this suggestion was presented in Chapter 7, my experience is that most people don't follow through and apply it without encouragement. If you want to develop refined profiling skills, this is something you cannot put off. A wise counselor/friend, who has your best interest at heart, can help you think through how others, like themselves, communicate, think, and so on with significant immediacy.

A Personal Story—My wife Sandy and I have been joyfully married for 39 years. She is God's greatest gift to me—and all our friends will testify to this fact. In the early years of our marriage we were trait opposites. She was an ACCOUNTANT/ARTIST–MANAGER and I was a SALESMAN/SERGEANT–INNOVATOR. We were opposites which is one reason we were attracted to each another; we each had something the other didn't have. And, like other couples, it was also one of the major reasons for disagreements and marital fights (and yes, I was usually the one in the wrong). Over time, though, I marveled at how she smoothly handled people and situations that for me were puzzling. For example, she always uses her NONASSERTIVE trait with care and understanding for the benefit of serving others. By training she was a labor and delivery nurse. Twenty-three years ago she founded The Festive Kitchen, one of Dallas's finest catering establishments, along with two gourmet-to-go shops.

Shortly after I developed the *KPS*, I realized anew who I had married and that Sandy was my opposite, and I regularly sought her advice on or about how she would approach a specific person or situation. That was then.

Today, I regularly think "how would Sandy do it?" She is my greatest ally in business and in all other facets of my life. I know that this is how the Lord intended marriage to be, but with time I appreciated those finest thinnest threads in her with even greater clarity. So if you have a wise mate or friend who is your opposite, treasure and hold in high esteem one of life's greatest gifts.

Reason #4: People Can Learn a Specific Action

As we've learned, people can learn an action outside their type that can cause misreads. For example, a teacher who is an ACCOUNTANT type, may have cultivated the ability to enthusiastically communicate a subject, an action usually associated with someone who is a SALESMAN. This action, however, may have been cultivated out of a desire to encourage students or it may have been learned as a youngster from a parent who was a teacher.

△ **Antidote**: Be certain your read isn't based upon just one read. Faithfully follow Rule #3 that promotes systematic accuracy— *Anything worth measuring once is worth measuring at least twice.* If you notice another action at some later point that seems to come from a different type or trait inventory, don't panic. Take more reads. Look at past behavior—the best predictor of future behavior. Eventually you'll flesh it out.

Reason #5: Life-changing Experience

This concept, noted in earlier chapters, is unfortunately becoming more common in most countries, principally driven by deteriorating social conditions. Other positive and negative factors such as marriage, birth of a child, death, illness, loss of job, demotion, or a move can also cause people to temporarily operate in a way that is inconsistent with their actual traits. In other cases, though, these kinds of events in a person's life can result in a permanent change of plot points, even moving a person from one side of a gauge to the other.

When hiring staff, this can be troublesome when you think you've hired someone who is a match for a position. A few months down the line, though, his plot point(s) changes and he is no longer suited for the position. The following antidote can help you minimize the chances of this happening—which benefits both you and the prospective employee. The themes described are also invaluable when developing new relationships to improve your ability to reach out to, counsel, cheer on, or be there for someone.

△ **Antidote**: To increase the accuracy and possible stability of a specific person's traits, look at past behavior and breaks in consistency from the actions of his trait(s) or type(s).

When a person has gone through a life-changing experience that has temporarily shifted his plot point, checking out past behavior is one of the best ways to determine where a person is likely to land after they have absorbed and dealt with the full impact of the experience. When we go through a situation that stretches us—like an elastic band—we can return to our old plot points.

To check your read, inquire about past actions whenever possible. And specifically, how he dealt with non-life-changing pressure in the past. Precisely how you do this during an interview should be reviewed with legal counsel because of laws constraining the types of questions that might be considered discriminatory, prejudicial, etc.

One possible tact that doesn't necessarily require an interview, however, would be to review a person's resumé and work history. See if there is a consistency between the candidate's profile and previous job descriptions. Look for patterns regarding in which the person did and didn't excel, which can reveal whether his profile was or wasn't suited for specific responsibilities.

For example, you have a research position open in a marketing group that is best suited for a person who is NONASSERTIVE. Ellen applies for the position, and during her first interview you believe she is NONASSERTIVE. When you review her resumé, however, it's apparent Ellen excelled in strategic sales environments, which required that someone have an ASSERTIVE trait. To be certain you didn't misread her NONASSERTIVE–ASSERTIVE trait, test your read.

Focus on how Ellen handled a stressful situation in her previous position(s). You might ask her to describe how she handled the restructuring of her group, which was the catalyst for her decision to seek new employment. As she describes her reaction and response, listen carefully to *how* Ellen communicates what she did because under pressure people typically show their actual trait. Listen for clues to specific past actions that might illuminate her NONASSERTIVE or ASSERTIVE trait. (Chapter 17 provides additional guidance when handling this kind of situation.)

Perhaps she succeeded in her previous position with a NONASSERTIVE trait because of preparatory skills and her ability to listen to and meet her client's technical needs. Or, you might discover that in those past situations she did use an ASSERTIVE trait, exemplified by how she negotiated important contracts.

There isn't a one-size-fits-all method to check out past behavior, only the principle that it should be a part of the process. Because so many people are going through changes in their lives where the ground is shifting under their feet, strategies that are within the law and professional ethical boundaries must be harnessed. (It is recommended that those charged with hiring responsibilities take a behavioral interviewing course providing strategies that satisfy the demands of current state and federal laws.)

Reason #6: Culture Masks Actual Traits

Cultures can suppress actions that can reveal a person's actual traits—from organizations to neighborhoods to countries. If you don't take a second look that includes unobtrusive reads, you can fall prey to misreads. Here are some examples.

In the military, enlisted men and women all wear the same uniform and salute in the same way. This can foster a stereotype that all individuals in a unit are CONVENTIONAL, even though there are many personality types in our armed forces.

In the 1970s, the corporate culture of one Fortune 500 company was known for its regimented style. Men and women typically wore blue or gray suits, and men's haircuts resembled military cuts, mirroring the image established by the company's founder. An outsider profiling this company's employees might mistakenly think that all were CONVENTIONAL and CONTROL because of the "corporate uniform."

A more complicated example of cultural suppression of traits is found in countries that experienced repression. I witnessed this first-hand in Poland, shortly after the fall of Communism, where I've lectured regularly at universities since 1992. In the early 2000s, the repressive and flattening effects of Communism were still physically evident by the many gray-boxed apartment buildings in Warsaw. You could also see a flattening effect in how people communicated. Unless you went into someone's flat, where they felt free to be themselves, you would mistakenly think that

Polish people were all CAUTIOUS/FEARFUL , CONVENTIONAL, CONTROL, and NONASSERTIVE.

> △ **Antidote**: To bypass the cultural facade, we make unobtrusive
> reads that are noninvasive in situations where people feel
> the freedom to be themselves while we look for breaks in
> consistency—leakage.

When profiling military personnel during basic training, we don't make reads based upon how they salute or stand at attention during a roll call. We make unobtrusive, noninvasive reads during a training exercise, relaxing in the barracks, or enjoying a dinner at a local restaurant. You observe them when they can be themselves—preferably in a way in which you don't intrude.

In the corporate culture of the Fortune 500 company referenced, one way to make unobtrusive reads was to look for leakage in attire. Men who were UNCONVENTIONAL or EXPRESS sometimes expressed their trait by wearing cuff links that had a unique flair. When in a critical meeting, they simply pulled the sleeve of their coat down, covering their "rebel" cuff links. When they went out to eat with colleagues at lunch, a tug of the sleeve, and voila...freedom of expression.

The women did it differently.

Some who were UNCONVENTIONAL or EXPRESS used earrings to express their trait. In meetings, their hair covered their lack of uniformity, and at lunch with the flick of a hand, they tossed their hair behind an ear to enjoy a small freedom of expression.

In other contexts, teachers can profile students in the hall or during a team assignment. Mom's can make reads when teens come over for a party.

In Poland in the early 1990s, I was able to see through the cultural façade by having dinner in someone's flat. On the street, people were still walking quickly with their eyes down, rarely showing emotion, not wanting to be noticed. As in other former Communist countries, standing out could draw the attention of the feared state police. I found, though, once you stepped into an apartment, color abounds and the real traits of Poles came to life and were revealed—even to a foreigner who couldn't speak the language. (Additional suggestions for profiling in a cross-cultural environment are provided in Chapter 16.)

Reason #7: Reading Past the Game Face

People can put on a game face subconsciously or deliberately. Yet, it is almost always possible to identify their actual traits by making additional unobtrusive reads or where there is a bit of stress involved. An example is Bill in the "Leaking Eyes and Smiles" story in Chapter 7. To be believed, he subconsciously restrained his EXPRESS trait, but *leaked* his trait when asked if his doctor thought he was healed, which applied a little pressure in the situation.

> △ **Antidote:** If we think someone is putting on a game face, we make unobtrusive reads or reads where there is a measure of stress as we look for leakage.

To begin, remember that it's easier for people to restrain traits they have than to manufacture a trait they don't have. The traits that are easiest to restrain, as earlier noted, are: EXPRESS, ASSERTIVE, UNCONVENTIONAL, and CONFIDENT. Here are common reasons people subconsciously restrain a trait and put on a game face and try to appear the *opposite* of each trait:

- **EXPRESS:** Want to appear CONTROL to be believed; don't want to draw attention.
- **ASSERTIVE:** Want to appear NONASSERTIVE so not to stand out; avoid the appearance of being self-serving or arrogant; make themselves accessible to people who aren't as strong (those who are NONASSERTIVE or FEARFUL).
- **UNCONVENTIONAL:** Want to appear CONVENTIONAL to be a part of a group; not put people off by being different.
- **CONFIDENT:** Want to appear NONASSERTIVE so not to stand out; avoid the appearance of being self-serving or arrogant; make them-

selves accessible to people who aren't as strong (those who are NONASSERTIVE or FEARFUL).

While not as common, here are reasons people subconsciously try to manufacture a trait *they don't have*. The reality is that when they do, it usually looks affected and is typically easy to spot. The trait see person has is specified first followed by why they try to appear like the opposite trait.

- **CONTROL:** Want to appear to EXPRESS to be a part of an EXPRESS group; wants to be believed about an emotional situation, especially if there is an imminent threat.
- **NONASSERTIVE:** Want to appear ASSERTIVE to increase stature; command a situation.
- **CONVENTIONAL:** Want to appear UNCONVENTIONAL to be accepted; not considered stuffy/staid/nonprogressive.
- **CAUTIOUS/FEARFUL:** Want to appear CONFIDENT to appear in control of the situation or their destiny.

Game Face by Choice—The other reason people put on a game face is that they've chosen to do so for a specific reason. Interview training and video aids for role-playing, for example, have taught people how to project an image to secure a position.

For example, a financial institution is looking for a person who can follow regulations for compliance. A critical factor to identify is how a candidate handled a fast-changing stressful situation in the past where compliance was mandatory. So a question might be: *Please describe a situation in the past where the Fed handed down new regulations that put time pressure on the situation, but you still had to complete your audit. In detail, please explain what happened.*

If the candidate did her homework, she knows this question might come up and may have a stock answer ready. If her response doesn't sound transparent, ask for up to *three more examples* that are similar in nature. This injects stress into the situation, as few people have multiple canned answers for critical questions, thus making it easier to hear/see her actual trait. This technique is so effective, that when this is role played in training by those who know the technique, the pressure still causes the actual trait to appear virtually every time.

Reason #8: Emotional Reads

We are vulnerable for misreads when we have a positive or negative emotional experience and then make a read based upon our emotions. Some examples:

- You had an exceptionally good or an exceptionally bad day.
- You've just been notified that your firm has been awarded a hard-fought contract.
- You've just been passed over for a career-advancing project.
- You've just come from your daughter's basketball game and her team pulled off a come-from-behind upset.

Any of these positive and negative situations can present an opportunity for our emotions to interfere with making an accurate read. This doesn't mean we should abandon our emotions. It's part of who we are. We just need to be sure that when we are placed in an important or unexpected situation, that we check to see if our reads have been misdirected by our emotions.

As noted in Chapter 3, one of the worst kinds of situations is when people make an inaccurate emotional decision—a read—and then try to justify and back it up with logic. Then prides creeps in and dominates as we defend our position. There is a better way.

△ **Antidote**: Recommit to read everyone based upon the extreme ends of your personalized gauges. In important situations when you are emotionally charged and an accurate read is essential, mentally step back. Use your wire. If it's CONTROL–EXPRESS, ask yourself: *Does her overall persona tilt toward Queen Elizabeth or Jim Carrey*—or whatever extreme examples you've chosen. Let the gauge be your guide. When you do, you'll find your intuition, which can be guided by your emotions, will sharpen—and, most importantly, you will know why it's sharper.

Reason #9: Combination Types

When a plot point is near the middle, it's common to misread people because they are combination types. You see them operating at one side of their range one moment and on the other side of their range hours (or days) later. For example, someone who is 1 EXPRESS and 3 NONASSERTIVE, might appear to be an ARTIST (EXPRESS) one day and an ACCOUNTANT (CONTROL) the next.

> △ **Antidote**: Commit to vigilantly apply Rule #3 that promotes systematic accuracy: Anything worth measuring is worth measuring at least twice.

Always take more than one read and test your reads. Don't ever assume your first or second read is accurate. Assume there will always be people who will fool you. Not because they are trying to trip you up, but simply because of their plot point.

Therefore, be especially vigilant when you think someone has a 2 plot point or less—when there is a strong possibility a person might be a combination type. People with extreme traits, around 4 or 5, usually won't fool you. Mentally, accept and prepare for the fact that you will need to take multiple reads for the 10–15% of those people you will meet who will be combination types. Accepting and applying this responsibility will not only increase your profiling accuracy of these people, but your overall profiling accuracy will improve because of your heightened awareness.

Also, remember entrepreneurs and those from small towns, as explained in Chapters 4 and 6, are more likely to have combination types than others.

Assignment #15

Goal: Be able to recall and apply the ideas in Chapters 7 and 11.
Time Required: 1 to 2 hours.

Type a short list of the reasons for misreads and their antidotes. On the back type a condensed list of the tips presented in Chapter 7. Carry this list as a quick reference guide, and do a review every few months.

CHAPTER 12

TWENTY
COMPREHENSIVE PROFILES

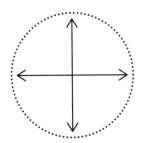

To this point, you've learned how to plot people on the four gauges and identify COMMUNICATION and PERFORMANCE types, which you can use as safety checks on your accuracy as well as to create SNAPSHOT and FINE-TUNED reads. You're now ready for the last step, combining COMMUNICATION and PERFORMANCE types together to reveal the COMPREHENSIVE profiles.

The COMPREHENSIVE profile not only provides a richer layer of insight into a person, but it also provides compact suggestions for the best ways to interact with someone. Each profile starts with a short summary paragraph and then includes:

- Strengths
- Shortcomings
- Other tendencies
- Trait indicators (which traits drive specific actions)

And, guidance for:

- Interaction tips
- Presenting and selling ideas, products, and services
- Handling confrontations and disagreements
- How to lead and motivate

The Three Benefits of Comprehensive Profiles

Increased insight and predictive ability—COMPREHENSIVE profiles give you more predictive accuracy because they show how COMMUNICATION and PERFORMANCE types interact when combined together. The COMPREHENSIVE profile is also invaluable for understanding your own profile and tendencies. After you've identified your profile, devote some time and journal how others perceive you as you reflect on past interactions.

You'll use the COMPREHENSIVE profiles in most important situations, such as negotiations, hiring or promoting a key person, coaching, calling upon a new client, critical investigations, teachers interviewing parents, family and personal relationships, and so on. The profiles not only provide more insight, but you can quickly see the differences between profiles, like a SERGEANT–MANAGER and a SERGEANT–INNOVATOR and how to interact with each.

For example, because a SERGEANT is CONTROL and ASSERTIVE, we might assume a SERGEANT can be depended upon in a crisis to give direction. But what if a person is a SERGEANT and a LOYALIST (CAUTIOUS and CONVENTIONAL). Now we have a SERGEANT type who may not be the best selection to provide consistent and confident direction under pressure. If your profile is a SALESMAN–INNOVATOR, for example, read the other profiles where just *one trait is different*, like the SERGEANT–INNOVATOR or ARTIST–INNOVATOR or SALESMAN–CAUTIOUS INNOVATOR. You'll note that similar profiles have some of the same or similar suggestions/observations because they *share traits*. This will also help you visualize the differences in profiles made by changing just one trait.

This kind of information can be critical when making long-term decisions about relationships or approaching some first-time interactions.

Compact suggestions for interaction—Each is formatted for easy reference (or you can use the app we'll discuss shortly). Unlike information provided by types, COMPREHENSIVE profiles also provide suggestions for how to interact with someone in specific contexts like how to lead and motive or how to defuse a confrontation or disagreement.

Your second safety check—COMPREHENSIVE profiles give you another layer of accuracy protection. Your first check on the accuracy of your reads are a person's type actions (Chapter 6), which you may want to review. Your second safety check is the twenty COMPREHENSIVE profiles. Just like you do with types, if the COMPREHENSIVE profile doesn't match, look at similar profiles that might be a match.

For example, perhaps you thought someone was SALESMAN and a MANAGER. When you read his COMPREHENSIVE profile, however, it's clear from the profile descriptors that you missed a read. So you may look at a similar profile, like the SALESMAN–INNOVATOR and find it's a match. This means you misread his CONVENTIONAL–UNCONVENTIONAL trait. If SALESMAN–INNOVATOR isn't a match, you might look at the SALESMAN–LOY-ALIST as the next option if you are certain you have the COMMUNICATION type accurate.

Four Predominantly Negative Profiles

As already stated, individual traits are not inherently good or bad, except for FEARFUL. There are, however, good and bad actions associated with each trait. Regarding sixteen of the twenty COMPREHENSIVE profiles, the same rule applies: There are no inherently good or bad profiles. People can use their profiles both positively and negatively. The exception are the four RANDOM ACTOR profiles.

As detailed in Chapter 9, people with the RANDOM ACTOR PERFORMANCE type are typically troubled individuals because of their FEARFUL trait (4 or 5). So it follows that the four RANDOM ACTOR COMPREHENSIVE profiles are also people who are struggling. Themes for how to interact with people with the RANDOM ACTOR profile are provided in Chapter 15 that augment the information provided in each RANDOM ACTOR profile in this chapter.

Three Helpful Suggestions

Evaluating the profile of someone who Is a combination type—If a person is a combination type, such as a SERGEANT/SALESMAN–MANAGER, you'll need to review the profiles of both the SERGEANT–MANAGER and the

SERGEANT–SALESMAN. (And, in some rare cases, in which someone is a combination type in both his COMMUNICATION and PERFORMANCE types, you will need to review as many as four profiles.) This will require some additional work to flesh out as you identify in which type someone prefers to operate based upon what type of situation.

Yes, this is an investment of time, but understanding the two (or up to four) arenas in which this person prefers to operate puts you much further ahead than if you didn't have any information at all. And, when you do take the time to understand them, you'll find appreciation and receptivity for your effort to understand and meet their complex needs.

Read both sell/present and confrontation suggestions—Two of the how-to-use-it paragraphs in each profile provide guidance to (1) Sell/Present or (2) Confront/Disagree. Be sure to read *both* paragraphs for *either* situation as they can overlap. In some Sell/Present situations there's the possibility of confrontation/rejection of ideas/products/services. And, to Confront/Disagree, you may need to sell an idea to a person to open up or to bring closure to a confrontation.

Review *both* COMPREHENSIVE profiles and FINE-TUNED reads—Of the two, the COMPREHENSIVE profile is a more powerful descriptor than the FINE-TUNED read. However, it is strongly recommended for critical situations that you review both a person's COMPREHENSIVE profile and his FINE-TUNED read. A specific action for a person's type might be an important ingredient when working with someone—an action that may not be in the COMPREHENSIVE profile.

For example, if a person is an ARTIST–INNOVATOR, observing a specific positive INNOVATOR action, such as *self-assured*, may indicate that this person will take action. Another action, *reckless*, might indicate he'll needlessly "rock the boat," an INNOVATOR shortcoming.

As reminded throughout, the word "typical" should not be interpreted as "always." These profiles are inventories of commonly seen actions for each combination of types, but they are not determinate. In addition to an individual's COMPREHENSIVE profile, you will need to take into consideration factors such as a person's unique combination of skills, intellect, culture, strategic positioning, and so on before interacting with that person.

Twenty Comprehensive Profiles

Below are the twenty different profile combinations. An important addition to this 2nd edition is the CAUTIOUS–INNOVATOR profile. Since our natural instinct is to read someone's COMMUNICATION type first, the combination of types are presented with the COMMUNICATION type listed first.

SERGEANT Types
- SERGEANT–MANAGER
- SERGEANT–INNOVATOR
- SERGEANT–LOYALIST
- SERGEANT–RANDOM ACTOR
- SERGEANT–CAUTIOUS INNOVATOR

ACCOUNTANT Types
- ACCOUNTANT–MANAGER
- ACCOUNTANT–INNOVATOR
- ACCOUNTANT–LOYALIST
- ACCOUNTANT–RANDOM ACTOR
- ACCOUNTANT–CAUTIOUS INNOVATOR

SALESMAN Types
- SALESMAN–MANAGER
- SALESMAN–INNOVATOR
- SALESMAN–LOYALIST
- SALESMAN–RANDOM ACTOR
- SALESMAN–CAUTIOUS INNOVATOR

ARTIST Types
- ARTIST–MANAGER
- ARTIST–INNOVATOR
- ARTIST–LOYALIST
- ARTIST–RANDOM ACTOR
- ARTIST–CAUTIOUS INNOVATOR

For specific profiles, which are more difficult to understand or where additional information is needed for interaction, more descriptors and suggestions are provided. The additional information, however, shouldn't be interpreted that one profile is more important than another. Every individual, regardless of one's profile, is important.

You'll also find that every profile that has the CAUTIOUS or FEARFUL trait (CAUTIOUS INNOVATORS and RANDOM ACTORS) will have some common observations/suggestions, such as mentoring to help make CONFIDENT decisions separate from one's area of competency (a concept explained in Chapter 14).

Using common and less common profiles to focus reads—In the 1st edition I explained that one way to decide where to focus your reads is to recognize that some profiles are more common than others. This strategy isn't stereotyping, rather it's utilizing this fact while still taking more than one read and testing your reads.

For example, let's assume you identified that Alice is an ACCOUNTANT. In the 1997 1st edition, a list of the most and least common profiles was provided, and it was more common to find ACCOUNTANT–MANAGERS than ACCOUNTANT–INNOVATORS. So, in the absence of an observable read, such as her likes and dislikes or her current employment, you could start with the hunch that Alice is more likely an ACCOUNTANT–MANAGER than an ACCOUNTANT–INNOVATOR and then test your hunch. This was a practical concept. Then extreme change occurred.

As explained in Chapter 9, cultures worldwide have severely shifted to the UNCONVENTIONAL trait and now we can't apply this principle as liberally. Today, it may be more likely to find people who are ACCOUNTANT–INNOVATORS rather than ACCOUNTANT–MANAGERS. The principle, though, is still useful, so long as you update your list based upon your observations in the cultures where you make your reads.

As a point of reference, a current list is provided as well as the original 1997 list. You'll note the CAUTIOUS INNOVATOR profiles have been added.

Common Profiles (Current)
- SERGEANT–MANAGER
- SERGEANT–LOYALIST
- SALESMAN–MANAGER
- SALESMAN–INNOVATOR
- SALESMAN–CAUTIOUS INNOVATOR
- ARTIST–INNOVATOR
- ARTIST–LOYALIST
- ARTIST–CAUTIOUS INNOVATOR
- ACCOUNTANT–LOYALIST
- ACCOUNTANT–INNOVATOR

Less Common Profiles (Current)
- SERGEANT–RANDOM ACTOR
- SERGEANT–INNOVATOR
- SERGEANT–CAUTIOUS INNOVATOR
- SALESMAN–RANDOM ACTOR
- SALESMAN–LOYALIST
- ACCOUNTANT–RANDOM ACTOR
- ARTIST–MANAGER
- ARTIST–RANDOM ACTOR
- ACCOUNTANT–MANAGER
- ACCOUNTANT–CAUTIOUS INNOVATOR

Common Profiles (1997)
- SERGEANT–MANAGER
- SERGEANT–CONFORMIST
- SALESMAN–MANAGER
- SALESMAN–INNOVATOR
- ACCOUNTANT–MANAGER

Less Common Profiles (1997)
- SERGEANT–RANDOM ACTOR
- SERGEANT–INNOVATOR
- SALESMAN–RANDOM ACTOR
- SALESMAN–CONFORMIST
- ACCOUNTANT–INNOVATOR

- ACCOUNTANT–CONFORMIST   • ACCOUNTANT–RANDOM ACTOR
- ARTIST–INNOVATOR   • ARTIST–MANAGER
- ARTIST–CONFORMIST   • ARTIST–RANDOM ACTOR

KPS App Is Available With All The Profiles

After several years of requests, an app is finally available that automates the *KPS* for use on cellphones (and soon computers) and contains all the profiles for instant access. It's called the Pocket PeopleReader®, and you can read about it at the back of the book or on the KoremAssociates.com website. It not only decreases your memory work, but the "suggestions for interactions" component can be customized for virtually any application, including: negotiations, leading teams, sales, coaching athletes, cross cultural interactions when you travel, and even selecting baby sitters.

The Twenty Comprehensive Profiles

SERGEANT–MANAGER

The SERGEANT–MANAGER has the following combination of traits:

- CONTROL–ASSERTIVE   • CONVENTIONAL–CONFIDENT

This common profile will typically be seen as a "strong" personality. Many are often labeled "strong executive timber" in the corporate world the stronger their traits. SERGEANT–MANAGERS often hold the CEO's chair in a large organization. The profile combines a dominant, controlled social style with a self-initiating, consistent PERFORMANCE type which is CONFIDENT. People with this profile can make a bold first impression and then show that they can "do what they say" over longer periods of time. While this profile is naturally suited for leadership roles, it isn't naturally suited for mentoring and it is also one that can turn callous and uncaring when negative actions aren't restrained.

Typical Strengths

- Combine emotional control and confidence.
- Perceived as being reliable to "deliver the goods" in almost any circumstances.
- Viewed as role models of how to maintain control.
- Viewed as "strong leaders."

Typical Shortcomings

- Can be rigid.
- Don't like change/unwilling to change.
- Over-dominate and over-control or stifle people who work with or for them.
- Often ineffective at developing/helping others.
- Can be poor listeners.
- Not effective when motivating diverse, complex teams that face creative problem-solving challenges.
- May have difficulty letting people work on their own. Often want to control and influence.
- May not be a natural "learner"; not particularly adaptive.

Other Tendencies

- Tend to hire "strong" people v. "growing" their successors or team.
- Prefer to let others learn on their own, but have difficulty letting others work on their own.
- Will make unilateral decisions when necessary to deliver final results.

Trait Indicators

- Shortcomings are most pronounced with high ASSERTIVE, CONFIDENT, or CONTROL traits.
- Strengths more pronounced when ASSERTIVE and CONFIDENT traits are stronger.
- Lower ASSERTIVE trait is the most likely indicator that they can overcome any listening deficiency and address shortcomings.

Interaction Tips

- Be direct and concrete in language.
- Focus on bottom line.
- When possible, help them adapt to ambiguity and the fact that they can't control all situations.
- Don't expect good "coaching" from them.

Sell/Present—Keep presentations short, crisp, and to the point. Use concrete language that displays a clear command of the facts and issues. Some emotional display is acceptable, but refrain from displays of emotions in place of facts. Don't try and "wing it" with fluff or you'll be shown the door. You may run into resistance if presenting a completely new concept, so try to link to similar products/services/strategies that were successful.

Confront/Disagree—When confronted, will typically turn to ASSERTIVE trait to respond. Be prepared with facts and hard, concrete language. Develop strategic control before and after engagement, but be especially respectful. They typically won't back down. The higher ASSERTIVE, CONFIDENT, and CONTROL, the more difficult to confront—the more preparation is needed. When possible, engage with a person whose ASSERTIVE, CONFIDENT, and CONTROL traits are stronger, or who has political capital that will cause this person to exercise restraint.

Lead/Motivate—They like challenges with clear objectives, without ambiguity, and tangible, non-abstract rewards. The higher the CONVENTIONAL and CONTROL, the fewer the words and displays of emotion should be used to lead and motivate. They must sense assertiveness in communication when being led and CONFIDENT during the mission. If you ask what motivates them, expect a direct answer; it's even better to anticipate and have a plan that matches their bottom line needs/desires.

SERGEANT–INNOVATOR

The SERGEANT–INNOVATOR has the following combination of traits:
- CONTROL–ASSERTIVE
- UNCONVENTIONAL–CONFIDENT

The SERGEANT–INNOVATOR'S profile is similar to the SERGEANT–MANAGER. The difference is the UNCONVENTIONAL trait. SERGEANT–MANAGERS prefer to be CONVENTIONAL while SERGEANT–INNOVATORS are UNCONVENTIONAL. This difference is why this profile is a significant source of entrepreneurs and others who lead in new and creative directions. SERGEANT–INNOVATORS have a COMMUNICATION type that allows them to "take charge" while their more open PERFORMANCE type will cause them to enjoy and thrive on change, risk-taking, and adventure, the higher their UNCONVENTIONAL and CONFIDENT traits.

Typical Strengths
- Comfortable with change and new and different ideas/appearances.
- Can be flexible in the amount of personal control they require in relationships.
- Can produce unique products and ideas.
- Tolerant of others' views and ideas. (This doesn't necessarily apply to tolerance of issues such as one's morals. Any of the profiles can be

tolerant or intolerant regarding moral issues.)
- Prefer to solicit ideas during the development stages of a new effort.
- Appear controlled and not inclined to "lose their cool."

Typical Shortcomings
- May over-control the delivery of final product or work effort—due to their creative bent.
- SERGEANT characteristics may dominate when deadlines approach.
- Relationships with others (and projects) may not be as consistent as SERGEANT–MANAGERS, and thus can cause more instability in the work environment.
- Like others with the UNCONVENTIONAL trait, may have trouble focusing and being consistent with follow-through, especially if high UNCONVENTIONAL.

Other Tendencies
- May be seen by others as erratic or eccentric—stronger UNCONVENTIONAL will magnify this quality/perception if not disciplined.
- Capable of developing a balance between career and outside interests.
- May appear inconsistent—may seek cooperation early in a relationship and then try to control later on.
- Will make unilateral decisions when necessary to deliver final results.

Trait Indicators
- Shortcomings are most pronounced when high UNCONVENTIONAL.
- Will appear more eccentric or hard to read the higher UNCONVENTIONAL, especially if negative actions are dominant.

Interaction Tips
- Don't be misled by open problem-solving style; will still try to dominate later in relationship.
- Anticipate "high drive" work style resulting from desire to control implementation of lots of ideas.
- Present range of ideas before you present specific recommendations.
- Watch confidence indicators closely; they will reveal strength of desire to control.

Sell/Present—Stay two or three steps ahead of anticipated questions, which will show your creative ability to keep up with their UNCONVENTIONAL trait. In this way you won't lose control of the situation, which they naturally seek. Also, infuse ideas that will trigger them to participate creatively, but in a predictable direction. Don't let creative dialogue get in the way of bringing closure to the sale or acceptance of a suggestion/idea.

Confront/Disagree—When confronted, they will turn to their ASSERTIVE trait, but with less predictability than the SERGEANT-MANAGER. They will typically rely upon a mix of creative thinking balanced by controlling emotions. It may be helpful to confront with two people—one who is ASSERTIVE and CONVENTIONAL and another who is ASSERTIVE and UNCONVENTIONAL, thus providing a balance. The person with the CONVENTIONAL trait can focus on fact issues and keep the dialogue on a more predictable course. The person who is UNCONVENTIONAL can engage the creative/abstract issues. If only one person is possible, use a person who is ASSERTIVE (preferably stronger than the person being confronted) and who is low UNCONVENTIONAL so he/she can cover the fact issues while not being intimidated by their UNCONVENTIONAL trait.

Lead/Motivate—The key to leading this profile is to provide a context in which discipline is created with rewards for timely performance. Unlike SERGEANT-MANAGERS who prefer tangible objectives and rewards, this profile may also value intangibles like ideals and opportunity for creative input/ownership. If you ask what motivates them, expect a direct answer, but it may be abstract. If lead by someone who is CONVENTIONAL, it's best if he/she is low CONVENTIONAL and has tolerance for the intangible.

SERGEANT–CAUTIOUS INNOVATOR

The SERGEANT–CAUTIOUS/INNOVATOR has the following combination of traits:

- CONTROL–ASSERTIVE
- UNCONVENTIONAL–CAUTIOUS/FEARFUL

The SERGEANT–CAUTIOUS/INNOVATOR profile can be confusing if not approached carefully because they are ASSERTIVE when they communicate, like to explore ideas, but are cautious when making decisions. Together, these traits can appear contradictory. This profile can be a productive player in a small group setting, especially technical, creative situations. Like other SERGEANTS, the higher the ASSERTIVE trait the easier they can be directive. When operating in their area of competency, may even be able to lead a small team with an innovative focus as long as not thrust into sudden change. Their cautious nature allows them to proceed carefully, weighing all the options, and their UNCONVENTIONAL trait is willing to consider new options. Like other CAUTIOUS/INNOVATORS they share many of the actions of INNOVATORS but are different in that they usually need more time to process decisions outside area of competency or when there is change.

Typical Strengths

- Comfortable with change and new and different ideas/appearances if given time to process.
- Can be flexible in the amount of personal control they require in relationships.
- Can produce unique products and ideas.
- Tolerant of others' views and ideas. (This doesn't necessarily apply to tolerance of issues such as one's morals. Any of the profiles can be tolerant or intolerant regarding moral issues.)
- Prefer to solicit ideas during the development stages of a new effort.
- Appear controlled and not inclined to "lose their cool" the lower their CAUTIOUS trait.

Typical Shortcomings

- May over-control the delivery of final product or work effort—due to combination of their creative bent and cautious nature.
- SERGEANT characteristics may dominate when deadlines approach.
- Relationships with others (and projects) may not be as consistent as SERGEANT–MANAGERS, and thus can cause more instability in the work environment.
- Like others with the UNCONVENTIONAL trait, may have trouble focusing and being consistent with follow-through, especially if high UNCONVENTIONAL.
- May not be suitable leaders because they lack personal confidence to quickly "take charge" in new or unfamiliar situations.
- Others may question their "value" or contribution to an organization or project if can't take action.
- May play the "devil's advocate" as a deflection because of FEARFUL trait to buy more time to make a decision; or use UNCONVENTIONAL trait to "explore" options/changes/ideas.

Other Tendencies

- May be seen by others as erratic or eccentric—stronger UNCONVENTIONAL will magnify this quality/perception if not disciplined.
- The higher the CAUTIOUS trait, the greater time required to process decisions and change.
- Capable of developing a balance between career and outside interests.

- May appear inconsistent—may seek cooperation early in a relationship and then try to control later on.
- More likely to make unilateral decisions when necessary to deliver final results the lower the CAUTIOUS trait (0–2) and if operating in area of competency.
- When communicating, more likely to be ASSERTIVE, the higher the trait, but more likely to seek consensus or have others make final decisions when working on a situation/project due to CAUTIOUS trait.
- Most effective in a less regimented/bureaucratic environment.
- What can cause them internal tension is their CAUTIOUS trait. They want to do something new, but caution is a restraint. This trait, though, can be applied as a positive restraint to test new ideas/concepts before taking action.

Trait Indicators

- Shortcomings are most pronounced when high UNCONVENTIONAL and high CAUTIOUS.
- Will appear more eccentric or hard to read the higher UNCONVENTIONAL and CAUTIOUS, especially if negatives of either trait are dominant.

Interaction Tips

- Don't be misled by open problem-solving style; may try to dominate the "discussion" the higher ASSERTIVE, but will put off making a decision.
- Don't be frustrated by their "mixed style" when they deal "up the chain of command" v. "down the chain of command." When they deal "down," they will tend to be more dominant the lower the CAUTIOUS trait, while they'll appear to be less dominant when they deal "up" the chain of command.
- Anticipate cautious work style as they work to implement lots of ideas.
- Present range of ideas before you present specific recommendations, and provide more time to process than with INNOVATORS.
- Watch confidence indicators closely; they will reveal resistance to make a decision, even if bright and seemingly in command of the facts.
- Allow time to gain approval of leaders.

Sell/Present—Stay two or three steps ahead of anticipated questions, which will show your creative ability to keep up with their UNCONVENTIONAL trait. In this way you won't lose control of the situation if they start playing the "devil's advocate." Infuse ideas that will trigger them to participate creatively, but without personal risk. Don't expect SERGEANT–CAUTIOUS/INNOVATORS to take risks. If you do ask them to take a risk, expect severe reversals later if their security is in any way threatened the higher the CAUTIOUS trait. They'll take in new ideas but will need time to make a decision. Best to find someone who is CONFIDENT to help them make a decision, especially outside area of competency. If not given time to evaluate decisions or something new, will lay the blame at your feet—or anyone else who is available.

Confront/Disagree—When confronted, they'll turn to their ASSERTIVE trait, to minimize their immediate fears, and then they take the offensive using their SERGEANT actions—but with less predictability than the SERGEANT–INNOVATOR because of the CAUTIOUS trait. They will typically rely upon a mix of creative thinking balanced by controlling emotions. Similar to SERGEANT–INNOVATORS, it may be helpful to confront with two people—one who is ASSERTIVE and CONVENTIONAL and another who is ASSERTIVE and UNCONVENTIONAL, thus providing a balance. The person with the CONVENTIONAL trait can focus on fact issues and keep the dialogue on a more predictable course. The person who is UNCONVENTIONAL can engage the creative/abstract issues. If only one person is possible, use a person who is ASSERTIVE (preferably stronger than the person being confronted), CONFIDENT, and who is low UNCONVENTIONAL so he/she can cover the fact issues while not being intimidated by their UNCONVENTIONAL trait or derailed by inability to make a decision.

Lead/Motivate—The key to leading this profile is to provide a context in which discipline is created with rewards for timely performance where they aren't asked to risk personal failure outside area of competency. Unlike SERGEANT–MANAGERS, who prefer tangible objectives and rewards, this profile may put a higher value on intangibles, like ideals and ideas. If you ask what motivates them, expect a direct answer, but it will probably be abstract and even vague the higher the CAUTIOUS trait. If lead by someone who is CONVENTIONAL, it's best if he/she is low CONVENTIONAL (2 or lower) and has tolerance for the intangible and patience for more time to reach decisions. As explained in Chapter 14 and *Snapshot*, mentor how to make small bite-sized CONFIDENT decisions separate from area of competency to expand capacity for increased confident decision-making.

SERGEANT–LOYALIST

The SERGEANT–LOYALIST has the following combination of traits:
- CONTROL–ASSERTIVE
- CONVENTIONAL–CAUTIOUS/FEARFUL

The SERGEANT–LOYALIST has the dominant, CONTROL-oriented interpersonal style of the SERGEANT, coupled with the "dutiful and loyal" PERFORMANCE type of the LOYALIST. This type is most easily characterized as the loyal, obedient middle manager, or lower level staff officer. Because of their caution-based motivations coupled with their social dominance and predictability, they will seldom risk new ideas or challenges or challenge others or the status quo. SERGEANT–LOYALISTS dislike sudden or unpredictable change, and they fear the personal consequences of such change. They do not want to be surprised or to surprise those who may control their future or their fate.

Typical Strengths
- Faithful "right-hand" people who will deliver results once the task is defined or initiated.
- Motivated by loyalty, not personal fame or recognition.
- Will be described by others as persistent and tenacious.

Typical Shortcomings
- Do not make good leaders because they lack personal confidence to "take charge" in new or unfamiliar situations.
- Likely to be "blindly loyal" the higher the CAUTIOUS/FEARFUL trait.
- Others may question their "value" or contribution to an organization or project.

Other Tendencies
- Seldom risk new ideas/challenges.
- Rarely challenge system or superiors.
- May appear as dictators and stiff autocrats to subordinates ("down the ladder") while appearing overly compliant to superiors or other "controllers" ("up the ladder").
- While socially strong, their PERFORMANCE type tends to be followers and not self-initiating.

Trait Indicators
- Higher CAUTIOUS/FEARFUL trait is typically associated with more risk-aversion and tendency to avoid challenging any aspect of the system or the environment.

- Lower ratings on ASSERTIVE and CONTROL will make them appear to be more consistent and easier to understand. The effect is a softer, less commanding SERGEANT.
- Higher ASSERTIVE and CONTROL traits combined with CAUTIOUS/FEARFUL is what makes them seem contradictory to others. (The effect is a strong directive in the talk but a weak showing in the walk.)

Interaction Tips

- Be sure to always deliver on promises and commitments.
- The higher the CAUTIOUS/FEARFUL trait, the more likely they are to point a finger at you when you are not to blame for a problem. Therefore, evaluate entering situations where risk is a significant factor. This can especially be difficult, the higher the ASSERTIVE trait.
- Expect rigid interpretations of rules; don't ask for compromises or exceptions.
- Allow time for SERGEANT–LOYALISTS to gain approval of leaders.
- Don't misinterpret a defense of the "status quo" for being CONFIDENT.
- Don't be frustrated by their "mixed style" when they deal "up the chain of command" v. "down the chain of command." When they deal "down," they will tend to be more dominant, while they will appear to be less dominant when they deal "up" the chain of command.
- Like all LOYALIST profiles, encourage them to recognize their natural tendencies toward loyalty and to consider carefully the integrity of those whom they serve so that their trusting nature isn't abused.
- Like other LOYALIST profiles, operate with them in their area of expertise.

Sell/Present—Use SERGEANT or ACCOUNTANT type with excellent verbal skills who knows content for presentation. Remove ambiguity in both presentation and in the expected outcome. Do not expect SERGEANT–LOYALISTS to take risks. If asked to take a risk, expect severe reversals later if their security is in any way threatened. They're not problem-solvers and will lay the blame at your feet—or anyone else who is available. Like other LOYALIST profiles, best to find another person in the organization to sell to or act as a support to undergird and strengthen any decision that is made or if this person later gets "cold feet."

Confront/Disagree—When confronted, they usually turn to their ASSERTIVE trait to minimize their immediate fears, and then they take the offensive using their SERGEANT actions. It can be helpful if the confronter is CONFIDENT and ASSERTIVE. Remember, when backed in a corner, they will be driven by FEAR when making decisions. So, tactically work to reverse fear during the engagement as well as after the engagement when they have time to reflect and may choose to retaliate. Other profiles that have a CONFIDENT trait, such as a SERGEANT–MANAGER, might accept a blow and move on. They are more likely, however, to plot retaliation because of their fear of rejection and loss of stature with others.

Lead/Motivate— Do not present with critical decisions or significant change. Lead with clear objectives without ambiguity and provide tangible, non-abstract rewards for dutiful, non-risk performance. Like SERGEANT–MANAGERS, the higher the CONVENTIONAL and CONTROL the fewer the words and displays of emotion should be used to lead and motivate. If you spontaneously ask what motivates them, expect hesitancy. If you give them time, expect a calculated answer that measures risk and stature first. What motivates this profile is tangible rewards for dutiful performance that is well mapped out and is a part of a team effort. As explained in Chapter 14 and *Snapshot*, mentor how to make small bite-sized CONFIDENT decisions separate from area of competency to expand capacity for increased confident decision-making.

SERGEANT–RANDOM ACTOR

The SERGEANT–RANDOM ACTOR has the following combination of traits:
- CONTROL–ASSERTIVE
- UNCONVENTIONAL–FEARFUL

SERGEANT–RANDOM ACTORS, while not a common profile, may be one of the most difficult and troubling of all the profiles. The COMMUNICATION type of SERGEANT–RANDOM ACTORS will cause them to initially appear much like the other SERGEANT-based profiles, but their performance will vary widely across time and situations. This is because they are motivated by extreme fear and their actions are UNCONVENTIONAL. It's not uncommon to find someone with this profile in leadership roles in organizations that have a deceptive theme consistent in their culture. In history, Adolph Hitler possessed this profile. The combination of his SERGEANT traits, ASSERTIVE and CONTROL, and his FEARFUL trait presented a rigid appearance; he used his ASSERTIVE trait to try to control others and control his fears.

SERGEANT–RANDOM ACTORS will seek to maintain the strong, controlling image of the SERGEANT, but will frequently disappoint others with their unreliability and their unwillingness to take responsibility for their circumstances. Their fear-based motivation will cause them to feel and act "out of control" while their COMMUNICATION type will drive them to maintain the appearance of CONTROL. This combination of traits will produce a tension that can result in anger, impatience, depression, moodiness, or authoritarianism, which shouldn't be confused as the EXPRESS trait. Additionally, when they have a strong ASSERTIVE trait, the illusion may be created of being high CONFIDENT. (Be sure to review general observations of RANDOM ACTORS in this chapter and Chapters 8 and 15.)

Typical Strengths

- Able to appear strong and dominant in short-term relationships like any of the SERGEANT-based profiles.
- Can be a strong "second in command" in situations requiring unswerving loyalty or in very controlled situations. (This may serve the purposes of their commanders, but produce a harrowing experience for those under them if their status is threatened.)
- Like other RANDOM ACTOR profiles, can have a positive front if operating in area of competency.

Typical Shortcomings

- No matter what their performance level, they will attempt to dominate and control others.
- Their unpredictability and fear-based motivations yield random actions that may have no relevance to the situation.
- They tend to act defensively, even when a threat isn't present.
- Susceptible to depression, neuroses, and risks of self-harm—even suicide the more extreme their PERFORMANCE traits.
- Lack the confidence of the INNOVATOR types to translate their unconventionality into creativity, unless someone else executes the plan, or to trust their judgment when acting outside standard operating procedure.
- Can be dangerous when placed in a position of unilateral and unmonitored power, especially the stronger their FEARFUL and ASSERTIVE traits and if extreme negative actions of each are present combined with the lack of a moral compass.
- Like other RANDOM ACTOR profiles, if asked to operate outside area of competency/expertise, FEARFUL trait can take over.

Other Tendencies

- COMMUNICATION type will appear as strong as other SERGEANT-type profiles, especially the higher ASSERTIVE, while performance indicators vary widely.
- This can be one of the more confusing profiles to read because even though they are ASSERTIVE, they are FEARFUL when making decisions.
- If has a moral compass, may be able to restrain volatile self-centered behavior, although daily actions may still be inherently destructive.

Trait Indicators

- How often they will be required to operate outside area of competency and the volatility of the FEARFUL trait will determine level of risk when dealing with them.
- Extreme UNCONVENTIONAL trait and associated negative actions trait should be considered carefully for pathological implications in combination with high FEARFUL trait.
- Can choose to move out of their RANDOM ACTOR type by learning to make small decisions out of confidence and trust, and can become CAUTIOUS/INNOVATORS, especially if they have a solid moral/ethical standard.

Interaction Tips

- Avoid implied threats or criticisms.
- Focus on building their self-confidence and providing structure to offset unpredictability.
- Focus on that which is positive that they can control.
- Avoid sudden changes in direction or plans.
- Do not give a lot of freedom when making decisions, especially where there is the threat of risk involved outside the area of their expertise/competency, as this will increase the possibility that they will rely upon guile to defend or conceal their position.

Sell/Present—Like all RANDOM ACTOR types, presenter should appeal to whatever positive actions are found in their COMMUNICATION type. Avoid making presentations to these people when risk is involved and/or if they are FEARFUL—especially if the interaction is long-term. Keep presentations direct and language clean/clear and unambiguous. When risk of failure is low, you can venture out to ideas as well, but otherwise, stick to the bottom line. Anticipate and prepare for swift reversals, even after they say "yes."

Confront/Disagree—First, be sure to review the guidelines for interacting with a RANDOM ACTOR detailed throughout the text. Because they possess a SERGEANT type, they will try to dominate. Therefore, be prepared to use a stronger ASSERTIVE trait when closure is sought. The higher the level the confrontation, the stronger the ASSERTIVE trait and the swifter the action required. Don't drag it out or they will try to dominate. Be swift. Appeal to some positive goal toward which the SERGEANT side of these people can direct their attention. When SERGEANT–RANDOM ACTORS threaten you, they will be overt, not subtle. As with other RANDOM ACTOR profiles, appeal to the positive actions you observe in their COMMUNICATION type.

Lead/Motivate—Lead and motivate them in their area of expertise and competency focusing on the positive actions you observe in their COMMUNICATION actions. Do not present with critical decisions. The higher the UNCONVENTIONAL trait the more likely will want norms and willing to try new ideas/ventures, but must be provided significant time for FEARFUL trait to absorb opportunity. Emphasize team effort and safety nets along the way. Only place them in a position to use their ASSERTIVE trait when operating in area of expertise/competency, and only for short periods of time. As explained in Chapter 14 and *Snapshot*, mentor how to make small bite-sized CONFIDENT decisions separate from area of competency to expand capacity for increased confident decision-making.

SALESMAN–MANAGER

The SALESMAN–MANAGER has the following combination of traits:

- EXPRESS–ASSERTIVE
- CONVENTIONAL–CONFIDENT

SALESMAN–MANAGERS are a common profile characterized by predictability and self-confidence as well as a salesman/communicator COMMUNICATION type. They are very similar to SERGEANT–MANAGERS except they have a more open communication style. They are perceived as "disciplined extroverts" who appear warm and open on first meeting, but demonstrate decisiveness, a willingness to take leadership roles, and a desire to deliver predictable performance. Because of these qualities, they are often in sales and marketing or managerial positions. In many ways, this profile may represent an ideal leadership/ambassador style, especially for larger organizations where both charisma and consistency in performance are required to meet the needs of a wide ranging constituency of investors, customers, and employees. They may even provide superior leadership when compared to the SERGEANT–MANAGER or SERGEANT–INNOVATOR because of their initial focus on open, positive personal relationships. The SALESMAN–MANAGER will approach people and situations with an open, direct style followed by a focused concern with delivering performance commitments. They can be particularly effective in leading strong teams who are facing complex problems that require diverse input to achieve a solution.

Typical Strengths
- Inspire confidence in others.
- Reliable.
- Able to maintain both open relationships and consistent performance trends at the same time.
- Will take unilateral action when required, but don't always need to be in control.

Typical Shortcomings
- May not be a natural "learner"; not particularly adaptive.
- Will base decisions on experience rather than creativity; not inclined to look for new and different ways to approach questions or relationships.

Other Tendencies
- Take a pragmatic approach to new, opportunistic situations.
- Will surprise those who stereotypically view the SALESMAN type as all "hot air."

Trait Indicators
- Ability to rely on more than past experience and performance increases with low CONVENTIONAL trait.
- High ASSERTIVE indicates less of a facilitator and more of a directive leader.

Interaction Tips
- Encourage them to consider alternative ideas and new solutions before settling on a given solution or answer.
- Provide clear, unambiguous directives.
- Be direct and open in all forms of conversation.
- Expect decisiveness, not extensive discussion.
- Sell new ideas based on their links to previous successes; build on experience.

Sell/Present—Sell the bottom line with a firm ASSERTIVE orientation. Reference past successes and how they predictably will lead to future successes. You may run into resistance if presenting a completely new concept, so try to link to similar products/services/strategies that were successful. If you use a NONASSERTIVE person for a presentation, be sure this person is articulate and well in command of the facts, because he won't be able to fall back on an ASSERTIVE trait to keep things moving forward if there is difficulty.

Confront/Disagree—Engage much as you would SERGEANT–MANAGERS, but use an open communication style. When confronted, will typically turn to ASSERTIVE trait to respond. Be prepared with facts and hard, concrete language. Develop strategic control before and after engagement, but be especially respectful. They typically won't back down. The higher ASSERTIVE, CONFIDENT, and the lower EXPRESS (2 or less), the more difficult to confront— the more preparation is needed. When possible, engage with a person whose ASSERTIVE, CONFIDENT are stronger and EXPRESS trait is lower, and who has political capital that will cause this person to exercise restraint. If appropriate, appeal to the EXPRESS trait to encourage open dialogue. Be careful, though, because this could increase volatility when there is tension. If resistance is present, detail the predictable results that will ensue if cooperation is not forthcoming. Focus on concrete issues, potential loss of stature, and their experiences rather than abstract ideas and concepts.

Lead/Motivate—Lead them as you would SERGEANT–MANAGERS, but use a more open social style—they have a higher tolerance for more dialogue/words. Apply greater emphasis on predictable results when presenting new concepts the higher the CONVENTIONAL trait (3 or higher). The higher the CONFIDENT trait, emphasize personal ownership for the task/project and that they will receive personal recognition for results. Like SERGEANT–MANAGERS, they like challenges, but make objectives clear without ambiguity and provide tangible, non-abstract rewards. The higher the CONVENTIONAL and the lower the EXPRESS trait (2 or less) the fewer the words and displays of emotion should be used to lead and motivate. If you ask what motivates them, expect a direct answer; it's even better to anticipate and have a plan that matches their bottom line needs/desires.

SALESMAN–INNOVATOR

The SALESMAN–INNOVATOR has the following combination of traits:

- EXPRESS–ASSERTIVE
- UNCONVENTIONAL–CONFIDENT

This profile shares many similarities with the SALESMAN–MANAGER, and is able to avoid a potential weakness of that profile: the negative side of UNCONVENTIONAL. Look for these people to be the creative sparks in a sales/marketing/communication arena. Entrepreneurs often possess this profile as well. The combination of confidence and unpredictability results in a personal PERFORMANCE type that is likely to be more creative and innovative than the SALESMAN–MANAGER. However, the creativity may be achieved at the expense of focus and discipline that is required in a leadership profile, which is why they aren't typically suited for sustainer roles of a corporate mission. SALESMAN–INNOVATORS have an extroverted COMMUNICATION type coupled with a "free-wheeling" PERFORMANCE type. They are typically enjoyable and productive team-players, quickly engaging in interpersonal interactions and at the same time willing to explore new ideas and creative solutions to problems. Depending on the level of ASSERTIVE (social dominance), they will either be a good facilitator of team activities or they may have a tendency to try to direct the team once the creative elements of the team's task are complete.

Typical Strengths

- Combine charisma with creativity and willingness to take risks.
- Can be good facilitators of problem-solving teams.
- Most effective in a less regimented/bureaucratic environment.
- Likely to be strong leaders in smaller, more entrepreneurial environments.
- Comfortable with change and new and different ideas/appearances.
- Flexible in the amount of personal control they require in relationships.
- Can produce unique products and ideas.
- Tolerant of others' views and ideas. (This doesn't necessarily apply to tolerance of issues such as one's morals. Any of the profiles can be tolerant or intolerant regarding moral issues.)
- Prefer to solicit ideas during the development stages of a new effort.

Typical Shortcomings

- Should not be called on to lead in situations where long-term, consistent, patterned results are the desired result, such as an

unchanging sales environment.
- Can appear "out of control" or "off the wall" when profile is extreme and accompanied by negative UNCONVENTIONAL actions.
- May be inclined to "job-hop" if not focused.
- Can be impulsive; usually not worried about the effects of impulsivity.

Other Tendencies
- May be described by others as always having a new idea or plan.

Trait Indicators
- The higher the ASSERTIVE trait the more likely they will have the ability to lead; the lower the ASSERTIVE trait the easier for them to be strong team players.
- "Out of control" style will be most noticeable when EXPRESS and UNCONVENTIONAL are high when there is lack of or resistance to discipline.

Interaction Tips
- Avoid assigning them long-term roles requiring routine performance.
- Focus on their tendency toward need for change and personal recognition.
- Give them leadership roles in problem-solving settings, not in solution implementation roles.

Sell/Present—Sell the benefit of ideas, innovations, and so on, rather than the bottom line. Presenter can use low NONASSERTIVE trait as long as verbal skill and/or ideas are good, though ASSERTIVE is preferable. The lower their ASSERTIVE, CONFIDENT, or UNCONVENTIONAL traits, the more likely they will seek advice from their team. Alternately, the higher these traits, the more likely they will feel comfortable taking action on their own. The latter may cause problems with their group, so it may be beneficial to include other members of their team in presentations, decision making, and so on.

Confront/Disagree—It is advisable to confront with a stronger ASSERTIVE trait. Also, either EXPRESS or CONTROL trait can be used. Focus on creative options that, if acted upon, will increase their personal stature. Alternately, when there is resistance, focus on how this can depreciate their stature, ideas, or creative input.

Lead/Motivate—Similar to SERGEANT–MANAGERS the key to leading this profile is to provide a context in which discipline is created with rewards for timely performance, but with a more open social style as they have a higher tolerance for more dialogue/words. Unlike SERGEANT/SALESMAN–MANAGERS who prefer tangible objectives and rewards, this profile may also value intangibles like ideals and opportunity for creative input/ownership. If you ask what motivates them, expect a direct answer, but it may be abstract. If lead by someone who is CONVENTIONAL, it's best if he/she is low CONVENTIONAL (2 or lower) and has tolerance for the intangible. Most prefer an open, relationship-driven environment to perform.

SALESMAN–CAUTIOUS INNOVATOR

The SALESMAN–INNOVATOR has the following combination of traits:
- EXPRESS–ASSERTIVE
- UNCONVENTIONAL–CAUTIOUS/FEARFUL

Like the SERGEANT–CAUTIOUS/INNOVATOR profile the SALESMAN–CAUTIOUS/INNOVATOR profile can be confusing if not approached carefully because they are ASSERTIVE when they communicate, like to explore ideas, but are cautious when making decisions. Together, these traits can appear contradictory. What makes them more accessible by comparison is their EXPRESS trait which creates a more open social style. They are typically enjoyable and productive team-players, quickly engaging in interpersonal interactions, and at the same time willing to explore new ideas and creative solutions to problems. This profile can be a productive facilitator in a small group setting—creative sparks in a sales/marketing/communication arena. While not natural leaders, when operating in their area of competency and have a low CAUTIOUS trait, may be able to lead a small team with an innovative focus for the short term as long as not thrust into sudden change. Their cautious nature allows them to proceed carefully, weighing all the options, and their UNCONVENTIONAL trait is willing to consider new options. However, creativity may be achieved at the expense of focus and discipline that is required in a leadership profile. Like other CAUTIOUS/INNOVATORS they share many of the actions of INNOVATORS but are different in that they usually need more time to process decisions outside area of competency or when there is change.

Typical Strengths
- Comfortable with change and new and different ideas/appearances if given time to process.
- Flexible in the amount of personal control they require in relationships.
- Can produce unique products and ideas.

- Tolerant of others' views and ideas. (This doesn't necessarily apply to tolerance of issues such as one's morals. Any of the profiles can be tolerant or intolerant regarding moral issues.)
- For short-term assignments and when operating in area of competency, can be facilitators of problem-solving teams.
- Comfortable with change and new and different ideas/appearances if given time to process.

Typical Shortcomings

- Like others with the UNCONVENTIONAL trait, may have trouble focusing and being consistent with follow-through, especially if high UNCONVENTIONAL.
- Should not be called on to lead in situations where long-term, consistent, patterned results are desired, such as an unchanging sales environment.
- Can appear "goofy" or "off the wall" when profile is extreme.
- May be inclined to "job-hop" if not focused.
- May play the "devil's advocate" as a deflection because of FEARFUL trait to buy more time to make a decision; or use UNCONVENTIONAL trait to "explore" options/changes/ideas.
- Others may question their "value" or contribution to an organization or project if can't take action.

Other Tendencies

- The higher the CAUTIOUS trait, the greater time required to process decisions and change.
- Capable of developing a balance between career and outside interests.
- Most effective in a less regimented or bureaucratic environment.
- May be described by others as always having a new idea or plan.
- Prefer to solicit ideas during the development stages of a new effort.
- What can cause them internal tension is their CAUTIOUS trait. They want to do something new, but caution is a restraint. This trait, though, can be applied as a positive restraint to test new ideas/concepts before taking action.

Trait Indicators

- Shortcomings are most pronounced when high UNCONVENTIONAL and high CAUTIOUS.
- Will appear more eccentric or hard to read the higher

UNCONVENTIONAL and CAUTIOUS, especially if negatives of
either trait are dominant.

- "Out of control" unfocused style will be most noticeable when EXPRESS
and UNCONVENTIONAL are high.

Interaction Tips

- Avoid assigning long-term roles requiring routine performance.
- Focus on their tendency toward need for change and personal
recognition.
- If given short-term leadership role, do so only in problem-solving
settings, not in solution implementation roles.
- Anticipate cautious work style as they work to implement lots ideas.
- Watch confidence indicators closely; they will reveal resistance to make
a decision, even if bright and seemingly in command of the facts.
- Allow time to gain approval of leaders.

Sell/Present—Sell the benefit of ideas, innovations, and so on, rather
than the bottom line. Presenter should be EXPRESS or ability to connect with
EXPRESS person; can use low NONASSERTIVE trait as long as verbal skill and/
or ideas are good, though ASSERTIVE is preferable. The lower their ASSERTIVE
or UNCONVENTIONAL traits and the higher their CAUTIOUS trait (2 or higher),
the more likely they will seek advice from their team. Alternately, the higher
the first two traits and the more CONFIDENT, the more likely they will feel
comfortable taking action on their own. The latter may cause problems with
their group, so it may be beneficial to include other members of their team in
presentations, decision making, and so on.

Confront/Disagree—It is advisable to confront with a stronger ASSERTIVE
trait. Also, either EXPRESS or CONTROL trait can be used. Focus on creative
options that, if acted upon, will increase their personal stature. Alternately,
when there is resistance, focus on how this can depreciate their stature, ideas,
or creative input.

Lead/Motivate—Like other CAUTIOUS/INNOVATORS, lead and motivate
them in their area of expertise and competency. Do not present with critical decisions outside area of competency. The higher the UNCONVENTIONAL
trait the more likely they will press norms and be willing to try new ideas/
ventures, but must be provided significant time for FEARFUL trait to absorb
opportunity. Emphasize team effort and safety nets along the way, and provide
an open, relationship-driven environment to perform. Similar to SERGEANT–

INNOVATORS the key to leading this profile is to provide a context in which discipline is created with rewards for timely performance, but with a more open social style as they have a higher tolerance for more dialogue/words. As explained in Chapter 14 and *Snapshot,* mentor how to make small bite-sized CONFIDENT decisions separate from area of competency to expand capacity for increased confident decision-making.

SALESMAN–LOYALIST

The SALESMAN–LOYALIST has the following combination of traits:
- EXPRESS–ASSERTIVE
- CONVENTIONAL–CAUTIOUS/FEARFUL

This profile combines the qualities of extroversion (SALESMAN) with obedience or a sense of duty (LOYALIST). The dominant COMMUNICATION type will almost always be noticed first, causing the more submissive side of the profile to be overlooked. The higher their ASSERTIVE trait, the more likely they will lead with their COMMUNICATION type. This profile is often suitable for routine sales positions, such as the classic order-taker, or other industries that require extensive people contact, such as customer relations. Do not count on them for high-powered creativity or initiative. When the SALESMAN type is combined with significant task competency, they may be able to operate in environments that require a little bit of risk-taking and significant attention to detail, such as a low-key but technical account manager salaried position. Other suitable roles are communication responsibilities which require a willingness to be directed, such as a low-key media broadcast position where one's strength is reading copy from a teleprompter rather than on-the-street reporting. SALESMAN–LOYALISTS are able to handle these kinds of low stress-provoking situations because they fall back on their ASSERTIVE trait during interactions, even though they aren't CONFIDENT.

Typical Strengths
- Display loyalty typical of LOYALIST type.
- Open, expressive, and endearing COMMUNICATION type.
- Well-suited for "rote" people-contact types of jobs (e.g., telephone sales, order-takers, customer service, etc.).

Typical Shortcomings
- Avoid risks in both social and performance arenas.

- Minimal leadership ability, other than ASSERTIVE trait.
- Lack creativity.
- Not strong problem-solvers.
- Lack strong personal initiative.

Other Tendencies
- Not as reactive as other SALESMAN profiles.
- Not a good second-in-command because they will be seen as only passing on the orders and directions of whoever is really in charge.
- Can be the "life of the party" the higher EXPRESS and ASSERTIVE but will have difficulty contributing to group problem-solving efforts.

Trait Indicators
- High ASSERTIVE trait can create impression of lacking in substance because of a lack of follow-through outside area of competency.
- High EXPRESS combined with strong LOYALIST traits will give appearance of being sympathetic, but ineffective in helping others solve problems—they can audit but not likely to find solutions.

Interaction Tips
- Don't expect big results quickly. They tend to be socially open, but move slowly.
- Give them explicit instructions about how they are to interact with others.
- Don't rely on their social skills to lead a group in problem-solving.
- Avoid quick changes that will be unsettling to their performance type.
- Like all LOYALIST profiles, encourage them to recognize their natural tendency toward loyalty and to consider carefully the integrity of those whom they serve so that their trusting nature isn't abused.
- Like other LOYALIST profiles, operate with them in their area of expertise.

Sell/Present—Create an open environment in which they can dialogue, as appropriate. Avoid presentations targeted toward making hard decisions. Rather, appeal to the fact that your idea seems to fit in with the norm—what is acceptable in their organization. Use ASSERTIVE trait with restraint, except when establishing friendly rapport. Then pull back ASSERTIVE trait a bit so that it doesn't provoke their CAUTIOUS/FEARFUL trait when they must make take a step forward. Like other LOYALIST profiles, best to find another person in the organization to sell to or act as a support to undergird and strengthen any decision that is made or if this person later gets "cold feet."

Confront/Disagree—To establish rapport, use EXPRESS trait to connect with their sociable SALESMAN style. Appeal to the status quo in which they feel comfortable operating. When confrontation is complex, work at obtaining concessions in small bites, so they don't overload due to their CAUTIOUS/FEARFUL trait. The lower their ASSERTIVE and EXPRESS trait the less likely for explosiveness. If retaliation does occur, it will probably be spontaneous, energized by their SALESMAN type. So, if tensions increase, appeal to their positive LOYALIST actions, to reduce potential explosiveness.

Lead/Motivate—Like other LOYALIST profiles, lead and motivate in their area of expertise and competency, and like other SALESMAN types they appreciate and respond to a more open social style as they have a higher tolerance for more dialogue/words. Do not present with critical decisions or significant change, but emphasize loyalty to the team/mission. If change is presented, must provide significant time to process and accept. Emphasize team effort and safety nets along the way. As explained in Chapter 14 and *Snapshot*, mentor how to make small bite-sized CONFIDENT decisions separate from area of competency to expand capacity for increased confident decision making.-

SALESMAN–RANDOM ACTOR

The SALESMAN–RANDOM ACTOR has the following combination of traits:
  - EXPRESS–ASSERTIVE   - UNCONVENTIONAL–FEARFUL

This profile is a picture of extroverted, dominant people who charismatically react to most situations out of their lack of self-confidence or fear of failure. It is not uncommon for cult leaders to possess this profile. David Koresh, the Waco, Texas, cult leader for example, or manic marketeers, who are given to bouts of severe depression. Their PERFORMANCE type causes them to appear unfocused and easily influenced by anyone or anything that might impact their fears. And when there is a focus, it is typically founded in an effort to derail their fears, except in their area of competency. In the workplace, this person often has the reputation for being a charmer and "hot air" with no substance when called upon to perform. Intellectual savvy coupled with manipulative control, however, can allow some to amass a following for a while, even though they inherently lack leadership. It works like this: Their SALESMAN COMMUNICATION type first captures the group, and then they reciprocally "capture" him because of their misguided needs/desires.

SALESMAN–RANDOM ACTORS typically move from one opportunity to another based solely on their need for variety and change, while trying to avoid any source of conflict or pain that will increase their fears. They look for the "greener pastures on the other side of the fence" in their professional and private lives, or, in the case of Koresh, create a paranoiac greener pasture—a compound—while inviting/directing others to join him in his misguided fear. (Be sure to review general observations of RANDOM ACTORS in this chapter and Chapters 9 and 15.)

Typical Strengths
- More easily led or motivated by most leadership styles the lower their ASSERTIVE and FEARFUL traits.
- Open, candid COMMUNICATION type.
- Always willing to risk emotions or tradition (but not willing to risk relationships).

Typical Shortcomings
- Will seek approval from or appease whoever is in control, especially when medium to low ASSERTIVE.
- More willing to lead others in misguided efforts the higher the ASSERTIVE trait.
- If they lead and attract others, it is through a combination of a strong ASSERTIVE and EXPRESS trait that sells fear and paranoia; thus, the group bands together for "protection."
- Lack both discipline and self-control.
- Susceptible to depression, neuroses, and risks of self-harm—even suicide the more extreme their PERFORMANCE traits.
- One of the most impulsive of all profiles because of the combination of UNCONVENTIONAL, FEARFUL, and EXPRESS.

Other Tendencies
- Can't keep secrets.
- Avoids confrontation or conflict; when extreme, build compounds (literally and figuratively).
- If has a moral compass, may be able to restrain volatile self-centered behavior, although daily actions may still be inherently destructive.

Trait Indicators
- Low UNCONVENTIONAL (3 or less) may indicate some ability to control impulsivity.

- High ASSERTIVE may indicate strong tendency to be "all talk and no do."
- Can choose to move out of their RANDOM ACTOR type by learning to make small decisions out of confidence and trust, and can become CAUTIOUS/INNOVATORS, especially if they have a solid moral/ethical standard.

Interaction Tips
- Get everything in writing!
- Don't tell them anything you consider confidential or a secret.
- To maintain consistent performance, maintain firm control of their rewards and penalties for failure to perform.
- Never expect them to present the whole truth, such as the negative side of the story.
- Focus on building their self-confidence and providing structure to offset unpredictability.
- Focus on that which is positive that they can control.

Sell/Present—Presenter with ASSERTIVE or low NONASSERTIVE trait should appeal to whatever positive actions are found in their COMMUNICATION type. Resist asking them to perform or act on something that is important, because they won't with any reliability. The higher the UNCONVENTIONAL trait, the more random their performance. Best advice: Find another place to do business. Anticipate and prepare for swift reversals, even after they say "yes."

Confront/Disagree—First, be sure to review the guidelines for interacting with a RANDOM ACTOR detailed throughout the text. Don't confront in front of their followers or peers. Their perpetual need and unpredictable methods for selling themselves or their agendas to others will negate rationale discussion. Find a strong ASSERTIVE and CONTROL person whom this person has trusted in the past to support your efforts. Bring closure swiftly. Before engaging, develop strategy for protecting yourself, as they will probably be inclined to retaliate the higher their FEARFUL and ASSERTIVE trait. When they attack you, it will be direct and loud, not subtle—"in your face." As with other RANDOM ACTOR profiles, appeal to the positive actions you observe in their COMMUNICATION type.

Lead/Motivate—Lead and motivate them in their area of expertise and competency focusing on the positive actions you observe in their COMMUNICATION actions. Do not present with critical decisions or put them in critical areas in a team as they can be disruptive. The higher the UNCONVENTIONAL trait the more likely will want to press norms and be willing to try new ideas/ventures, but must be provided significant time for FEARFUL trait to absorb opportunity. Emphasize value of their value-add ideas, competencies, and outcomes, but don't let them use this as a platform to lead. As explained in Chapter 14 and *Snapshot*, mentor how to make small bite-sized CONFIDENT decisions separate from area of competency to expand capacity for increased confident decision-making.

ACCOUNTANT–MANAGER

The ACCOUNTANT–MANAGER has the following combination of traits:
- CONTROL–NONASSERTIVE   • CONVENTIONAL–CONFIDENT

This common profile is an interesting combination that initially looks similar to the SERGEANT–LOYALIST profile. Like the SERGEANT–LOYALIST, ACCOUNTANT–MANAGERS prefer that which is predictable and CONVENTIONAL and will not seek change for change's sake. Be careful, though. Don't confuse their NONASSERTIVE trait for being cautious and unwilling to take risks or challenge the system. It's common for finance, audit, and engineering groups to have someone with this profile running a division. The ACCOUNTANT–MANAGER will typically analyze a problem carefully before advocating or implementing a solution. Thus, the combination of predictability and asking/analysis will give an initial impression similar to the predictability-fear combination of the LOYALISTS. However, the important distinction between these two profiles is their willingness to act independently in their areas of expertise, driven by their CONFIDENT trait, once they have analyzed a given problem. The ACCOUNTANT–MANAGER possesses a level of confidence that allows independent action when seeking predictable and stable results or performance. The LOYALIST-based profiles lack this element of personal initiative.

Typical Strengths
- Analytical.
- Detail-oriented.
- Deliberate/Prudent.
- Perform confidently and consistently after completing necessary analysis.
- Typically good listeners.
- Better adapted to develop/mentor others.
- Sharp, understated wit.

Typical Shortcomings
- May be unable to be directive or dominant when they communicate.
- Can get bogged down in details rather than face the challenge of leading.
- May initially appear overly cautious, averting "risk" situations.
- May avoid direct confrontation.
- Can be pessimistic, rigid, and stuffy

Other Tendencies
- Not inclined to challenge the system or assume risk-taking roles where they must communicate confidently.
- Prefer "calculated risks."
- Will control work/performance, but not social situations or relationships.
- Some may view these people as nondirective, and not inclined to be autocratic, especially when compared with the SERGEANT–LOYALIST, who possesses an ASSERTIVE trait.
- Weak COMMUNICATION type that possess few strong positive actions may cause others to underestimate their ability to deliver results.

Trait Indicators
- High NONASSERTIVE, accompanied by negative NONASSERTIVE actions, will cause this profile to appear more like the LOYALIST profiles; this same effect can appear when CONFIDENT is low.
- High CONTROL and high negative actions of CONVENTIONAL (like staid and stuffy) may indicate avoidance of all risks, overriding their level of confidence.
- Strong MANAGER traits should be interpreted as indicator of ability to deliver on commitments.
- Ability to develop others will be highest when CONTROL and CONVENTIONAL ratings are lower (3 or lower) and CONFIDENT rating is high.

Interaction Tips
- Allow time for analysis and detailed discussion of issues.
- Avoid putting ACCOUNTANT–MANAGERS in roles that require strong, directive interpersonal control or exchange, but can be invaluable as the listener/behind-the-scenes/"quiet leader."
- Be ready to back up recommendations with significant detail.
- Keep things neat and in order.
- Don't underestimate their ability to deliver.

Sell/Present—Presentations should be concise with unambiguous language. Use low EXPRESS or CONTROL when communicating. It's okay to use ASSERTIVE trait because of this profile's CONFIDENT trait, but don't stray too far with ideas. You may run into resistance if presenting a completely new concept, so try to link to similar products/services/strategies that were successful in the past, and suggest a low UNCONVENTIONAL person on his/her team to shoulder the new initiative. Keep agenda neat and orderly. Don't be discouraged by the request for details. Expect it, and prepare. Don't be fooled and think that a lack of verbal participation or lack of emotion means a lack of interest. Listen carefully to input because it may only come selectively. When you ask a question, don't interrupt. Allow for their nondominant ACCOUNTANT style of communicating, but don't be fooled when final decision is CONFIDENT-based.

Confront/Disagree—Have your details down and your approach well organized. These people do not like confrontations because of their NONASSERTIVE trait, which may necessitate a less direct, asking open-ended questions approach. The stronger the CONFIDENT trait—and associated positive actions—and the greater the presence of positive PERFORMANCE type actions, the greater the likelihood they will accept personal responsibility. Confront with a person who is stronger CONFIDENT and who can move between ASSERTIVE and NONASSERTIVE styles of communicating: NONASSERTIVE, when moving dialogue along, and ASSERTIVE when bringing closure (if strength is needed at closure).

Lead/Motivate—Like SERGEANT–MANAGERS, they prefer CONVENTIONAL challenges where objectives are clear without ambiguity but provide tangible, non-abstract rewards. The higher the CONVENTIONAL and CONTROL, the fewer the words and displays of emotion should be used to lead and motivate. They don't require a CONTROL person to lead them, just someone who is lower NONASSERTIVE and who is CONFIDENT during the mission. If asked what motivates them, expect an answer after reflection.

ACCOUNTANT–INNOVATOR

The ACCOUNTANT–INNOVATOR has the following combination of traits:

• CONTROL–NONASSERTIVE   • UNCONVENTIONAL–CONFIDENT

ACCOUNTANT–INNOVATORS have a somewhat paradoxical and uncommon profile. While not usually dominant, they're comfortable taking risks and trying new and different ideas. This profile is best represented by the soft-spoken inventor genius or the "technical guru or wizard" often found in key research or staff roles. They often create technical or professional innovations but lack the social style typically required of a leader, executive, or manager. ACCOUNTANT–INNOVATORS are unlikely to move beyond the "director of" level in most organizations, although their contributions are often crucial to solving problems that require an innovative flair.

Typical Strengths
• Comfortable being in the background, playing support roles.
• Creative.
• Easily motivated by creative challenge.
• Curious.
• Able to separate emotional issues from tasks; not likely to "lose their cool."

Typical Shortcomings
• Impact of their contributions may be overlooked because their COMMUNICATION type isn't assertive.
• If they don't have technical credibility, can experience significant loss of value/standing in an organization because of their NONASSERTIVE trait.
• May appear intensely motivated by creative challenges, but unconcerned about delivering timely results.

Other Tendencies
• Survival in organizations is dependent upon ongoing intellectual contribution.
• Like other INNOVATORS, may be viewed as unfocused, eccentric, erratic, or the "absentminded professor type" the stronger their UNCONVENTIONAL trait.
• When communicating, may appear less "results-oriented" than other profiles that have ASSERTIVE or CONVENTIONAL traits.
• Plays the "devil's advocate" due to INNOVATOR traits to explore ideas.

Trait Indicators

- High UNCONVENTIONAL may indicate inability to implement practical ideas, especially if combined with high NONASSERTIVE tendencies, but doesn't negate ability to make innovative/creative contribution if competent.
- High CONTROL and NONASSERTIVE will cause some to appear aloof.

Interaction Tips

- Give ACCOUNTANT–INNOVATORS autonomy and freedom to work on their own.
- Reward with professional recognition and acclaim, more than money or positions of power.
- Team up ACCOUNTANT–INNOVATORS, who are NONASSERTIVE, with SERGEANT–INNOVATORS, who are ASSERTIVE and direct the team to achieve creative results in a timely manner.
- Prepare for "eccentric" social style (especially when high UNCONVENTIONAL) and avoid impatience when listening to ACCOUNTANT–INNOVATORS.

Sell/Present—Although these people are NONASSERTIVE, a SALESMAN (ASSERTIVE–EXPRESS) type can do well as long as the focus is on ideas and personal rewards for acting on good ideas. When inquiring and seeking input, use nondirective, questioning style and open-ended questions. After asking a question, wait. When an important question is answered, wait some more. They are likely to offer additional information, as they are probably still processing the question and have more to say due to their INNOVATOR type. As with other ACCOUNTANTS, a lack of verbal rapport doesn't necessarily mean a lack of interest.

Confront/Disagree—They are likely to defend personal turf and ideas indirectly and even ramble under pressure. Look for playing the "devil's advocate" as a deflection device to "explore ideas." Using a moderate ASSERTIVE trait, keep them focused on the issues at hand, and give them an opportunity to think through the issue(s) presented. Remember, they are UNCONVENTIONAL, and are unlikely to be direct in their "taking action" process due to their desire to think through all the issues. SALESMAN or SERGEANT types, as a counterpoint, are more likely to tell you immediately what they think in response to a confrontation. ACCOUNTANT–INNOVATORS are also less likely to become hostile the lower their UNCONVENTIONAL and CONFIDENT traits. Conversely, the higher these traits, aggression is more likely to be indirect and in a negative context, scheming. If the latter is the case, anticipate and prepare for the unexpected.

Lead/Motivate—Like other INNOVATORS, a key to leading and motivating is to provide a context in which discipline is created with rewards for timely performance. Regarding rewards, intangibles, like ideals, and opportunity for creative input/ownership may be more highly valued than the usual compensations. When communicating, use a firm delivery that is low CONTROL or EXPRESS and avoid "pep rallies." If lead by someone who is CONVENTIONAL, it's best if he/she is low CONVENTIONAL (2 or lower) and has tolerance for the intangible.

ACCOUNTANT–CAUTIOUS INNOVATOR

The ACCOUNTANT–CAUTIOUS/INNOVATOR has the following combination of traits:

- CONTROL–NONASSERTIVE   • UNCONVENTIONAL–CAUTIOUS/FEARFUL

The ACCOUNTANT–CAUTIOUS/INNOVATOR can be invaluable on a team when operating in their area of competency—especially where creative/innovative technical skills are required. They don't require as much social interaction as those who are EXPRESS trait, and they prefer to thoughtfully consider new initiatives and not dominate the discussion. The unique combination of their traits allows them to stay more focused than most INNOVATORS, and the tendency to lose focus occurs the higher the UNCONVENTIONAL trait. While not natural leaders, their contributions are often crucial to solving problems that require an innovative flair. Like other CAUTIOUS/INNOVATORS they share many of the actions of INNOVATORS but are different in that they usually need more time to process decisions outside area of competency or when there is change.

Typical Strengths
- Comfortable being in the background in support roles.
- Creative/innovative.
- Will rarely challenge an order or directive.
- Easily motivated by creative challenge, if given time to process.
- Curious.
- Listen well, and appear interested in others.
- Able to separate emotional issues from tasks; not likely to "lose their

cool," especially if low UNCONVENTIONAL.

Typical Shortcomings

- Impact of their contributions may be overlooked because their COMMUNICATION type is not assertive and doesn't show emotion, which can be misinterpreted as a lack of conviction or enthusiasm.
- If they don't have technical credibility, can experience significant loss of value/standing in an organization because of their NONASSERTIVE trait.
- May appear interested or motivated by creative challenges, but lack ability to make necessary decisions when delivering results.
- Avoid leadership roles.
- If significant negative ACCOUNTANT actions apparent, more likely to be withdrawn, reclusive, disinterested in others.

Other Tendencies

- Survival in organizations is dependent upon ongoing intellectual contribution.
- Like other INNOVATORS, may be viewed as eccentric, erratic, or the "absentminded professor type" the stronger their UNCONVENTIONAL trait.
- May appear less "results-oriented" than other profiles that have ASSERTIVE or CONVENTIONAL traits.
- May play the "devil's advocate" as a deflection because of FEARFUL trait to buy more time to make a decision; or use UNCONVENTIONAL trait to "explore" options/changes/ideas.
- What can cause them internal tension is their CAUTIOUS trait. They want to do something new, but caution is a restraint. This trait, though, can be applied as a positive restraint to test new ideas/concepts before taking action.

Trait Indicators

- High UNCONVENTIONAL may indicate inability to implement practical ideas, especially if combined with high NONASSERTIVE tendencies.
- High CONTROL and NONASSERTIVE may cause to appear aloof.

Interaction Tips

- Reward with professional recognition and acclaim, more than money or positions of power.
- Pair them up with SERGEANT–INNOVATORS (who are ASSERTIVE) to achieve creative results in a timely manner.

- Prepare for "eccentric" social style if high UNCONVENTIONAL.
- Avoid references to your own power, position, or confidence.
- Avoid issues that could force them to reveal emotions; deal in nonemotional arenas.
- Like ARTIST or ACCOUNTANT–LOYALIST, don't ask them to give others negative or critical feedback.

Sell/Present—Focus on ideas/concepts and how similar results have been delivered in the past. Use a laid back, nonurgent approach that zeroes in on ideas and personal rewards for acting on good ideas that naturally evokes an "I am comfortable" response. When inquiring and seeking input, use non-directive, questioning style and open-ended questions. After asking a question, wait. When an important question is answered, wait some more. They are likely to offer additional information, as they are probably still processing the question and have more to say due to their CAUTIOUS/INNOVATOR type. As with other ACCOUNTANTS, a lack of verbal rapport or overt enthusiasm doesn't necessarily mean a lack of interest. Identify someone they trust who is CONFIDENT to reinforce the decision.

Confront/Disagree—Less likely to become hostile the weaker their UNCONVENTIONAL and CONFIDENT traits. Conversely, the higher these traits, aggression is more likely to be indirect and scheming. If the latter is the case, anticipate and prepare for the unexpected. They are likely to defend personal turf and ideas indirectly and even ramble under pressure. Look for playing the "devil's advocate" as a deflection device. Using a low ASSERTIVE trait, keep them focused on the issues at hand and give them an opportunity to think through the issue(s) presented. Don't be as direct with one's confrontation as one would with other related profiles, such as an ACCOUNTANT–MANAGER or a SALESMAN–LOYALIST. They have little to fall back on, such as a SALESMAN–LOYALIST who can retreat to his ASSERTIVE trait. Work quickly to bring closure before they freeze up and resist taking action.

Lead/Motivate—Like other CAUTIOUS/INNOVATORS, lead and motivate them in their area of expertise and competency with more assertiveness than their NONASSERTIVE trait. Do not present with critical decisions but emphasize team effort and safety nets along the way with a focus on ideals and ideas. The higher the UNCONVENTIONAL trait the more likely they will press norms and be willing to try new ideas/ventures, but must be provided significant time for FEARFUL trait to absorb opportunity. As explained in Chapter 14 and *Snapshot*, mentor how to make small bite-sized CONFIDENT decisions separate from area of competency to expand capacity for increased confident decision-making.

ACCOUNTANT–LOYALIST

The ACCOUNTANT-LOYALIST has the following combination of traits:
- CONTROL–NONASSERTIVE   • CONVENTIONAL–CAUTIOUS/FEARFUL

ACCOUNTANT-LOYALISTS perform their tasks and make decisions in ways that avoids risk or potential negative reactions from other people. They are indecisive, while simultaneously keeping their emotions passively "locked up" inside. ACCOUNTANT-LOYALISTS will ask questions in social relationships, but they seldom share anything about themselves or make declarative statements of any kind. The higher their CAUTIOUS/FEARFUL trait, the more they will fit the classic "frightened subordinate," who does whatever he is told and rarely expresses any emotion or feelings—suitable support people, as long as they aren't required to provide significant input or assume responsibility.

Typical Strengths
- Will perform most any detail job without "grumbling."
- Will rarely challenge an order or directive.
- Do not tire of repetitive, mundane tasks.
- Listen well, and appear interested in others the less extreme the ACCOUNTANT actions.

Typical Shortcomings
- Seldom assert themselves, even when surrounded by people who have no influence over their situation or future.
- Avoid leadership roles.
- Likely to be viewed as one of the most neurotic of all profiles the higher the CAUTIOUS/FEARFUL and CONTROL traits.
- Seldom expose self or emotions, even in close relationships.

Other Tendencies
- Are often unable to develop close friendships because of the combination of their NONASSERTIVE and CAUTIOUS/FEARFUL traits. This is due to their inclination to be socially reserved because they lack an ASSERTIVE trait. (Some SERGEANT-LOYALISTS can develop these relationships because their ASSERTIVE trait enables them to more easily

overcome their CAUTIOUS/FEARFUL trait and engage in dialogue. They lead relationships with their ASSERTIVE trait.)
- Can be viewed by others as "led around by the ring in his nose."

Trait Indicators
- More likely to demonstrate some type of independence if they have a low CONTROL or CAUTIOUS/FEARFUL trait.
- Follower orientation most pronounced when LOYALIST traits are strong.

Interaction Tips
- Refrain from asking them to speak in public or make "presentations."
- Look for ways to reduce fear if you want them to speak up on an issue.
- Avoid issues that could force them to reveal emotions; deal in nonemotional arenas.
- Avoid references to your own power, position, or confidence.
- For long-term relationships, gently place them in moderately challenging situations, combined with your encouragement, to help them move toward CONFIDENT.
- Like ARTIST–LOYALIST, don't ask them to give others negative or critical feedback.
- Like all LOYALIST profiles, encourage them to recognize their natural tendencies toward loyalty and to consider carefully the integrity of those whom they serve so that their trusting nature isn't abused.
- Like other LOYALIST profiles, operate with them in their area of expertise.

Sell/Present—If what you are presenting is important, a presentation for these people is likely to be frustrating. This is because they operate out of fear and you won't get much feedback when their CAUTIOUS/FEARFUL trait is coupled with their NONASSERTIVE trait. Only sell essentials that don't spark fear, or find someone else in whom they trust and whom you can depend upon to assist in the decision-making process. Adopt a very laid back, nonurgent approach. Make sure the presentation naturally evokes an "I am comfortable" response. Otherwise, don't expect them to volunteer to make decisions.

Confront/Disagree—If a response isn't needed quickly, use a NONASSERTIVE person for the confrontation who is CONVENTIONAL and can operate at the low end of CONFIDENT. This will put them at ease. Don't be as direct with one's confrontation as with other related profiles, such as an ACCOUNTANT–MANAGER or a SALESMAN–LOYALIST. They have little to fall back on, such as a SALESMAN–LOYALIST who can retreat to his ASSERTIVE trait.

When a quick response is needed, use a person who can build trust and who is medium to strong ASSERTIVE, CONFIDENT, and CONVENTIONAL traits. Work quickly to bring closure before they freeze up and resist taking action.

Lead/Motivate—Can be led by those who are more ASSERTIVE and CONFIDENT. This includes someone who is lower NONASSERTIVE and is CAUTIOUS, but is lower CAUTIOUS. Lead and motivate in their area of expertise and competency. Do not present with critical decisions or significant change. If change is required, must provide significant time to process and accept. The higher the CONVENTIONAL trait the more likely they will resist change, so emphasize loyalty to the organization and provide time to absorb opportunity. Emphasize team effort and safety nets along the way. As explained in Chapter 14 and *Snapshot*, mentor how to make small bite-sized CONFIDENT decisions separate from area of competency to expand capacity for increased confident decision-making.

ACCOUNTANT–RANDOM ACTOR

The ACCOUNTANT–RANDOM ACTOR has the following combination traits:
- CONTROL–NONASSERTIVE
- UNCONVENTIONAL–FEARFUL

This uncommon profile possesses some paradoxical combinations that must be carefully understood. Usually, people who are FEARFUL and are inclined to CONTROL their emotional reactions will periodically "slip" and display aggressive reactions against their social environment that will appear to be EXPRESS. However, in the case of the ACCOUNTANT–RANDOM ACTOR, the lack of social dominance (the NONASSERTIVE trait) makes it difficult for these people to "act out" their emotional reactions. This combination can result in a potentially volatile profile the higher the FEARFUL trait. This will cause them to suffer significant psychological tension, acting out their reactions only when the tension becomes so great they can no longer tolerate the situation. Or, they will release their anger through cleverly plotted schemes or through passive aggression by what they don't say. In an organization, this type person may be found in corporate support roles, such as finance and human resource functions. It's possible for this person to rise up through the ranks by relying upon his ACCOUNTANT type and/or unquestioning loyalty. But if there is extreme pressure, this person often disintegrates. In the criminal arena, it is not uncommon to find that "mousy" child molesters will have the ACCOUNTANT–

RANDOM ACTOR profile because their NONASSERTIVE style of communicating is appealing to young, trusting children. Additionally, Ted Kaczynski, dubbed the "Unabomber" for his series of letter bombs sent to numerous people during the 1980s and 1990s, possessed this profile. He resisted face-to-face confrontations, and instead made meticulously crafted, hand-carved, wood-encased bombs that he sent through the mail. (Be sure to review general observations of RANDOM ACTORS in this chapter and Chapters 9 and 15.)

Typical Strengths
- Appear reserved and under control in most situations.
- Able to listen to others and accept input.
- Will have a higher tolerance for emotional or psychological "pain."

Typical Shortcomings
- The higher their FEARFUL trait, will seek to avoid face-to-face confrontations over important issues in order to maintain emotional control.
- May employ "passive-aggressive" behaviors to deal with psychological tension.
- When ability to tolerate tension is surpassed, may be unpredictably volatile and reactive.
- Likely to express anger through scheming plans.
- Susceptible to depression, neuroses, and risks of self-harm—even suicide the more extreme their PERFORMANCE traits.

Other Tendencies
- Because of ACCOUNTANT COMMUNICATION type, may initially be misread as stable and consistent. Remember, it is from the COMMUNICATION type—the "talk" part of his life—that a RANDOM ACTOR will display positive actions. Ask this person to take action, however, and the actions of the RANDOM ACTOR can take over.
- If has a moral compass, may be able to restrain volatile self-centered behavior, although daily actions may still be inherently destructive.

Trait Indicators
- Strong RANDOM ACTOR traits are key indicators of volatility and reactiveness.
- Strong ACCOUNTANT traits indicate ability to delay RANDOM ACTOR responses because of their inability to vocalize and express themselves. They won't yell, like SERGEANT–RANDOM ACTORS; they must first

carefully think through how to carry out their plans, which may delay their taking action.

- Can choose to move out of their RANDOM ACTOR type by learning to make small decisions out of confidence and trust, and can become CAUTIOUS/INNOVATORS, especially if they have a solid moral/ethical standard.

Interaction Tips

- Watch for signs of "buried" emotions and "pent-up" feelings.
- In a less directive context, help them to talk about issues and then focus on resolving fears and concerns.
- Watch for passive-aggressive responses as clues to concerns or potential "trigger" issues that will later cause them to "erupt."
- Focus on building their self-confidence and providing structure to offset unpredictability.
- Focus on that which is positive that they can control.

Sell/Present—Because of their COMMUNICATION type, don't ask ACCOUNTANT–RANDOM ACTORS to buy into situations that require their personal interaction with others—only behind-the-scenes environments that are carefully controlled. It is easy to be initially fooled into thinking that they are compliant because of their ACCOUNTANT type, but the higher the FEARFUL trait, the greater the chance that swift and unannounced reversals will be carried out indirectly, to avoid a face-to-face confrontation—so anticipate and be prepared. When possible, bring closure quickly, because the longer the time for reflection, the greater the chance they will renege on a commitment.

Confront/Disagree—First, be sure to review the guidelines for interacting with a RANDOM ACTOR detailed throughout the text. Be prepared strategically. Make your case and bring closure quickly. Don't give them advance notice. And don't be misled by their low-key, ACCOUNTANT style of communicating. Look for preemptive scheming plans to resist you rather than relying upon the force of their personalities, like a SERGEANT or SALESMAN–RANDOM ACTOR. Appeal to the positive actions you observe in their COMMUNICATION type. Don't expect much emotional leakage to help you determine what is going on in their minds, but rather develop insight from past history—the best predictor of future behavior. You will probably only get one opportunity to confront them, as they will tend to withdraw the higher their NONASSERTIVE and FEARFUL traits. Regarding the confronter, it may be useful for this person to possess an ASSERTIVE trait, provided he can modulate his ASSERTIVE trait and even employ a NONASSERTIVE style for communicating. Then, at the moment of opportunity, this person can naturally employ the strength of his ASSERTIVE trait to demand closure or the truth. Finally, if they attack you, they will do it indirectly—a letter bomb sent through the mail, a magistrate embarrassingly serving you with papers at work, an attack on your credibility by placing cleverly layered lies in places that you don't think are important, and so on.

Lead/Motivate—Lead and motivate them in their area of expertise and competency and the positive actions you observe in their COMMUNICATION actions. Do not present with critical decisions. The higher the UNCONVENTIONAL trait the more likely they will press norms and be willing to try new ideas/ventures, but must be provided significant time for FEARFUL trait to absorb opportunity. Emphasize team effort and safety nets along the way. Only place them in a position to use their ASSERTIVE trait when operating in area of expertise/competency, and only for short periods of time. As explained in Chapter 14 and *Snapshot*, mentor how to make small bite-sized CONFIDENT decisions separate from area of competency to expand capacity for increased confident decision-making.

ARTIST–MANAGER

The ARTIST–MANAGER has the following combination of traits:
- EXPRESS–NONASSERTIVE
- CONVENTIONAL–CONFIDENT

An uncommon profile that can be a bit of a paradox, and can fool people. From a performance perspective, ARTIST–MANAGERS are CONFIDENT and CONVENTIONAL. They predictably perform and act based on their self-confidence in their ability to accomplish a task and make decisions. Their COMMUNICATION type, however, is an ARTIST, which often results in a tendency to ignore their leadership potential (MANAGER PERFORMANCE type) because of their ARTIST actions when they communicate. The ARTIST–MANAGER's tendency to be emotionally expressive, however, is counterbalanced by the MANAGER's tendency towards predictability and avoiding sudden change. An example of this profile is the amiable advertising executive who combines an artistic COMMUNICATION type with performance actions necessary to lead a group of creative people and bring a project in on-time and within budget. The head of a research medical staff is another common place to find this profile.

Typical Strengths

- Dependable.
- Creative when communicating.
- Can bridge the gap between creative and hard-nosed business demands.
- Comfortable and open in initial meetings.
- Usually a warm, optimistic initial outlook.

Typical Shortcomings

- May use poor judgment when trying to avoid conflict or confrontation with others due to their NONASSERTIVE-EXPRESS combination.
- May be insensitive to the fact that the combination of their expressive/ creative communication flair and MANAGER type will confuse people.
- May be self-centered and/or compulsive when they have a creative agenda, which they may conceal with their NONASSERTIVE trait.

Other Tendencies

- Typically better facilitators of teams than strong leaders of large, diverse organizations; an exception is noted under "Trait Indicators."
- Present a good balance between the predictability of a MANAGER and the ARTIST'S appreciation and sensitivity for change.
- May surprise subordinates with contrast between amiable COMMUNICATION type and more task-oriented PERFORMANCE types.

Trait Indicators

- Low MANAGER traits will quickly detract from performance effectiveness due to the impression created by their ARTIST COMMUNICATION actions.
- NONASSERTIVE trait coupled with high MANAGER traits can create strong team leader profile that can accomplish much through others in environments that do not require a strong directive (ASSERTIVE) leadership style. This is particularly helpful in creative/innovative environments where team players must have the freedom to experiment and create, such as software systems development, advertising and design, education, and so on.

Interaction Tips

- Be open and expressive in initial meetings.
- Allow extra time in meetings/work plans for ARTIST–MANAGERS to "warm up" to people.

- Once a task or project is started, realize that the MANAGER characteristics will make the ARTIST–MANAGER a more demanding taskmaster.
- To promote team welfare, encourage them to explain to others why their profile might be confusing—and beneficial.

Sell/Present—One should adopt a laid-back approach that presents predictable results. Expressing emotions is helpful, but not crucial. Also, either NONASSERTIVE or ASSERTIVE presenters can be effective, provided that NONASSERTIVE presenters are CONFIDENT, and ASSERTIVE presenters provide time for them to process questions. One can shift between bottom line and "idea" issues, but don't be surprised if they show some creative and bottom line tendencies simultaneously because of their COMMUNICATION type. The balance between creative and bottom line elements in your presentation should be evaluated based upon the respective strengths of their ARTIST and MANAGER traits.

Confront/Disagree—For volatile situations, avoid using much EXPRESS as this may trigger their desire to display negative EXPRESS actions, unless expressing sympathy or compassion toward someone or something is an essential factor. Either a NONASSERTIVE or an ASSERTIVE person can be employed for the confrontation, provided that the ASSERTIVE person doesn't override the ARTIST's need to process thoughts before responding. Approach them in a way that drives them toward sensitivity (their COMMUNICATION type) and away from the potential negative MANAGER action of self-centered.

Lead/Motivate—Like SERGEANT–MANAGERS, they prefer CONVENTIONAL challenges where objectives are clear and are provided tangible, non-abstract rewards. In relationships, though, they are more tolerant of ambiguity. The lower the CONVENTIONAL and the higher EXPRESS the more relational and open one should be to lead and motivate. They don't require an EXPRESS person to lead them, just someone who is more ASSERTIVE and who is CONFIDENT. If asked what motivates them, expect an answer after reflection.

ARTIST–INNOVATOR

The ARTIST–INNOVATOR has the following combination of traits:
- EXPRESS–NONASSERTIVE   • UNCONVENTIONAL–CONFIDENT

The ARTIST–INNOVATOR is a common source for great creative genius, and they are usually easy to read. Here the ARTIST COMMUNICATION type combines with self-confidence and unconventionality to produce the open, free-thinking style required to challenge the status quo, while simultaneously remaining attuned to the emotional impact of their actions. This type of person can be characterized as being completely in touch with his personal needs and desires as well as with the needs of the people and the situations around him. Look for these people in research and development, small creative shops, creative start-up companies, medical environments that require exploratory risk-taking, etc. A significant difference between ARTIST–INNOVATORS and ARTIST–MANAGERS is that ARTIST–INNOVATORS who are 3 or higher UNCONVENTIONAL and lack discipline, shouldn't be called upon to lead others over a sustained period of time—no matter how impressive their intellectual prowess.

Typical Strengths
- Creative.
- Self-confident and willing to trust own ability/judgment.
- Will personally deliver results.
- Good listener.

Typical Shortcomings
- Lack desire for control; will not manage or dominate in situations when they should.
- May be viewed as "unorthodox" or unwilling to "play by the rules."
- May cause unexpected conflict because they are not afraid to "rock the boat," which isn't apparent because of the NONASSERTIVE trait.
- May not be a strong leader.

Other Tendencies
- Willing to try almost anything once.
- Open to people and ideas.
- Can be the pure "artist"; work only for art's sake.
- Little concern for detail, order, or consistency.
- Can appear idealistic or naive.
- Like the ACCOUNTANT–INNOVATOR, may play the "devil's advocate."

Trait Indicators
- High EXPRESS coupled with high UNCONVENTIONAL trait can produce extreme "agitator" profile. They will tend to challenge the current system or proposal.
- High NONASSERTIVE may be best assurance that they are able to link

ideas and reactions (abstract) to real world (concrete) situations, as they are more inclined to "take in" information and process it before they communicate or take action.

- The higher the UNCONVENTIONAL trait, the less likely they are suitable for even short-term leadership roles.

Interaction Tips
- Expect lots of challenges and criticisms.
- If detail or precision is required, it must be provided by someone other than the ARTIST–INNOVATOR.
- Provide realistic balance to their idealism.
- Don't place in a leadership position that requires strong control-oriented leadership, even when they have the leading-edge ideas on a team.

Sell/Present—Don't be afraid to show emotion during presentations and appeal to the new creative venues that will be created. Bottom line issues are secondary. An ASSERTIVE person can do the job here as long as he is stimulating ideas and not stifling their ability to respond (due to their NONASSERTIVE trait). Remember, it may take these NONASSERTIVE people, who are INNOVATORS, longer to respond as they weigh all the creative options. So ask for a response, and wait—and, wait some more, even after they offer their first response. Bring closure by focusing on vibrant ideas with which they will be associated.

Confront/Disagree—Use a low CONTROL and NONASSERTIVE person who can reach out to their EXPRESS trait as necessary to allow them to open up. Appeal to the opportunities for understanding, feelings that will be settled or restored, new creative venues, etc. that will remain open or be created by coming forward or resolving the conflict. The higher the UNCONVENTIONAL trait, the greater the likelihood of a rebellious and/or frivolous attitude, such as a taunting devil's advocate response. Keep the attention focused on the nonpersonal to avoid triggering their EXPRESS trait, which cause them to tilt toward the illogical/irrational; the exception is when an appeal to positive ARTIST actions is needed, such as sympathetic/compassionate.

Lead/Motivate—Use an open, non-overbearing leadership style that provides tangible and intangible rewards for timely completion of objectives. The higher the UNCONVENTIONAL trait the more likely they will press norms and be willing to try new ideas/ventures. A SERGEANT–INNOVATOR who is low CONTROL and low ASSERTIVE can be an ideal leader to strike the right balance between moving forward and staying on task without stifling creativity.

ARTIST–CAUTIOUS INNOVATOR

The ARTIST–INNOVATOR has the following combination of traits:
- EXPRESS–NONASSERTIVE
- UNCONVENTIONAL–CAUTIOUS/FEARFUL

Like the ARTIST–INNOVATOR, the ARTIST–CAUTIOUS/INNOVATOR is a common profile in research and development, small creative shops, creative start-up companies, medical environments, graphic arts, advertising, software development, and other technical disciplines that require creative insight. The distinguishing characteristic from the ARTIST–INNOVATOR is they aren't suited for sustained leadership roles as they need more time to make decisions and process change. Their ARTIST COMMUNICATION type combines with caution and unconventionality to produce the open, free-thinking style required to challenge the status quo, while simultaneously remaining attuned to the emotional impact of their actions. This profile can be characterized as being moderately in touch with their personal needs and desires as well as with the needs of people and situations around them. Like other CAUTIOUS/INNOVATORS they share many of the actions of INNOVATORS but are different in that they usually need more time to process decisions outside their area of competency or when there is change.

Typical Strengths
- Comfortable being in the background in support roles.
- Creative/innovative.
- Will rarely challenge an order or directive.
- Easily motivated by creative challenge, if given time to process.
- Curious.
- Listen well, and appear in touch and interested in others.

Typical Shortcomings
- Lack desire for control; will not manage or dominate in situations when they should.
- If they don't have technical credibility, can experience significant loss of value/standing in an organization because of their NONASSERTIVE trait.
- May be viewed as "unorthodox" or unwilling to "play by the rules."
- If significant negative ARTIST actions apparent, more likely to be withdrawn, moody, reclusive, disinterested in others.

- Easily intimidated by those "in control."

Other Tendencies
- Open to people and ideas.
- Can be the pure "artist"; work only for art's sake.
- Little concern for detail, order, or consistency.
- Can appear idealistic or naive.
- May play the "devil's advocate" as a deflection because of FEARFUL trait to buy more time to make a decision; or use UNCONVENTIONAL trait to "explore" options/changes/ideas.
- Survival in organizations is dependent upon ongoing intellectual contribution.
- What can cause them internal tension is their CAUTIOUS trait. They want to do something new, but caution is a restraint. This trait, though, can be applied as a positive restraint to test new ideas/concepts before taking action.

Trait Indicators
- High UNCONVENTIONAL may indicate inability to implement practical ideas, especially if combined with high NONASSERTIVE tendencies.
- High EXPRESS coupled with high UNCONVENTIONAL trait can produce extreme "agitator" profile. Will tend to avoid important assignments or undermine moving forward the higher the CAUTIOUS trait.
- High NONASSERTIVE may be best assurance that they are able to link ideas and reactions (abstract) to real world (concrete) situations, as they are more inclined to "take in" information and process it before they communicate.
- The higher the UNCONVENTIONAL trait, the less likely that they are suitable for even short-term leadership roles.

Interaction Tips
- Don't confuse expertise/competency with CONFIDENT decision making outside area of competency. Positive ARTIST actions can innocently exaggerate this impression.
- Provide realistic balance to their idealism.
- Don't place them in a long-term leadership position, even when they have the leading-edge ideas on a team. Short-term leadership assignment is an option only if they are low CAUTIOUS, and are well respected for expertise, and team is willing to rally around them.

- Prepare for "eccentric" social style if high UNCONVENTIONAL.
- Avoid references to your own power, position, or confidence.
- Like ARTIST or ACCOUNTANT–LOYALISTS, don't ask them to give others negative or critical feedback.

Sell/Present—Best to engage with an ARTIST or SALESMAN type who is low NONASSERTIVE who focuses on ideas and concepts. Use a slow, deliberate NONASSERTIVE style, while preemptively preparing for any potential fear-provoking, need-to-take-action points. Bottom line issues are secondary. An ASSERTIVE person can do the job here as long as he is stimulating ideas and not stifling their ability to respond (due to their NONASSERTIVE trait). Remember, it may take these CAUTIOUS and NONASSERTIVE people longer to respond as they weigh all the creative options. They have a natural tension between doing something new and different (which they like) and making a decision. So ask for a response, and wait—and, wait some more, even after they offer their first response. Bring closure by focusing on vibrant ideas with which they will be associated as a part of a team.

Confront/Disagree—Use a low CONTROL person who can reach out to their EXPRESS trait as necessary to allow them to open up. Appeal to the opportunities for understanding, feelings that will be settled or restored, new creative venues, etc. that will remain open or be created by coming forward or resolving the conflict. The higher the UNCONVENTIONAL and CAUTIOUS trait, the greater the likelihood of a rebellious and/or frivolous attitude, such as a taunting devil's advocate response. Keep the attention focused on the nonpersonal to avoid triggering their EXPRESS trait, which may cause them to tilt toward the illogical/irrational; the exception is when an appeal to positive ARTIST actions is needed, such as sympathetic/compassionate.

Lead/Motivate—The focus is on rewarding this person with tangible and intangible rewards for creative/innovative timely performance. Do not present with critical decisions. SERGEANT–INNOVATORS (who are low ASSERTIVE and low CONTROL) are a good candidate to lead this profile through a combination of being directive and connecting on a creative level. SALESMAN–INNOVATORS, who have demonstrated disciplined performance, are another option, as they can connect through the shared EXPRESS trait. The higher the UNCONVENTIONAL trait the more likely will they press norms and be willing to try new ideas/ventures, but must be provided significant time for FEARFUL trait to absorb opportunity. Emphasize team effort and safety nets along the way. As explained in Chapter 14 and *Snapshot*, mentor how to make small bite-sized CONFIDENT decisions separate from area of competency to expand capacity for increased confident decision-making.

ARTIST–LOYALIST

The ARTIST–LOYALIST has the following combination traits:
- EXPRESS–NONASSERTIVE   • CONVENTIONAL–CAUTIOUS/FEARFUL

People with this profile have the COMMUNICATION type of an ARTIST— open, expressive, and sensitive. What is seemingly contradictory is they aren't UNCONVENTIONAL. They are open in relationships, but prefer more conventional tasks. Because this profile's PERFORMANCE type is characteristically compliant and obedient (CAUTIOUS/FEARFUL and CONVENTIONAL), these people don't translate their emotional sensitivity into new, creative, or unique performance. This seeming contradiction between their COMMUNICATION and PERFORMANCE types can result in tension for some that can create neurotic actions the stronger their CAUTIOUS/FEARFUL and EXPRESS traits; they're sensitive and want to step forward, but they are stymied by their fear.

This uncommon profile demonstrates the need to avoid preconceived stereotyping. While we tend to expect ARTISTS to take some risks in personal relationships because of their willingness to express emotion, we find that for these ARTISTS that their "talk" doesn't match their "walk." In this case, ARTIST–LOYALISTS extinguish their potential because they demand predictability in their performance and demand a safe, risk-free environment for managing their lack of confidence. This is very different from ARTIST–INNOVATORS, for example, who are willing to accept risk and try new ventures, taking advantage of their creative capacity.

Typical Strengths
- Open COMMUNICATION type coupled with willingness to loyally follow; a very yielding COMMUNICATION type.
- Has potential for combining a precise work ethic with a creative bent.
- Not likely to overreact like other ARTIST types, because they are restrained by their LOYALIST type.

Typical Shortcomings
- Won't try new ideas and adventures, despite open COMMUNICATION type.
- Avoids risks that might endanger relationships with others, even in the face of opportunity.

- Under emotional stress, inclined to be impulsive when they communicate and then "take back" what they have said or done.
- While appear open and easy to understand, they make decisions in ways that appear mundane or boring, earning the label of "underachiever."

Other Tendencies

- Can be hard to read because of contradictions in COMMUNICATION and PERFORMANCE types.
- Can serve as good "eyes and ears" for SERGEANT types who want to be more "in touch" with others; may be seduced into informant role.
- Avoid conflict.

Trait Indicators

- High NONASSERTIVE makes this profile most useful "eyes and ears."
- High EXPRESS may produce implosive reactions.
- High FEARFUL will cause profile to appear untrustworthy to peers and to those not in control.

Interaction Tips

- Don't force into quick decisions or reaction situations.
- Like ACCOUNTANT–LOYALIST, don't ask them to give others negative or critical feedback.
- After an agreement is reached, allow time for it to "settle in" before assuming it is a "done deal."
- Like all LOYALIST profiles, encourage to recognize their natural tendency toward loyalty and to carefully consider the integrity of those whom they serve—without paranoia—so that their trusting nature isn't abused.

Sell/Present—Like other LOYALIST profiles, resist approaching with important decisions the higher their CAUTIOUS/FEARFUL trait. ARTIST–LOYALISTS require a lot of time to process requests, and the strategic use of a person with a low or moderate ASSERTIVE trait may be helpful to get them to "move." (However, the longer the process, the greater the likelihood that their CAUTIOUS/FEARFUL trait will kick in as they mull over the options. Additionally, ASSERTIVE presenters will typically be ineffective in reaching them over a long, sustained period of time.) Avoid too much EXPRESS, which may trigger more irrationality in their CAUTIOUS/FEARFUL decision-making process. Best advice: Find backup support, such as one of their colleagues, to bolster their lack of decision-making initiative.

Confront/Disagree—You are confronting people who have both fear and sensitivity and will retreat into themselves. For this reason, these people usually aren't dangerous or highly volatile. Use an ARTIST or an ACCOUNTANT (who is low CONTROL) to establish dialogue and trust and a low ASSERTIVE person to encourage a decision or bring closure, but only if the NONASSERTIVE person isn't successful. Finally, in most cases, ARTIST–LOYALISTS won't attempt crippling or life-threatening retaliation.

Lead/Motivate—Can be led by those who are more ASSERTIVE and CONFIDENT. This includes someone who is lower NONASSERTIVE and is CAUTIOUS, but is lower CAUTIOUS. Lead and motivate them in their area of expertise and competency. Do not present with critical decisions or significant change and provide tangible rewards. The higher the CONVENTIONAL trait the more likely will resist change, so emphasize loyalty to the organization and provide time to absorb opportunity. Emphasize team effort and safety nets along the way. Remember, even though you may connect with their EXPRESS trait, this doesn't mean they are on board. As explained in Chapter 14 and *Snapshot*, mentor how to make small bite-sized CONFIDENT decisions separate from area of competency to expand capacity for increased confident decision-making.

ARTIST–RANDOM ACTOR

The ARTIST–RANDOM ACTOR has the following combination of traits:
- EXPRESS–NONASSERTIVE
- UNCONVENTIONAL–FEARFUL

ARTIST–RANDOM ACTORS are an uncommon profile who usually fool most people who meet them. They operate out of the same fear-based, UNCONVENTIONAL PERFORMANCE type as the other RANDOM ACTOR profiles, but like the ACCOUNTANT–RANDOM ACTOR, they fool people because of their NONASSERTIVE trait, appearing less threatening than a RANDOM ACTOR with an ASSERTIVE trait. When they communicate, their EXPRESS trait can evoke emotive empathy and portray interest in others, like a doctor with a good bedside manner. But, this is only when they communicate—the talk part of their life. If dangerous (remember not all are), their EXPRESS trait can cause their predatory nature to express itself by preying upon feelings and a sense of beguiling warmth. They will operate to protect themselves while placing little emphasis on conventionality or "appropriate" behaviors. A common place that we find ARTIST–RANDOM ACTORS are in the arts and media, and software development; to the extreme, in the role of cult follower, where they can be led down destructive paths due to blind loyalty, or the pedophile who uses his ARTIST type to gain intimacy. This profile's ARTIST type also makes them extremely susceptible to depression and expressions of a fatalistic bent. (Be sure to review general observations of RANDOM ACTORS in this chapter and Chapters 9 and 15.)

Typical Strengths
- Open and sensitive to others.
- Capable of being creative.

Typical Shortcomings
- Susceptible to depression, neuroses, and risks of self-harm—even suicide the more extreme their PERFORMANCE traits.
- Can become fatalistic.
- Potential for severe mood swings.
- Easily intimidated by those "in control."
- More likely to be blindly loyal than SERGEANT– or SALESMAN–RANDOM ACTORS.

Other Tendencies
- May struggle unsuccessfully to hide emotions from others.
- If has a moral compass, may be able to restrain volatile self-centered behavior, although daily actions may still be inherently destructive.

Trait Indicators
- Lower FEARFUL rating an indicator of ability to express creativity like ARTIST–INNOVATOR.
- FEARFUL trait can change creative genius into "insanity" or instability.
- Can choose to move out of their RANDOM ACTOR type by learning to make small decisions out of confidence and trust, and can become CAUTIOUS/INNOVATORS, especially if they have a solid moral/ethical standard.

Interaction Tips
- Be prepared for spontaneous and open displays of emotion, both positive and negative.
- Because this RANDOM ACTOR profile has the EXPRESS trait, focus on minimizing fear-producing events or discussions, which might emotionally trigger self-inflicted harm.

- Do not put them in "sensitive" or politically complex relationships.
- Focus on building their self-confidence and providing structure to offset unpredictability.
- Focus on that which is positive that they can control.

Sell/Present—Like all RANDOM ACTOR profiles, avoid making presentations that require important decision-making. Find another person in the organization to either make your case or help undergird their fears, such as the ARTIST–INNOVATOR. When making presentation, presenter with an EXPRESS trait is ideal who should focus on ideas rather than bottom line issues, using a slow, deliberate NONASSERTIVE style, while preemptively preparing for any potential fear-provoking, need-to-take-action points. Anticipate and prepare for swift reversals, even after they say "yes."

Confront/Disagree—First, be sure to review the guidelines for interacting with a RANDOM ACTOR detailed throughout the text. Like the other RANDOM ACTOR profiles, try and operate based upon the positive actions in their COMMUNICATION type. Reduce fear with soothing reassurances that keep their EXPRESS and FEARFUL traits in check. Only as a last resort should a person with a moderate to high ASSERTIVE trait be employed. Appeal to their desire to be amiable and respectful. That is, appeal to the positive actions you observe in their COMMUNICATION type and vocalize with a reassuring tone. When they seek to harm you, they will often try to get in close, playing off your "feelings" and intimacy. So, be careful what you give away about yourself personally.

Lead/Motivate—Lead and motivate them in their area of expertise and competency as well as the positive actions you observe in their COMMUNICATION actions. Do not present with critical decisions. If decision is necessary, provide significant time and support to process and accept. The higher the UNCONVENTIONAL trait the more likely will want to press norms and try new ideas/ventures, but must again be provided significant time for FEARFUL trait to absorb opportunity. Emphasize team effort and safety nets along the way. Remember, even though you may connect with their EXPRESS trait, this doesn't mean they are on board. As explained in Chapter 14 and *Snapshot*, mentor how to make small bite-sized CONFIDENT decisions separate from area of competency to expand capacity for increased confident decision-making.

CHAPTER 13

USING THE COMPREHENSIVE PROFILES

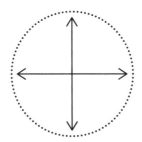

In this chapter we will examine four different cases in which COMPREHENSIVE PROFILES were integral in solving problems. Each case is based upon an actual situation in which I either acted as a consultant or closely observed. Two assignments are provided at the end to help you put the profiles to work in your professional and personal life.

Case #1—An outside consultant, Michael, is working with a creative work group in the audit industry. Every time the consultant makes a proposal that the staff wants to initiate, the group's manager, Thomas, throws up illogical roadblocks that nearly derail the project. What course of action should the consultant take to save the project?

The first step Michael took was to profile the manager. He based his read upon correspondence he received from Thomas, phone conversations, and a face-to-face meeting with the entire staff. He determined that Thomas was a SERGEANT–LOYALIST. Here are some excerpts from Thomas's COMPREHENSIVE PROFILE.

- Because of their fear-based motivations coupled with their social dominance and predictability, they will seldom risk new ideas or challenges and they will seldom challenge others or the status quo.

- SERGEANT-LOYALISTS dislike sudden or unpredictable change, and they fear the personal consequences of such change. They do not want to be surprised or to surprise those who may control their future or their fate.

- The higher the CAUTIOUS/FEARFUL trait, the more likely they are to point a finger at you when you are not to blame for a problem, so evaluate entering situations where risk is a significant factor. This can especially be difficult, the higher the ASSERTIVE trait.

- Expect rigid interpretations of rules; don't ask for compromises or exceptions.

- Do not be frustrated by their "mixed style" when they deal "up the chain of command" versus "down the chain of command." When they deal "down," they will tend to be more dominant, while they will appear to be less dominant when they deal "up" the chain of command.

First, it is pretty obvious that whoever hired Thomas to be the manager of this group didn't do a very good job. Rarely, if ever, do you want a SERGEANT-LOYALIST to manage a creative group because he has a natural aversion to new ideas and risk, which is an integral part of a successful creative process. Still, Michael has to get the job done. He knows, though, that all blame will be placed on his desk by Thomas if anything doesn't perform as expected—even if it isn't his fault.

To overcome this fear-driven profile, Michael first looked for two team members who were CONFIDENT and at least one who was UNCONVENTIONAL. He wanted those with the CONFIDENT trait to undergird Thomas's CAUTIOUS/FEARFUL trait, and he wanted someone with the UNCONVENTIONAL trait to navigate the creative project for Thomas. The strategy was: (1) Only present bottom-line decisions to Thomas, (2) After all ambiguity and risk had been minimized and assessed.

Michael selected Mark and Joy for their expertise and because both were about 3 CONFIDENT and not risk-adverse. Mark was low ASSERTIVE and wasn't afraid of verbally articulating a position, while Joy was NONASSERTIVE and demonstrated her confidence in the project through her actions rather than through dialogue. She was also UNCONVENTIONAL and was suited to shoulder the changes that always pop up during an innovative project. Together, Michael relied upon them to keep the project moving forward.

When Thomas threw down unnecessary objections, Michael provided responses through Mark and Joy. He provided Mark with oral responses when a verbal response was necessary, and he provided strategic direction to Joy when a written response was needed, such as a revision to a proposal or to a strategic point. In this way, they kept Thomas's CAUTIOUS/FEARFUL trait "propped up" and he didn't have to facilitate creative elements.

By relieving Thomas of the majority of the decision-making process when modified actions had to be taken, Thomas's CAUTIOUS/FEARFUL trait was minimized, the project was completed, and Michael's reputation remained intact and untarnished.

Michael also took action to protect his integrity if any phase did not perform due to factors out of his control. He wanted to avoid the usual "Well, you promised..." type of comments from Thomas.

One strategic step he took was regularly forwarding to Thomas written updates. This provided a vehicle through which anyone—Thomas's superiors, team members, or prospective future clients—could easily track the progress of the project. Each update also included observations about changes in delivery and completion dates, changes in strategy, etc. that were not directly communicated by Mark or Joy. He didn't let them accumulate. In this way, the bumps and obstacles that all creative projects face were presented in small doses, which can prevent fear-overload by LOYALIST profiles.

Similarly, Joy navigated the changes in the project. Only bottom line performance was reported to Thomas, a tactic that can minimize a severe reaction from a manager's superiors if the manager is forced to present several unexpected changes at one time. This is important for a SERGEANT-

LOYALIST like Thomas, as his superiors are less likely to exert overloading pressure on him which Thomas might be tempted to redirect at Michael.

Keeping Thomas regularly informed of changes also aided the communication process. As a SERGEANT–LOYALIST, Thomas's natural tendency is to be firm with subordinates (using his ASSERTIVE trait), while he is more likely to retreat (because he is CAUTIOUS/FEARFUL) if confronted by superiors, which can result in the derailing of a project, needless posturing, and so forth.

Case #2—Marc and his staff were pursuing a lucrative contract with XYZ Inc., a Fortune 1000 company. However, Marc encounters an unusual challenge. The CFO of XYZ requests an exploratory meeting with his staff before moving forward. He tells Marc, though, that under no conditions may any of Marc's staff make contact with anyone at XYZ before this meeting. Then, the day of the meeting, the CFO slams the boardroom door shut and screams at his subordinates, while Marc and his staff are standing outside the door within earshot of the CFO's loud barks. What action did Marc take, based upon the CFO's actions, that increased his company's chances of securing a future contract?

Sometimes it is just as beneficial to know when not to press forward as when you should move forward aggressively to secure a contract. When the decision is made not to move forward because of inopportune factors, the same resources can be directed toward a more productive opportunity or you can wait until the time is right to resume sales and marketing efforts. This case is an example.

Marc profiled the CFO as a SERGEANT–RANDOM ACTOR. He based this upon the reads of technical support people in his organization and observations of outside vendors who had done business with the CFO. Marc tested these reads during his first interactions with the CFO on the phone and during a prior meeting. Unfortunately, everyone was on target: the CFO was extremely volatile and manipulative.

Here are highlights of the SERGEANT–RANDOM ACTOR profile.

- SERGEANT–RANDOM ACTORS will seek to maintain the strong, controlling image of the SERGEANT, but will frequently disappoint others with their unreliability and their unwillingness to take responsibility for their circumstances. Their fear-based motivation will cause them to feel and act "out of control" while their COMMUNICATION type will drive them to maintain the appearance of CONTROL. This combination of traits will produce a tension that can result in anger, impatience, depression, moodiness, or authoritarianism.

- No matter what their performance level, they will attempt to dominate and control others.

- Their unpredictability and fear-based motivations yield random actions that may have no relevance to the situation.

- This may be one of the most difficult profiles to read because of the strong contrast between the COMMUNICATION and PERFORMANCE types. Even though they are ASSERTIVE, they are FEARFUL when making decisions.

Even to the uninformed, a quick glance at these tendencies says: Do not enter into long-term relationships with volatile RANDOM ACTORS unless you are willing to deal with the consequences. (Remember, not everyone with the RANDOM ACTOR profile is volatile; but most are troubled because of their extreme FEARFUL trait.)

Given the CFO's profile, Marc has two reasons for not doing business with XYZ. First, the key player is volatile, paranoiac, and unstable. Second, when SERGEANT–RANDOM ACTORS exit their senior level positions, housecleaning often follows. This often includes the cancellation of contracts, termination of relationships, etc. Taking this into consideration, Marc still wanted to eventually do business with XYZ, so he took three courses of action.

First, during the meeting, that eventually started after the CFO slammed the boardroom door shut, Marc politely disengaged his staff from negotiations using nonthreatening, open-ended language. Marc didn't want to needlessly create an enemy. Second, he instructed his staff to quietly develop strategic relationships with technical staffers at XYZ so that if and when the CFO exited, they would be positioned to move forward again—but with helpful alliances in place. Third, he directed his staff to focus their time and resources on other accounts.

Did Marc get the account? No. But, he made a wise decision for maximizing his resources and positioning his company for a better day in the future with XYZ.

Case #3—Katie is an independent negotiator who brings documentary producers and cable networks together. For two months she tried to purchase the rights to an historically significant documentary series made by a British production company. Scott, her contact, was very difficult to pin down; it was the first time he negotiated a contract for his company. One day the deal was on, the next day it was off. Her only contact with Scott was through correspondence and telephone conferences. She thinks he is a CAUTIOUS INNOVATOR, and she is willing to do whatever is necessary to secure this important documentary. What course of action did she take in order to secure the contract?

Katie profiled Scott as an ARTIST–CAUTIOUS INNOVATOR whose UNCONVENTIONAL and CAUTIOUS/FEARFUL traits were about 2 or 3. Some of the highlights of this profile are:

- Lack desire for control; will not manage or dominate in situations when they should.

- If significant negative ARTIST actions apparent, more likely to be withdrawn, moody, reclusive, disinterested in others.

- Easily intimidated by those "in control."

- Use ARTIST or SALESMAN type who is low NONASSERTIVE who focuses on ideas and concepts. Use a slow, deliberate NONASSERTIVE style, while preemptively preparing for any potential fear-provoking, need-to-take-action points. Bottom line issues are secondary.

Unlike Marc's situation in the previous case, Katie pursued her contract with Scott because he wasn't high FEARFUL and she wasn't entering into a long-term relationship with Scott; it was short-term. Once the deal was signed, there would be no more obligations or action points with Scott. Additionally, she believed that working with Scott was an acceptable risk because his UNCONVENTIONAL and CAUTIOUS/FEARFUL traits were only about a 2.

Tactically, it was crucial that Katie do whatever was necessary to drive down Scott's fears/apprehensions because it was his first major contract. His future reputation was on the line, and he would almost singularly be motivated by the opinions of his superiors. Driving down Scott's fears in this pressure situation was also more likely to make his actions more predictable, but only in the short-term.

So what did Katie do?

She flew to England for a face-to-face meeting with Scott. She was determined to identify the positive traits in Scott's ARTIST type and operate with him on that level. As they communicated, she wanted Scott to see with his own eyes that she could be trusted and that her first desire was to see Scott shine in the eyes of his superiors. Was her costly trip guaranteed to work? No. But she was confident that her US client was the best vehicle for Scott's documentary series. She also felt that if Scott would trust her, both would end up winners.

The result?

Scott signed, and his company's documentary series aired with much acclaim in the US. Scott also increased in stature in his company. And yes, Katie was able to discuss future projects with Scott because his trust in her was established—the key in successfully operating with CAUTIOUS INNOVATORS. She made sure, however, that none of the transactions required a long-term commitment on Scott's part.

Katie put to work the essence of thoughtful profiling: *I know who you are. Good for me, better for you.* It's the art of treating people right the first time.

Profiling with this attitude does work.

Case #4—All teenagers become odd in different ways when they go through "the change." In our family we call it "lala land." Kids can't help it, just like you and I couldn't help it when our hormones ravaged us. Pimples, new hair, rearranging of body parts . . . it's all a part of the mutation/transformation.

Robert and Sharon have two teenage boys. They are convinced that the reason God created puberty was so that they would have an easier time letting go of their sons when they became men. They love their boys, who are both competitive with very different profiles, but nurturing and disciplining is a challenge. Here are some ways that they used profiling to keep the lines of communication wide open.

Their oldest son, Brandon (16), is an ARTIST/ACCOUNTANT–INNOVATOR. Jake (14) is a SALESMAN/SERGEANT–MANAGER. Both boys, who are combination types, are extremely competitive, driven by their high CONFIDENT traits, which were nurtured by their parents and a handful of very caring teachers.

The difference in the two boys was humorously apparent by the time they were three and five. Jake, the MANAGER, could completely dress himself, shirt tucked in. Everything coordinated. Brandon, the INNOVATOR, who was two years older, was lucky just to get out of bed. From the time Jake was three, he actually dressed and critiqued his older brother, morning after morning, until Brandon was seven.

By the time the boys started their lawn-mowing business, Jake, now 10, was the organizer, and Brandon, 12, had the warm, winning smile that endeared his neighbors to give them a chance.

When discipline was necessary, their parents took a slightly different approach with each son. For both sons they first reviewed the facts of the infraction, the punishment, and their expectation for change. When confronted with a huge error by Brandon (the Innovator), his dad would have Brandon write a paper to be sure the expectation for change was concrete and unambiguous in Brandon's idea-driven mind.

When disciplining Jake (the MANAGER), they followed the same initial process: review the facts of the infraction, the punishment, and their expectation for change. But when a specific situation needed to be emphasized, he was usually given a specific task that was a direct counterpoint of how he ineffectively handled/managed himself. For example, if Jake failed to take out the bathroom garbage for the second time in a week, his punishment went as follows: First, he empties the garbage from each bathroom into a large container in the garage. Second, he then returns each container to its respective bathroom. Third, he recollects the containers from each bathroom. Fourth, he replaces the emptied garbage that is in the large container in the garage back into each bathroom container. Finally, Jake must return each container back to its original bathroom with its original garbage. For emphasis, the whole process is then repeated about a half-dozen times.

In Robert and Sharon's house, both boys had to obey the same rules. They used two very different approaches, however, to help each boy learn his lesson in a way that matched his profile. They applied the same kind of thinking in all other important situations, such as times of encouragement, teaching, making "suggestions," and so on. The boys almost always sensed that Mom and Dad understood and took a unique interest in their successes and failures, their missteps and their maturing steps forward. Yes, this requires time, but it is parenting with a legacy of blessings.

Assignment 16

Goal: Learn how to use the COMPREHENSIVE PROFILES to solve a professional problem.
Time: Approximately two hours.

Think of a problem that you encountered in your professional life which ended in an unsuccessful resolution but which might have been tackled successfully if you had known how to profile. Now do the following:

1. At the top of a legal pad, write a summary statement of your hoped-for outcome at that time. Be specific.

2. Write a summary statement of the actual outcome underneath your initial anticipated outcome.

3. Identify the profile of each person who was involved.

4. Review each person's profile, and record their specific actions that had a direct bearing on the outcome.

5. With a blue or black pen, catalog on a separate legal-sized sheet of paper the facts on a vertical time line of what occurred. The simplest way to do this is to write down the sequence of events—one event on each line. In the left-hand margin, provide the time of each event, when appropriate.

6. After compiling the time line, record the tendencies/actions of each profile that, if addressed differently, might have changed the outcome.

7. Review your personal profile and make notes about how your specific tendencies may have affected the outcome.

8. Using the sequence of events you prepared in Step #5, create another time line on another sheet of paper as follows: For each specific event that you wouldn't have changed how you interacted, write these in blue or black ink—one event for each line. After carefully reviewing the mix of profiles that were involved in the situation, both yours and the profiles of others, record how you would modify specific interactions, actions, and directives if faced with the same situation. Write these modifications on your time line in red pen. Be sure to be specific and not ambiguous. In some cases you may be looking for a completely successful outcome, while in other cases you will only be able to minimize damage.

9. Now review the entire modified time line, taking note of your suggestions (which are in red). Evaluate and then reevaluate your modifications. When possible, ask another person who possesses wisdom and insight to review your suggestions.

10. Finally, write out specific lessons and insights you have gained by applying profiling to this situation and how you will tackle future situations which are similar. Don't just talk this last step out. Write out your thoughts. You will find that even as you put your ideas down on paper that you will probably gain an additional insight or two.

Assignment 17

Goal: Learn how to use the COMPREHENSIVE PROFILES to solve a personal problem.
Time: Approximately two hours.

For this assignment, think of a minor personal problem that you had with another person which had an unsuccessful resolution but which you might have been able to resolve successfully if you had known how to profile. Start with a less-than-volcanic problem to avoid unwanted intrusion of your personal emotions at this point. Only after you have practiced this exercise on a couple of less explosive situations should you consider examining a volatile and/or life-changing event.

Follow the ten steps provided in ASSIGNMENT 16. Addressing a personal situation can sometimes be more difficult than examining a professional problem. Therefore, be sure you set aside sufficient reflective time so that you won't be interrupted. Seek impartial and wise input when necessary. Once you have thought through and learned from one situation, try another. Resist tackling difficult situations until you have gained some experience.

If you are reviewing a situation together with a spouse, be patient. Let grace be the operative word. We all have strengths and deficiencies. Don't clobber your mate with newfound understanding and knowledge which you have gained from your profiling skills. One of the best pieces of advice I have ever received was from my colleague, Dr. James Reese, who wrote the foreword for this book. He said: If you really care, would you ever want to see your best friend fail and lose in life? Of course not. Well, it's the same with your spouse, especially in an argument. Don't hound the person you love until you win and he or she fails. That's a pretty shallow and hollow victory. Be on your spouse's side so that he/she wins and doesn't fail.

Again, the philosophy introduced in Chapter 2 must be made to prevail: *I know who you are. Good for me, better for you. It's the art of treating people right the first time.*

Assignment 18

Goal: Learn how to use COMPREHENSIVE profiles to interact with precision and/or succeed in a future situation.
Time: Approximately two hours.

Think ahead to professional and personal situations that you know you will probably encounter in the *future*. Then apply the following steps.

1. Identify a future situation, such as how you will:
   - Refine a presentation for a previously puzzling client.
   - Encourage a student who needs to tackle a new challenge.
   - Help your team better interact, respecting each other's strengths.
   - Attempt to defuse the anger of a colleague who must be confronted.
   - Conduct an interview so fears are not unnecessarily provoked.
   - Change your consultation approach so a client acts on your recommendations.
   - Provide a patient with appropriate counsel.
   - Show your spouse that you respect his or her unique style for communicating and performing.
   - Communicate your vision for a project to a group.

2. Write a summary statement of your anticipated outcome.

3. Identify the profile of each person that will probably be involved.

4. Review each person's profile and record the tendencies/actions which might have a direct bearing on the outcome.

5. Review your personal profile and make notes about how your

cific tendencies/actions may affect the outcome.

6. Write out a time line, referencing how you will interact, direct, listen, etc. with each individual.

7. Write specific goals of what insight you hope to attain by using profiling in this situation.

A LIFE-CHANGING TOOL . . . AND, RESPONSIBILITY

Forty years ago, people generally had a better sense of who they were in relationship to everyone else. Families were more stable. For most of us there was at least one person who helped instill in us our internal and external bearings. That's changed. It's almost like we're starting all over—rediscovering who we are and how we are put together. Durable homespun wisdom is now uncommon. We can no longer draw upon the durable resident memories that previous generations could draw from.

All of my children could rapid-fire profile by the time they were fourteen by virtue of their father's work.

When my oldest son, Erik, was sixteen, he was selected by his classmates to be a "peer helper" at his high school, which had over 1,500 students. The twenty-five peer helpers, who were carefully interviewed and screened by counselors, offered an alternative for troubled youths who want help. They could go to a responsible peer for guidance. The training for peer helpers was rigorous, combining students from four high schools at a weekend retreat. Many schools across North America still use this valuable resource.

During one exercise, Erik and his new friends experienced what it's like to be stereotyped. For the demonstration, Erik and four other students were selected from the one hundred trainees and given a headband to wear. On the headband was a label and a command. Erik nor his four colleagues were allowed to look at what was printed on their own headbands.

For the next fifteen minutes, the five teens treated one another as per the label and command on their headbands. Their ninety-plus peers observed the five youths interact. Then the five students sat down in chairs in front of the rest of the group. They were asked to guess what was written on their headbands.

Erik said, "I think my label is Nerd and the command is *make fun of me*." In fact, Erik quoted the label and command verbatim. His profiling skills kicked in. He didn't miss a word. His peers were amazed and they cheered at his insight. But the cheering was short-lived.

The counselor pointed out how Erik, a six-foot-two, two-hundred-and thirty-five-pound football player, appeared confident before the exercise. His body was erect. His head and gaze were steady. As he was derided, however, he changed. When Erik was asked to take a seat in his chair, he was slightly slumped forward. His ever-present smile gone from his face.

When asked how he knew what was on his headband, he said, "When I was ten, I was overweight and kids made fun of me. I hadn't grown yet. It didn't take much to remember how people used to treat me."

No one likes to be treated based upon callously applied labels. Shallow stereotyping.

Erik was fortunate. He grew and the derision faded. But what about other people we know on whom someone has placed a label that we insensitively read and react to? People whom we don't take the time to profile and treat them based upon who they really are.

You've learned how to profile and with it you've taken on a life-changing responsibility. Use it wisely. Others are depending upon you.

CHAPTER 14

BUILDING CAPACITY FOR CONFIDENT DECISION MAKING & LEADING CAUTIOUS INNOVATORS

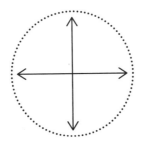

During the last thirty years, there has been a severe decline in people's ability to make confident decisions separate from their area of competency or giftedness. In the early 1980s, I came face to face with this trend when investigating the root causes for several destructive social trends. It first appeared in the youth trends, and then as they became adults, the trend became entrenched in the adult population. Why this trend is here and how to build capacity for confident decision-making are the core of this chapter (adapted from a Chapter 15 in *Snapshot*). The capacity-building technique which has been successfully used with thousands of students, athletes, and private sector professionals. You'll learn how to help anyone increase their capacity for confident decision-making—one of the greatest gifts you can give someone. In fact, it can be used with anyone who wants to increase their capacity to make CONFIDENT decisions.

We will also look at how to lead people who have the CAUTIOUS-INNOVATOR profile, introduced in Chapter 9. It is the fastest growing profile in most developed countries, which has caused significant confusion because of their desire to innovate, create, and adapt to change, while simultaneously restrained by CAUTIOUS decision making.

Confidence Vanishes for a Multitude

The attorney was bright, gifted with insight, but couldn't profile. When Barry encountered Louisa, he found her contradictory and was at a loss how to lead her professionally. She was bright, and she easily engaged others in dialogue. When performing tasks, she was UNCONVENTIONAL but was a CAUTIOUS decision maker. The latter two traits, the desire to try something different but cautious when making decisions, created tension. She wanted to move forward, but her caution put on the brake, and he didn't know how to get her past it to lead her. In Barry's profession, time is critical, which is one reason he wanted to learn the *KPS*. A day after he learned the four gauges, I asked him if he had any insights into how he could help Louisa.

"I guess I would use my ASSERTIVE trait to reassure her and also educate her longer on the task at hand," he surmised. Unfortunately, this usually won't work.

Louisa is an example of the fastest growing profile—the CAUTIOUS INNOVATOR, and you probably know people with this profile and may have experienced Barry's confusion about how to help. Complaints by organizational leaders who were confused and teachers struggling to lead students caused me to realize that this was a critical "muscle" to develop in any organization or classroom.

The seeds of fear—In the 1950s, the majority of Americans were confident decision-makers. We fought through two world wars, a depression, and won. Then something happened. Families began to disintegrate at a frightening rate, where now more than one out of every two first-time marriages ends in divorce. For marriages with children (in addition to the millions of kids in dysfunctional or abusive homes or whose parents have never married), this increased FEARFUL decision-making in youth who carry this into their adult lives. In the minds of the thousands of youth I interviewed and observed for my research, the theme was the same: *Mom* *and Dad said "I do" when they pledged their wedding vows. Now they say "they don't." Who can I trust?* Fundamental trust is undermined.

This has propagated large populations of youths and adults who can't discern good from evil, who can they trust, or how to make a commitment and keep it. Collectively, this has increased the number of people who make decisions toward the CAUTIOUS/FEARFUL side of the confidence wire. While obviously not everyone on this side of the gauge has experienced severe family difficulty as a child, my experience is that the majority have.

When researching why affluent youths from suburbs and small towns were forming gangs for the first time in world history in sizable numbers for my book, *Suburban Gangs—The Affluent Rebels* (1995), I found that of 54 million youth, over 40 million were from homes where there was divorce, separation, physical or sexual abuse or where at least one parent was severely dysfunctional, as with alcoholism. Thirty-two million alone were from single parent homes—that's almost the population of Canada. That was in the early 1990s, and the numbers are even greater today.

The full compliment of divorce, separation, family dysfunction, and more has created uncertainty in millions of young people. At the extreme end of this at-risk trend, we witnessed the sudden emergence of significant numbers of students with the RANDOM ACTOR traits.

At the less extreme end were students who were UNCONVENTIONAL and CAUTIOUS—not high FEARFUL. The first to see this trend were of course teachers.

I've researched and written extensively on how other violent youth trends emanate from this factor, like the school massacre trend such as the attacks at Columbine High School (1999) and Virginia Tech (2007). Virtually any group of educators or law enforcement officers anywhere in the world will voice the same opinion because they see the effect of it every day. When kids are insecure and the world is shifting under their feet, so goes their confidence in making decisions.

The shift toward the CAUTIOUS/FEARFUL is even more significant than the Earth's shift to the UNCONVENTIONAL trait. In a typical school forty years ago, about 75% of the students were CONFIDENT decision makers.

Today, it's 50% or less in middle- and upper-middle class neighborhoods—and even higher in the inner city. Even those who are from stable homes are affected, as some slide to CAUTIOUS/FEARFUL as they are influenced by their friends.

Related to the culture at large, as they enter the workforce, there is now a potentially crippling effect that is a part of the corporate landscape: the inability to make CONFIDENT decisions when decisions and changes are needed to compete and keep up with changes in markets and technology. This can be crippling when decisions have to be made quickly. Some of you are struggling with this right now and wondering what you can do.

The traditional method of providing more competency training by itself won't work when change is needed—when people have to make decisions *outside* their area of competency. A common example is the severe changes in technology that force people to find new careers and organizations to retool or change focus to remain competitive.

This inability to make CONFIDENT decisions is a stymying factor that keeps kids to adults from reaching their potential or leading fulfilled lives.

Building Capacity to Make Confident Decisions

CONFIDENT decision making is like a muscle you exercise. It is something we have a choice to use or not use, regardless of our circumstances. Even those who are low CONFIDENT (0–2 on the CONFIDENT side of the wire) can move to higher levels of confidence.

All schools and workplace teams should include building this capacity as a sustained best practice. Even more powerful is for families to self-apply. Two or three families can even join together. It's something that we did instinctively with kids in our neighborhood when my children were growing up.

There are five common-sense steps to help someone increase their CONFIDENT decision-making muscle. These steps—themes—have been taught to thousands who have helped adults and students. These steps can be applied one-on-one or in a group setting. If you need help, find someone who has basic insight into others for input into the best approach for each step. I've never found a group of folks who couldn't find a way to apply the steps.

1. Develop trust. For someone to follow your guidance, there must be trusting communication. For most people, this can be done quickly. If trust has been violated, it may take time to reestablish. For kids, establishing trust usually occurs within a shorter time than for an adult—even as short as one meeting. If you are helping a single individual, explain the need to be able to make CONFIDENT decisions separate from his or her area of competency, especially in changing times.

2. Acknowledge need to make CONFIDENT decisions. Regardless of someone's plot point on the CONFIDENT–CAUTIOUS/FEARFUL wire, have them plot themselves on the wire. This is important so that they take ownership of the process. For those who are on the CAUTIOUS/FEARFUL side of the gauge, this is powerful as they are making a CONFIDENT decision to trust someone with important information about themselves.

You can also ask them to write a paragraph or a one-pager on how their day, career, personal relationships, etc. might be different if they can move just 1 or 2 points toward the CONFIDENT side of the wire—or move higher on the CONFIDENT side, if they're low CONFIDENT. This allows them to articulate what this might look like. (For those who are 5 on the FEARFUL scale, more is provided in the next chapter.)

For organizations, the idea must be clearly explained that your *team* must build capacity for making CONFIDENT decisions *separate* from one's competency so you can compete when change is required due to changing markets, technology, etc. You can even point to examples of organizations that have failed because they couldn't pull the trigger. The key is that it's presented as a team competency, rather than just helping one or two individuals.

A positive of increasing CONFIDENT decision-making capacity in a group setting is it builds team leadership and pulls along those who might not otherwise participate. I watched this occur over a period of time in the company of one of my clients.

Patricia, the president, had a number of team leaders who were single women, divorced by men with significant personal issues. Most were CAUTIOUS decision makers. Patricia regularly had them make small decisions outside their area of competency. Over time, they grew in decision-making confidence. More importantly, when new staff came on board, they conveyed to someone who was struggling that they could do it, too, like they did. They literally became a team that left no one behind.

3. Make a CONFIDENT decision that day. Once someone expresses a desire to make more CONFIDENT decisions, guide them toward a decision they can make, immediately, on the spot. The qualifications for a decision are:

- Concrete—not abstract
- Nugget-sized
- Time-compacted (for an immediate result)
- Specific—not expansive
- Short duration—not drawn out

The idea is to help them decide on an immediate CONFIDENT decision over which they have control and which has quick closure. Just "doing better on the job" or "getting a better algebra grade" doesn't qualify. It's vague, general, and not time compacted. Spending an additional ten minutes a day for a week when preparing a report or homework assignments is better.

Also, it's best if they come up with the decision(s). Providing a list of decisions doesn't offer them control of the process—it puts you in control, which may be part of the problem. You should act as a guiding sounding-board. For example, you could point them toward specific task areas in which they can make decisions, but they must wrestle with the concept of making confident decisions and how it directly applies to their life, career, and so on. This ensures that they internalize the process and take ownership.

One starting-point option is to have them recall a confident decision they made in the past that they felt good about. Ask them why they knew it was a good decision and if they would like to have that same kind of confidence today. (In extreme cases where someone is high FEARFUL, though, postponing this type of question might be advisable as they might not be able to recall a CONFIDENT decision and become despondent.)

Remember, what we *aren't* looking for is how a person communicates, such as talking confidently, but rather specific actions that indicate CONFI-

DENT decision making.

In an organizational setting, the team can decide on decisions and you can have some "back-ups" if they get stuck. The idea is that the decisions do not capitalize on group, organizational, or individual competencies. The tasks in which they must make decisions, though, must add value to the daily work process. It may be as simple as working for just half a day with someone they don't usually get along with or assisting in an area of the company for a day where they don't have competency, but awareness of how that unit operates will help them in their responsibilities. (The CBS TV series, *Undercover Boss*, is a good source of inspiration for ideas and is available in various formats.)

4. Regularly provide encouragement and guidance to make simple, time-compacted decisions out of confidence. New decisions must be selected and acted upon monthly, weekly, or even daily (especially for kids). Remember, they are exercising a decision-making muscle. Neglect only leads to atrophy. It's one reason why leaders universally know that if you aren't moving forward you are moving backward.

5. Over time, encourage to make decisions that are more challenging, complex, and take longer to complete. Just like athletes in training who increase the weights they lift with increased reps, decisions should become more challenging and take longer.

A simple, time-compacted decision in the beginning might be: Work with Jennifer (something he dislikes) on a project for a day. A more challenging decision might be: Work with Jennifer for two weeks and find at least two positive things you like about her. While there is no set list of suggestions for more complex decisions, be guided by common sense, feedback, insight from others, etc.

Teaching young people how to strengthen their decision-making muscle. When kids are taught this concept, they grab onto it. As an experiment, I trained over fifty high school students how to profile. Here are some of the small and big confident decisions they made within two weeks of using the *KPS*.

- I decided to apply to a college that I did not think I could get into.
- I waited to do a report. I made a B, but I know I could have done the work better to make an A. Now I am mad at myself.
- I have made some better decisions at work.
- I've made some better decisions in sports since I've been trained.
- I can tell I have made better decisions in the way I think.
- I am analyzing things more before I make a decision now.
- I am more confident now that I have made the right decision.
- I have used this to get along with my parents—I stay at both of their houses at different times.
- I decided to go for a role in the musical—now I am ready to commit to it.
- I decided to tell someone something very important—I didn't want to.
- I studied for a test and it was a good decision—I did well.
- I have eliminated two colleges I was thinking about.
- I've decided to work hard for my future, even if my parents don't want to help me with it.
- This has really helped me decide what school to go to.
- I decided where to go and now I am going with more confidence.
- I decided to go to a different church retreat than my own. Now I met new friends and am very glad I did.

Pulling the trigger when it counts. One of America's premier coaches told me that he estimated that, approximately 20% of the time, impact players *can't* pull the trigger and make a play. I asked him for his personal take on this inability to perform.

He said that 10% of the time, it's because of a lack of instinct. More importantly, he said that 10% of the time it's behavioral. As we drilled down, I asked him if this was the inability to make a CONFIDENT decision in an unfamiliar situation. He had never thought about it in those terms, but he said that was probably it.

He estimated that if athletes could increase their ability to make CONFI-DENT decisions, their margin of error could probably be reduced by 10% or more. From his perspective, that can translate into a championship season instead of just a winning season.

Be careful when using the word ego. Don't confuse CONFIDENT decision making with being egotistical. The phrase, *he has a big ego*, usually implies that a CONFIDENT person is also self-directed or absorbed. It is stereotyping to denigrate another by saying they have a big ego because they can make CONFIDENT decisions, as if only the selfish can do that.

Unfortunately, we don't have a word for confident decision-making that is others directed. For me, the word *noble* is a descriptor that is close, such as she has a noble presence.

Leading and Working with Cautious Innovators

As you've learned, there has been a severe shift to the UNCONVENTIONAL trait and the CAUTIOUS/FEARFUL trait. The first is because of the injection of technology and the latter because of family deterioration. As a result, the fastest growing profile in the culture is the CAUTIOUS INNOVATOR, like Louisa, whom you met at the beginning of the chapter. She wants to venture out and try new and different ideas, adventures, and more. But, her CAUTIOUS decision making tends to build tension in her. Sometimes she doesn't move forward. Other times she does, but only after careful evaluation. For those not savvy to the profile, it seems contradictory, confusing, and leads to crossed signals when trying to lead them that sound like this: *She says she wants to do something different, so why doesn't she do it? ... or ... Why does it take her so long to make up her mind?*

To get a picture of how many youth and adults have this profile, remember that up to 75% of every class of students now have the UNCONVENTIONAL trait. Then, add those who are CAUTIOUS, which can be up to 50%. Now you have an idea of how many might have this profile.

People with this profile can be invaluable on a team where change is occurring. They can act as a check on whether or not the change is a positive, should be pursued, etc. because of their CAUTIOUS trait.

There is nothing inherently problematic with the CAUTIOUS INNOVATOR profile, but you must recognize the following simple themes.

Themes for Leading CAUTIOUS INNOVATORS

1. Don't interpret the desire to try something new (UNCONVENTIONAL) with the action of making a decision to move forward (CAUTIOUS).

2. They may require *additional time to process a decision outside area of competency.* When operating within their area of competency, though, they may be able to make a CONFIDENT decision.

3. As with others with the UNCONVENTIONAL trait, provide change, variability, flexibility while emphasizing innovation between the lines with discipline. Without discipline and a positive recognition of following basic rules, codes of ethics, etc. the negative UNCONVENTIONAL actions are likely to appear. (More on this in *Snapshot.*)

4. Like all others on a team, build capacity to make CONFIDENT decisions *separate* from area of competency.

5. It is possible due to life-threatening or, altering stressors that a CAUTIOUS INNOVATOR may spike out to 4 or over on the FEARFUL gauge and operate in the RANDOM ACTOR quadrant. If the stressors diminish, the person usually reverts to their CAUTIOUS INNOVATOR type.

CHAPTER 15

RANDOM ACTORS
CAN CHANGE

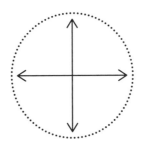

As noted in Chapter 9, those who commit mass suicide terrorist attacks, school shootings/bombings, postal and company shootings, as well as serial killers, typically have the RANDOM ACTOR profile. Additionally, we are seeing an increase in these type of acts and they aren't expected to diminish in our lifetime because of the number of people with this profile (currently 6% of all K–12 students and approximately 4–6% of adult populations). While most people with this profile won't commit acts of violence, they often lead troubled lives because of their high FEARFUL trait (paranoia)—either professionally, personally, or both.

For this reason, I've provided condensed overviews of insights about the profile, themes for prevention and intervention, and the three-point strategy that guides most out of this profile. This content is adapted from *Rage of the Random Actor—Disarming Catastrophic Acts and Restoring Lives*. There is obviously more complexity than what can be presented here, but I strongly recommend this 500-page resource if you need amplification. At the end of each section in this chapter, I've noted the chapters in *Rage of the Random Actor* that provide more details, cases, documentation, and data sources.

If you require more information related to preventing violent RANDOM ACTOR attacks by youths, like the Columbine Massacre, I recommend *If Only I Had Known: The Life-Saving Solution That Thousands Have Used to Stop School Massacres* by William H. Dodson, Ph.D. He was the first school superintendent who experienced a devastating school attack that started the global trend. He chose the title because he didn't know that the research I developed quantifiably stops attacks.

The positive is that the intervention themes work and have proven their mettle in schools, the workplace, and in combat. Not only have major incidents been averted, but more importantly, the majority of adults and youths with the RANDOM ACTOR traits who aren't violent, but who have received assistance, do better and even move out of the profile. Additionally, many people have self-identified themselves as having the traits, applied the themes, and guided themselves out of the profile and away from destructive behavior.

Why the Two Traits Spark

By themselves, the two traits, FEARFUL and UNCONVENTIONAL, aren't inherently combustible, although paranoia when making decisions is troubling for anyone. But, when the traits are combined, there is always the potential for severe internal tension.

Imagine that you like to be UNCONVENTIONAL, always trying something new and different, distinguishing yourself from the crowd. But, then you are chained by indecision rising from your paranoia, which sets off all kinds of contradictory behavior. Separate yourself from your natural skills and talents, and you can't escape your deepest fears when you make decisions—unless you are in total control. You want to do something, but your decision-making is always saying, *not so fast . . . you know they're against you . . . you know they want you to fail.* You feel cursed and trapped.

Those who are not violent regularly find themselves immobilized because they are afraid to commit—to a new career, a personal relationship, to anything where they don't have control. Some retreat where no one is an eyewitness to their insecurities, and of these, some fall into groups that directly or indirectly promise relief and safety from their own insecurities—from faddish groups to gangs to cults to terrorist cells. Those who have an adept or pleasing communication side to their personality, use their COMMUNICATION actions to hide their turmoil—commonplace in media and arts-related industries, like reporter Jason Blair of the *New York Times* who plagiarized dozens of stories from 1999–2002 through deception and manipulation to achieve undeserved recognition.

For others, tensions escalate and verbal and non-lethal acts erupt; some have a short fuse and others don't, depending upon the frequency of contact with those they perceive as a threat, impact of successes and failures, number of distractions in their life, and so on. When people seek to take advantage or achieve an advantage over them, they consider it apocalyptic. For example, in marketplace competition, where competitors are trying to beat your price: You *know* they want more than your profits; you believe they want to control you—own your very soul. Or, when you fail to deliver a project on time and on budget, you explode that the client is out to destroy your reputation and you lie to cover your inadequacy or misstep.

Lethal rage erupts when paranoid decision-making collides with the extreme dark side of the UNCONVENTIONAL trait—actions that are reckless, rebellious, and anarchistic. You don't care about rules or laws, you just want your way, and you want it now before someone steals it from you. This becomes calamitous when mixed with intense selfishness—narcissism. You want your own way, period. Dictators, cult leaders, and leaders of RANDOM ACTOR bands of killers or terrorists are found here. (*Rage*, Chapter 3)

Why the RANDOM ACTOR Descriptor

The term, RANDOM ACTOR, was selected to create a picture of a person who is extremely FEARFUL but would use the UNCONVENTIONAL trait and "random act" and "do whatever it takes" to create the impression of being confident. The original request to develop the *KPS* came from presidents of companies who needed a system for negotiations. The RANDOM ACTOR descriptor was selected as a quick picture of someone with whom you didn't want to negotiate because of instability.

While RANDOM ACTORS who kill indiscriminately commit "random acts of violence," this fact was just coincidental when selecting the descriptor. (There are also RANDOM ACTOR attacks that are deliberate, like 9–11, which required require planning, but killed indiscriminately. And, there are RANDOM ACTOR attacks that target a specific person, like the assassination of Austrian Arch Duke Franz Ferdinand, that triggered World War I, or the 2011 shooting attack on U.S. Rep. Gabrielle Giffords.) (*Rage*, Chapters 3 and 17)

How Hard Is It to Identify a Volatile RANDOM ACTOR?

It's isn't difficult at all. The reason for this is that their traits are extreme. And, as you've learned, people with extreme traits are easy to identify, like Jim Carrey (EXPRESS) or any of the other extreme examples provided for each trait. We have never received a call from the 15,000 educators we trained where a student was identified as having the RANDOM ACTOR traits who didn't. (Ways to prevent false positives are noted throughout *Rage of the Random Actor.*)

Who They Like and Don't Like and Why

In the early 1990s, members of the Society of Human Resource Management asked if the *KPS* could be used to identify mass company shooters, which was an emerging trend and started with postal shootings. I asked them for a list of cases, and when they were reviewed, I noticed that virtually all the killers were RANDOM ACTORS. I then asked: Who else is in the delivery business that *doesn't* have these attacks? That's when the pattern emerged. UPS and FedEx rarely if ever had an attack.

As I looked at mass company shootings and bomb threats, again the same pattern: all were RANDOM ACTORS. More importantly, I found that these incidents occurred in the accounting departments and on assembly lines *but not the art department or public relations.*

Then I profiled UPS/FedEx v. the post office as well as accounting/ assembly lines v. art departments/public relations. That's when it became clear. The post 0ffice/accounting/assembly lines represent the MANAGER quadrant while UPS/FedEx/art departments/public relations represent the INNOVATOR quadrant. Why is this significant?

RANDOM ACTORS who are violent typically dislike and attack their *behavioral opposite*—anything that represents the MANAGER quadrant. They share nothing in common behaviorally. In the mind of a person with RANDOM ACTORS traits, the stiff, autocratic, depersonalizing post office represents the MANAGER quadrant but not FedEx, which emphasizes change, variability, and flexibility and inclusive team management. For RANDOM ACTORS, FedEx represents the INNOVATOR quadrant. This doesn't mean every post office or accounting department is poorly run, but this is how these environments can be perceived by someone with the RANDOM ACTOR traits. Please review ILLLUSTRATION 1 which shows the RANDOM ACTOR and MANAGER and INNOVATOR connection.

Illustration 1

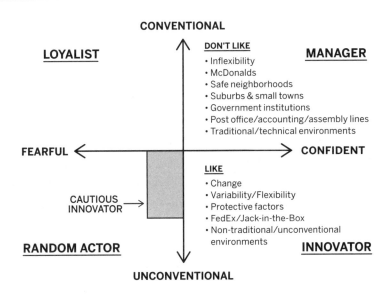

What's important to note is that there are people working at FedEx and UPS who have the RANDOM ACTOR traits, but it's not inherently antagonistic to them like some post offices. And, statistically the majority of RANDOM ACTOR postal attacks are committed by those who work *inside* jobs (where there is less change, variability, and where paranoia can be set off if they get isolated) versus those who are mail carriers (who have significantly more change and variability). I also found the same connection related to attacks and bomb threats on iconic McDonalds restaurants (MANAGER), but rarely Jack-in-the-Box *which is out-of-the-box* (INNOVATOR). The former head of investigations for one of North America's largest financial institutions found that all who were making serious bomb threats against the institution were RANDOM ACTORS.

When I identified this connection, I was also doing research for my book *Suburban Gangs—The Affluent Rebels* (1995). That's when I saw a statistically significant number of students with the "postal" RANDOM ACTOR profile in suburbs and small towns. When I used the postal-FedEx equation, I was able to predict that school massacres, like Columbine and Virginia Tech, were going to occur and, with almost 100% accuracy, where they would occur and not occur and why.

In addition to explaining my findings at numerous national education and law enforcement conferences, I wrote about this in *Suburban Gangs* and the first edition of *The Art of Profiling* which was released in June, 1997. Three months later, the first RANDOM ACTOR school attack occurred in the sedate suburban community of Pearl, Mississippi. Globally, virtually every school attack occurs in MANAGER quadrant communities—usually statistically safe suburbs and small towns. This sounds counterintuitive because these are also the *safest* communities, while rarely if ever are there RANDOM ACTOR attacks in poor, inner-city communities, where there is always a lot of chaos (the UNCONVENTIONAL trait). In fact, I characterized these as *a new form of terrorism*.

Similarly, suicide terrorists typically come from educated, affluent communities and are very difficult to recruit from poor neighborhoods. The 9–11 suicide attackers, for example, were all from middle- and upper-middle class communities. (*Rage*, Chapters 4 and 18–24)

Psych Ward Effect

After the 1999 Columbine massacre, over 10,000 North American schools were closed because of RANDOM ACTOR threats. Unprecedented numbers of threats against all kinds of institutions also occurred after 9–11. Beginning in 1997, I predicted in speeches that this would happen, and we called it the "Psych Ward Effect."

Imagine a psychiatric ward with thirty stabilized patients. Then, place a destabilized patient on the ward, and the rest of the ward can be destabilized with all kinds of severe behavior.

This is what happened after Columbine and 9–11. It was a unique type of *contagion of fear* that affected people with the RANDOM ACTOR traits.

They witness a horrific incident, and their paranoia is set off, resulting in all kinds of erratic, irrational behavior, including threats. It was *not* "copycat" behavior. I personally observed this in many schools. Many who made these threats couldn't even articulate why they did it.

No school threats in an entire region of US—More important, after 9–11, the northeastern region in Texas, which educated over 50,000 students, didn't have *any* RANDOM ACTOR threats, while similar districts around them did. It was the only large populated region in the US that didn't have threats. The reason for this was that over 2,500 specially trained education professionals applied the RANDOM ACTOR violence prevention strategies. They provided the three–point intervention with students who had the RANDOM ACTOR traits. (*Rage*, Chapters 10, 20, and 21)

Bunker Syndrome

When cornered, volatile RANDOM ACTORS will often commit suicide. I coined the term from when Hitler, a RANDOM ACTOR surrounded by the Soviets, went in his bunker and committed suicide. This is a common pattern.

When Jim Jones, the cult leader, felt authorities closing in, he and his cult committed suicide in Jonestown, Guyana, in 1978, the largest mass suicide in recent history, claiming 918 lives. David Koresh committed suicide at the Branch Davidian cult in Waco, Texas, in 1993 along with 75 others, including 20 children. The Columbine killers killed themselves at the end of their rampage. Most homicide-suicide attackers during the Iraq and Afghanistan wars (2003 until the present) had the RANDOM ACTOR profile.

A major factor why they commit suicide is their FEARFUL trait, which is an accelerant on their extreme irrationality and despair. By applying the themes in this chapter, it is possible to prevent this from happening. In combat, Major Pedro Rosario, who applied these strategies and concepts during the Iraq war, wrote, "I used them in Iraq to protect those in my charge and even save the lives of over fifty insurgents who wanted to kill."

So if you have to engage/confront someone who has the RANDOM ACTOR profile and you suspect extreme volatility, first do whatever you can to drive down their fear. It will reduce irrationality and make their actions more predictable. Second, get help: mental health, law enforcement, etc. Whatever is appropriate for that situation. (*Rage*, Chapter 11)

Why So Few Violent Women RANDOM ACTORS?

The crux of the reason is women are not as likely to commit *any* type of violence, as evidenced by crime reports, incarceration rates, etc. This doesn't mean that women are less likely to have the profile, rather they are less likely as a group to act out violently. Cases where this occurs and why, including serial killers and suicide terrorists, are detailed in *Rage of the Random Actor*. (*Rage*, Chapters 11 and 23)

Hiring Someone with the RANDOM ACTORS Traits

I know of many cases where people with the RANDOM ACTOR profile were hired and made a valuable contribution because of their expertise, work ethic, etc. What is essential, though, is applying the three-point intervention described in this chapter.

Related to their work responsibilities, do not place them in ongoing assignments/responsibilities where there is severe repetition and a lack of change as this will inherently create stress, tension, and even alienation. Along with this, be certain they are on a team that has an inclusive approach so they don't become isolated, which will aggravate their FEARFUL trait. Significant sections in *Rage of the Random Actor* address workplace issues. (*Rage*, Chapters 13–15 and 18)

Themes for Interactions

The following are reminders for interactions, some of which are suggested in the COMPREHENSIVE profiles and others expanded throughout *Rage of the Random Actor.*

- The more extreme the UNCONVENTIONAL trait accompanied by the negative actions of this trait, the greater need for caution when interacting with this person.
- Most people with the RANDOM ACTOR traits have some positive COMMUNICATION type actions. Be sure to identify their positive actions and steer interactions so they are activated. Therefore, it is best to operate with them on a communication level and not put them into a position in which they must "perform" in an area outside their area of expertise and trigger their FEARFUL trait.
- Another source of positive actions is when they are operating in their area of competency.
- Avoid long-term interactions with those who are extremely volatile.
- When one must interact, carefully monitor activities.
- When you must confront, work tactically to drive down fear so that actions will become more predictable. (If and when this tactic works, it usually only works for short-term durations.)
- Remember, they can change and move out of the profile by learning to make CONFIDENT decisions outside their area of competency as explained and by being guided through the three-point intervention explained later.

Are RANDOM ACTORS Psychopaths?

In a profiling workshop, an FBI profiler asked me, *Do you think that a* RANDOM ACTOR *is a sociopath?* The term sociopath is often used interchangeably with psychopath. Robert D. Hare, one of the foremost experts on psychopathic behavior, explains the confusion over the two terms:

In many cases the choice of term reflects the user's views on the origins and determinants of the clinical syndrome or disorder ... some clinicians and researchers—as well as most sociologists and criminologists—who believe that the syndrome is forged entirely by social forces and early experiences prefer the term sociopath, whereas those—including this writer—who feel that psychological, biological, and genetic factors also contribute to development of the syndrome generally use the term psychopath. The same individual therefore could be diagnosed as a sociopath by one expert and as a psychopath by another.[1]

I personally accept a bit of both, as I believe that social and psychological factors work together to shape this individual coupled with choices that this person makes. But, I use the term psychopath, as most people do have a choice whether or not to commit heinous acts.

To evaluate the answer to the agent's question, we reviewed several quantitative assessment lists associated with psychopathic/sociopathic behavior. One well-accepted list, provided below, was developed by Hare.[2]

• Impulsive	• Egocentric and grandiose
• Lack of remorse or guilt	• Lack of empathy
• Deceitful and manipulative	• Glib and superficial
• Need for excitement	• Shallow emotions
• Poor behavior controls	
• Lack of responsibility	
• Early behavior problems	
• Adult antisocial behavior	

The actions on the left are those that are either identical (such as impulsivity and irresponsibility) or very similar to the actions of a RANDOM ACTOR (such as the need for excitement, which can be reflective of someone who is UNCONVENTIONAL). In effect, these actions are PERFORMANCE actions. Please note, however, that the other behaviors, such as glib, egocentric, grandiose, and shallow emotions are more reflective of

COMMUNICATION actions associated with ASSERTIVE, CONTROL, etc. This is important, as I have investigated and observed numerous psychopaths who are not glib, egocentric, or possessing shallow emotions when they communicate (although they don't have empathy for those whom they harm). One individual was an ACCOUNTANT–RANDOM ACTOR who had threatened to bomb abortion clinics. He was not glib, or grandiose, but he certainly operated from a seared conscience, was impulsive, deceitful, and so on.

Lastly, I think that a psychopath is actually a *subset* of the RANDOM ACTOR type. The difference is that a psychopath is *without affect*. They know the difference between right and wrong, they just don't think it applies to them. They have committed terrible acts for so long that there is no emotive response. (*Rage,* Chapter 16)

INTERVENTION THEMES

The Three–Point Strategy: "Doing the FedEx Thing"

Three themes have been identified that, when applied, not only stop attacks and threats, but help most people move out of the RANDOM ACTOR profile and into the CAUTIOUS INNOVATOR or INNOVATOR profile. Not only have these themes been used in companies to prevent massacres, but virtually every school system since 1997 that has applied these themes saw their RANDOM ACTOR threats and building evacuations stop, while similar schools around them continue to vacate their facilities at a cost of millions to taxpayers in every state every year. Schools call this *doing the FedEx thing.* (While you can't always prove that a specific person with the RANDOM ACTOR traits who received intervention didn't commit an attack on a specific day, you can prove *that threats stop.*) (*Rage,* Chapters 13–16)

Theme 1: Change, Variability, Flexibility—A person with the RANDOM ACTOR traits has the UNCONVENTIONAL trait. Providing change, variability, and flexibility accommodates their trait and isn't inherently antagonizing like the CONVENTIONAL trait—especially the negative actions like stiff, dismissive, bureaucratic, and arrogant.

And, it's the right thing to do for *anyone* who is UNCONVENTIONAL.

While FedEx and art departments carry out this theme intuitively, it can seamlessly be adapted into any school or organization. In education, we found something stunning in a specific population of schools that, like FedEx, uses the three themes intuitively.

Alternative education K–12 schools don't have RANDOM ACTOR attacks. What is amazing is that these schools (several thousand nationwide) educate students who by definition are all "at risk." They've committed a crime, gotten in a fight, done drugs, etc. *After 9–11, none of these schools had* RANDOM ACTOR *threats.* What is the significance? *The schools that have the highest risk population of at-risk students are the safest from an attack when educated in behaviorally appropriate ways.* This isn't the case in the rest or our schools where the atttacks take place. Currently, 100 times a day, North American youths are found with guns, bombs, and plots to take out their schools—and virtually all these students have the RANDOM ACTOR profile. (For more on alternative education, as there are various types, and threat reduction, see *Rage*, Chapters 4, 13, and 21.)

Theme 2: Protective factors are put in place—In a school this means no bullying or allowing a student to get isolated. In a company, this means inclusive team leadership and not exclusive, which will antagonize the paranoia of someone with the FEARFUL trait and create an us-against-them mentality.

Alice Guy, a board member of the Washington, D.C., Chapter of the Association of Threat Assessment Professionals, applied these themes and averted a company attack, de-escalated other incidents, and turned around a severely at-risk New Jersey school. In 2006, the school averaged five to six incidents a week where a student threatened to hurt or kill another student. She wrote: "Since the training and research were applied, there has not been a single threat [for over one year]. I'm taking this to the state board of education."

Theme 3: Mentor how to make CONFIDENT decisions—This theme, explained in the last chapter, has a profound impact on a person with the RANDOM ACTOR traits. For students, the deterioration of paranoia usually takes place within weeks. For adults, it takes longer, but often immediately mitigates the potential for those who might be violent.

For Extreme Cases: Journal Life's Positive Experiences

Some people with the RANDOM ACTOR traits have experienced extreme trauma in their past. For many, it's almost inconceivable that anything is a positive in life as they replay past incidents, are shackled with guilt, or are terrified of trusting others, many times with reason. To help mitigate these experiences, I have found that the following daily exercise can have a profound impact on their lives.

They keep a daily journal of positive, selfless acts others have done for them, they've seen others do for others, or they themselves did for someone else. This practical exercise over time helps deteriorate paranoia, promote trust, and strengthen their "reminder muscle" that there is good in life, there are people who are beneficent, and it is possible to trust.

Most Common Reason Someone Seeks Help

The most common reason I've found that a person self-identifies as having the RANDOM ACTOR traits and they work to apply the three–point intervention is that he or she makes a new or renewed spiritual commitment. This wasn't something I anticipated.

As they articulated their thoughts, it became clear. When someone trusts God with their struggles, while doing his or her part to move for-ward, it is a powerful step toward *confidence*. Similarly, while researching youth gangs, I discovered that turning to God in faith was one of the most common reasons why a youth exited from a gang, even in the face of death threats for leaving the gang. I have found this faith factor consistent across over twenty countries where I have done on-the-ground research.

As explained to me by one man struggling to deal with his RANDOM ACTOR traits, he said he was trusting in his Creator, who created healthy traits, and that he would trust God to chart a new course to restore his traits to health so he could refrain from harm and destruction, and instead, focus on serving others.

If you consult *Rage of the Random Actor* for additional insight, please remember that the descriptors for two of the gauges have changed from

ASK–TELL to ASSERTIVE–NONASSERTIVE and PREDICTABLE–UNPREDICTABLE to CONVENTIONAL–UNCONVENTIONAL.

And when reaching out to those who are troubled or trying to prevent catastrophic incidents, this verse from the Scriptures can keep you focused on why you are giving your time selflessly for someone else.

> *Do not be overcome by evil, but overcome evil with good.*
> *Romans 12:21*

CHAPTER 16

ADVANCED STRATEGIES AND APPLICATIONS

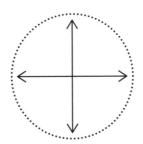

Now that you've learned how to use the entire *KPS* you're ready to learn some powerful concepts that you can immediately use. (If you've skipped ahead to this chapter without learning the *KPS*, the value of these techniques will be minimized.) These concepts will help you rapid-fire profile faster, smarter, and with more precision. But before reading this chapter, please review the concepts in Chapter 7 as some of them are further developed in this chapter.

Here is a brief summary of what is covered:

- **Three-question strategy:** Dramatically shortens time to make reads.
- **Profiling people before you meet them:** Invaluable and a time saver.
- **Profiling groups:** How to do it and tendencies of how people interact in groups.
- **Cross-cultural profiling without stereotyping:** Key principles that work in any culture.
- **Team profiling to produce measurable results:** How teams can pool resources to profile people before meeting them to produce quantifiable results with lightning speed. Especially valuable for teams/orga-

nizations in a competitive environment.

- **A hiring strategy:** Integrating profiling into your hiring process.
- **Learning actions that aren't in your type:** Guidelines how to do it.

The Three-Question Strategy

Anne's attorney was full of energy and confidence as she explained to Anne that there was a good case for negligence against XYZ, a multibillion dollar company. This meant significant punitive damages for Anne in addition to her loss. XYZ sold Anne tainted goods that were mandated to be pulled from the shelves by a Federal recall. This hit Anne's small company with a loss of several hundred thousand dollars. XYZ admitted they sold her tainted goods, but callously didn't even reimburse her for what she paid for the product. XYZ did, however, sue *their* supplier who sold them the tainted goods. For Anne, thankfully there was no question about XYZ's liability, one of the most important factors to prove in this type of case.

Anne's attorney, Jacqueline, had previously done light work for Anne. Jacqueline was a person of integrity who had provided sound counsel, but this was a major lawsuit. Anne now has to determine if Jacqueline is a strong enough personality to stand up against a battery of "big company" lawyers. Second, Anne has to know if Jacqueline is a tough and thorough strategist for an important trial who does her homework and examines all the options. To evaluate Jacqueline, Anne needs to profile Jacqueline's talk *and* walk.

If you were counseling Anne, where would you direct her to quickly focus her reads to identify Jacqueline's profile? Time is short, and there are many factors in the mix: the facts of the case, the players and relationships involved, options how to proceed, and so on.

That's where this powerful three-question strategy is invaluable. It's one of the most important concepts in this book.

The strategy uses three questions that will quickly remind you in a fast moving situation where to look to identify a specific trait or type. These questions will help you when making rapid-fire, on-the-spot reads as well as looking at someone's past history. The questions are:

1. How does a person handle *situations*? (PERFORMANCE traits)

2. How does a person handle *people*? (COMMUNICATION traits)

3. What do they do for a living, do they like it, and *why*? (All four traits)

Like most reads, when stress/pressure is involved as a factor (Chapter 7), the accuracy of your read usually increases.

How does someone handle *situations*?—This question points you toward PERFORMANCE traits, because it focuses attention on how people handle tasks, problems, challenges, make decisions, and so forth. A situations can be anything during which people have to *do* something—take action. It can range from: rejection/failure/success related to a specific project or task; how they prefer to handle a task; how they handle change, like moving to a new neighborhood or a merger or acquisition; how they make a decision.

If you look at how someone handled a *previous* restructuring process, you might find out that he welcomes change and adapts easily, suggesting that perhaps he is UNCONVENTIONAL. If, however, he is uncomfortable in that kind of situation, then he is more likely CONVENTIONAL. You make the read by asking him how he handled the situation, or you can use the observations of others, both of which must be checked for accuracy and bias.

Regarding Jacqueline's suitability for Anne's case, careful questioning should include Jacqueline's previous cases that were brought to trial, their complexity, strategies developed for each one, etc.

Anne profiled Jacqueline as a strong INNOVATOR—both traits were about 4. The negative INNOVATOR action, "not thorough," was a specific action that was unacceptable for Anne's case which required attention to detail. To test Jacqueline, Anne gave her a major news article with a critical piece of information to see how she would handle and analyze it. Jacqueline decided to pass it to another attorney in the firm. A few days later when Anne asked her about the facts and its implications, Jacqueline hadn't reviewed the facts and provided errant counsel. Quickly and dispassionately, Anne identified that Jacqueline had the negative INNOVATOR action which was a deal killer for the case. Anne liked Jacqueline as a person and knew she was honest, but her action demonstrated she wasn't a match.

How does someone handle *people*?—This question points you toward COMMUNICATION traits because it focuses on personal interactions. If, for example, Anne observes that Jacqueline is emotional and sensitive when she interacts with others, she is most likely EXPRESS, but if she is private and introverted, she is probably CONTROL. Like other reads, you can use your observations or the reads of others. For Anne, if she asks Jacqueline how she handled/interacted with a specific person, she can make a read of Jacqueline's COMMUNICATION traits as she *describes* the situation, which acts as a check on her read.

Anne profiled Jacqueline as SALESMAN whose traits were about 4. While Anne saw that her SALESMAN traits could easily communicate with strong-arming attorneys in a mediation, she was not suitable for a more complex trial environment that required being thorough and strategic.

Using the first two questions helped Anne dispassionately make an informed decision to protect her company's future.

What do you do for a living, do you like it, and *why*?—This last question, which is actually three, can help you identify any of the traits. You can ask a person these questions directly or ask others for their opinion. The most important part of this trio of questions is that you drill down past the surface. The "why" part of the question is where the profile pops out. It tells you who people are and their relationship to what they like and don't like and why.

When using this question, it is important to distinguish the overall nature of the job from other factors, such as whether or not someone likes a specific project, a specific boss, or their work environment. These factors can be impacted by downsizing, poor market conditions, and so on, which may color someone's opinion about their current position. What you're looking for is if someone likes the nature of his work, apart from internal or external factors that may affect one's attitude.

When people don't like the nature of their job description, this might indicate a poor match of traits with the needs of the job. For example, if Jenn is involved in sales, but doesn't enjoy selling herself or her product, even though she likes her product, then this might indicate that she is NONASSERTIVE and/or possibly CONTROL, as sales personnel often rely upon ASSERTIVE and/or EXPRESS traits.

Or, if Lee, an engineer, likes the nature of his work, it's likely that his traits are a good match for what he does. So, if Lee enjoys engineering, you can start with a hunch that he's CONVENTIONAL, CONTROL, and possibly NONASSERTIVE—common traits in engineering groups.

When asked the "why" part of the question, he might tell you that he likes to work in a profession where precision is important, which would confirm the CONVENTIONAL read. If, however, he said he likes to innovate on an engineering team, then probably UNCONVENTIONAL.

Or, if Debra enjoys being the director of marketing, ASSERTIVE and CONFIDENT are possible starting points. But when asked why she likes her job, she says she likes leading teams behind the scenes as a mentor. Then NONASSERTIVE would be a better hunch for her COMMUNICATION trait.

Using the last question with students—Teachers have to communicate with students *and* they have to assign tasks and help increase performance. When we trained thousands of teachers how to use the *KPS* to improve the classroom experience, I adapted the three-question strategy for educators. This enabled them to sharpen how they communicated with students as well as modify assignments to match a student's PERFORMANCE type. They also used the *KPS* to pair up students with complementing profiles on teams to improve team assignments. As expected, the effect of using this skill was an immediate increase in student comprehension and retention.

We showed the teachers a modified version of the last questions when talking about a student's future. They asked, "If you graduated from college today, what would you do for a living, would you like it, and why?" Not only did this provide insight into a student's aspirations, which a teacher can elevate, they also learned the student's profile. We also gave them other questions they could use like: Who is your favorite teacher and why? What's your favorite subject and why?

To demonstrate how easily these questions can be applied, I video recorded short interviews I did with twenty students. I asked them these questions, and in every case, the why part of the question popped their profile right out.

One student, Don, was extremely NONASSERTIVE, high CONTROL (an ACCOUNTANT) and a LOYALIST. He said wanted to be a criminal attorney, but it was obvious by his softspoken tone of voice that this wasn't a fit. So I asked him, "So you wouldn't mind getting up in front of a group of complete strangers and forcefully and passionately making your case, and if you failed, an innocent person might go to jail for the rest of his life?"

Don's eyes almost glazed over as he was lost in thought, imagining himself in time and space. "No, maybe not," he said cautiously.

"What about being a corporate attorney and carefully preparing contracts?" I asked.

"Yeah, that sounds better," he replied with a relieved exhale of air.

Don over time would have probably figured out that a trial attorney wasn't a fit unless he improved his communication skills, but a little insight and a thoughtful suggestion may have saved him years of pursuing the wrong path.

Additional Suggestions For Focusing Reads

Be specifically intentional—Anne used common sense to focus her reads. First she profiled Jacqueline's COMMUNICATION type, and then she focused on Jacqueline's INNOVATOR actions—and specifically if she had the negative action of not being thorough. Here are other common sense examples.

If you are in a social environment, the ASSERTIVE–NONASSERTIVE trait may be the most important trait to identify, enabling you to communicate sensitively with someone. As one of my sons says, "No one turns away from the NONASSERTIVE man/woman." It's often best to be a little more restrained with someone who is NONASSERTIVE to put them at ease.

If you are negotiating a contract, you may want to identify the NONASSERTIVE–ASSERTIVE trait first, enabling you to identify someone's communication tendencies. Your second choice may be the CONFIDENT-CAUTIOUS/FEARFUL trait, so that you can identify how someone makes decisions. (By reading these traits first, you also avoid confusing the

ASSERTIVE trait for CONFIDENT, as discussed in Chapter 11.)

If you're the team leader on a newly assembled volunteer committee, you may need to delegate two tasks: a "greeter" and an "implementer," who likes to work behind the scenes and make sure details are facilitated. For the greeter, you've decided that a thoughtful NONASSERTIVE greeter would work best; you need someone with a kind, servant spirit. So you first observe how everyone is interacting with each other, then talk to the couple volunteers who appear more NONASSERTIVE and observe who is the most thoughtful and the best listener. It's quicker to find someone by looking for NONASSERTIVE first and then the specific action of altruistic. An ASSERTIVE person can be kind, but assertiveness may unintentionally be subtly intrusive for the occasion.

For the implementer, you look at the list of your volunteers, their professions, and specifically professions that attract detailed CONVENTIONAL people. Then, talk to each briefly about what they do for a living and why they like it, focusing on how they handle *situations*. Like Anne did, if there is a specific negative action that is unacceptable, focus your read a bit deeper in that direction.

Identify key individuals, responsibilities, and what is important to each—When meeting with a group of people in any context, it's wise to identify key people, their position, responsibilities, and what is important to each. This insight usually shortens the time it takes to profile. For example, the manager/leader of a group is more likely to be CONFIDENT, while someone whose focus is more creative/research/development oriented is more likely to be CONFIDENT and UNCONVENTIONAL. Also, by identifying positions and responsibilities of leaders and subordinates, as well as what is important to each, one can begin to create hunches about which person's traits are likely to influence others in the group, and when and how a person is likely to exert his influence.

Profiling People Before You Meet Them

When interviewing people for a documentary or a book, I've always made it a best practice to profile them before I meet them. It's more efficient to prepare questions, interpret perspective, and meet a person's needs—especially victims of crime—based upon their profile than to just show up.

In the last 1980s, a con artist was running a scam where he seemingly healed people using "psychic surgery." I caught up with him in a small town in upstate Washington, where most people were NONASSERTIVE. Like other "psychic surgeons" who were making the circuit in the US, he used sleight of hand to create a convincing illusion that he could remove tumors from people. When he was caught and arrested, people complained that he should be released. It's not uncommon for people who see healers to have an emotional "high" that releases the body's natural pain inhibitors, masking their pain, and they think they're healed, when in fact their lives are still at risk.

In response, the editor of the local newspaper wrote that people should be able to practice their religion even if deception were involved. A young woman, who was a medical technician and dying of a terminal lung disease, had returned home from Los Angeles to give away her children before she died. She agreed to assist law enforcement when the healer convinced her foster parent, who was like a natural father to her, that he was healed of cancer of the bladder.

At the time I was investigating a number of healing scams and had already obtained a full on-camera confession from another psychic. The Washington case was unique, though, so I decided to interview the victims of the scam and their families and ask them: *Do you think it's acceptable to lie to a dying person?* Taking into consideration the NONASSERTIVE trait of the people I'd be interviewing, I softened the question so it was less direct: *When if ever is it acceptable to lie to a dying person?*

The results of those interviews were stunning, and the insights they shared helped save lives. If I hadn't used profiling and modified my question, I'm certain that they wouldn't have been as reflective and transparent.

To profile people before meeting them, we make reads of their past actions. You'll use all the concepts you've already learned, like the three-question strategy or the tip that under pressure people usually show their actual trait (Chapter 7). The difference is that you won't read them on the spot. Rather you'll look at their past behavior, especially if there was stress. With practice, you'll find that your accuracy will be 60–70% or higher, which is a real time-saver and allows for significant preparation. You of course check your reads when you first meet that person, but the time required will be significantly less than making all four trait reads cold.

Here are some additional guidelines to help you focus where to read past behavior. In the next chapter the five sources for making reads is explained in more detail.

Profile of organization and past history—Questions should be answered, including: Does an organization have an identifiable group profile? Does the organization's profile impact the profile of specific work groups, such as marketing or systems? Can the profile of key decision-makers be identified from past interactions, input from outside vendors, or past reactions to mergers and acquisitions? How has the organization made decisions in the past? Did an individual's decision-making in the past reflect an individual or group persona?

If you're a parent trying to profile your child's new teacher, you can look at the kinds of subjects he/she taught in the past, the community/school where they last taught, opinions of other teachers or parents, and so on.

Identify positions of key players, responsibilities, and what is important to each—If you're profiling several people in a group, the idea here is the same as just explained when focusing your reads, but you are reading *past* behavior.

Identify opportunities for making unobtrusive reads—As you learned in Chapter 7, unobtrusive reads are some of the most effective reads, especially if profiling someone before you meet them, such as:

- Observe someone on the job without calling attention to yourself.
- Observe how someone interacts with others.
- Insight from a colleague who dealt with this person in the past.
- Input from the assistant of the person you are profiling.
- Review of past correspondence, especially if written under pressure.
- Observations from outside vendors or competitors.
- A teacher who instructed a student the year before.

Each situation and work environment will dictate when and where unobtrusive reads can be made. Care must be taken not to violate ethical codes of conduct, or make observations in a way that inappropriately fuels suspicions/resentments. One's attitude should be the same that has been promoted throughout the text: *I know who you are. Good for me, better for you. It's the art of treating people right the first time.* If your method for obtaining a read violates this philosophy, don't use it.

Traits revealed when confronted with stress in the past—Because past behavior, particularly under pressure, is the best predictor of future behavior, make inquiries about past situations in which stress was a factor. Some common examples are:

- Organizational downsizing or restructuring.
- Reactions to shifting markets.
- Reaction to performance evaluations.
- How a patient handled a past diagnosis.
- How a parent reacted to their child's difficulties in a prior class.

Correspondence, articles, video, online presence—Any of these can be used to make reads, but must be approached cautiously as there are often slanted opinions, people can put on a game face, and so on. The latter is especially true for when someone wants to create an impression. The act of writing can reveal a person's traits, but because it is a passive activity and not physically engaging a person, people can intentionally or unintentionally create an illusion of a trait that they don't have.

Five clue sources for making reads—There are clue sources where we make reads of people. In the next chapter you'll learn how to use them to enhance your ability to make reads before you meet someone.

Profiling Groups & Leadership Tendencies

Here's a puzzle…

The Festive Kitchen, my wife's catering company, catered a posh Christmas company party for about one hundred guests, and she and her staff watched something odd.

One of the treats of the buffet-style feast was a giant, richly garnished silver punch bowl filled with jumbo shrimp on ice. With great amusement, they watched as every guest did exactly the same thing on each of their plates. After consuming a shrimp, they lined up the tails—about six to ten a plate—in a precise arc around the edge of their plate. Virtually none of the one hundred-plus employees deviated, and there was no "shrimp-tail conspiracy" amongst the company employees to line up the tails.

Now the question is: What was the profile of the company?

The company was a software company primarily comprised of software engineers and technicians. The profile of the typical staff member was an ACCOUNTANT–MANAGER or LOYALIST—people who are fastidiously detailed and precise. Placing the tails in a neat arc on their plates was an unconscious expression of being precise. The chain reaction was most likely initiated when one colleague subconsciously observed another colleague line up the tails on his plate. He then copied his colleague's actions because he possessed the same fastidious profile. The rest of the staff followed suit in the relaxed setting because being precise was something that felt natural and comfortable.

Even though individuals in an organization have individual profiles, when collectively compiled together, a work group often takes on a group profile, and it will display many uniform actions. This is because the majority of the members of a group have a similar mix of traits. The company that Sandy observed is just one humorous example.

Other common examples of work groups that often adopt a group type or profile are:

- **Research and development**—INNOVATOR
- **Sales and marketing**—SALESMAN
- **Administrative staff at a hospital**—ACCOUNTANT
- **Education administrators**—LOYALIST

This doesn't mean that everyone in the group will possess the same type(s) as the group because individuals will have their own unique profile. At the party, for example, Sandy noted about half a dozen plates that came back where the tails were tossed helter skelter without a pattern on the plates. Curious, she identified this handful as the company's wild banshee type marketers and designers. As a group, though, the company tilted toward CONVENTIONAL.

In audit groups, for example, ACCOUNTANTS or SERGEANTS are the most common COMMUNICATION type (those who are CONTROL) and either MANAGERS or LOYALISTS PERFORMANCE type (those who are CONVENTIONAL). If the unit is large enough, though, there are usually one or two INNOVATORS who work on innovating/creating new systems.

Identifying a group's profile is invaluable for gaining insight into how a group as a whole prefers to interact and operate. Identifying the group profile is also useful for evaluating how a specific person may or may not operate in a given situation.

Also, the stronger the influence of the group and the greater the desire of an individual to get along and be a team player, the more likely that he'll tip toward that side of his range. So, if Michael is an INNOVATOR, but his group operates as a MANAGER, look for Mike to use his UNCONVENTIONAL trait at the lower end of his range—toward CONVENTIONAL.

Alternately, if Michael isn't an integral part of the team and/or isn't motivated because of poor leadership, he may react against the group and move toward the extreme end of his range that is the farthest from the group's trait(s).

When identifying profiles and considering how groups and individuals interact, we are looking at typical preferences for communicating or performing. We aren't making reads when people make important moral or ethical decisions. As already noted, even those who are extreme FEARFUL can choose, as an act of character, to operate with, against, or without a group.

Up or down the ladder—Another factor to consider is where someone is on the organizational chart, similar to what was briefly discussed in Tip #7 (Chapter 7). The further down the organizational chain of command an individual's position, the more likely that the group profile will affect the individual's profile. Alternately, the higher up the chain of command, the less likely the group's profile and tendencies will impact an individual's preferences for operating.

For example, Thomas, the SERGEANT-LOYALIST in the last chapter (first case), was the head of his group. The group's profile didn't affect his decision-making, rather his paranoia simply made the group more neurotic. A positive counterpoint to Thomas are CONFIDENT leaders who inspire those in their charge to operate at the end of their range that tilts toward optimum confidence. In this case the group may take on a more CONFIDENT flavor due to leadership from the top.

Cross-Cultural Profiling

Winterthur, Switzerland. My host, a Swiss police officer, suddenly turned reserved. On the train ride up from Zurich, Monika had been fairly expressive and open. The moment we entered the chandeliered ballroom in the quaint hotel, where I was to give a speech to local business leaders on why there was a new increase in juvenile crime, she became high CONTROL and NONASSERTIVE like those assembled. When I gave my speech, I simply stated my theory and presented the facts without fanfare. I learned that in Switzerland you don't begin a speech with a personal story, as is common in the US; it's considered too personal. I also restrained my EXPRESS and ASSERTIVE traits, and it was apparent that they appreciated it—I wasn't *too* American.

Christmas was a couple of weeks away, Winterthur was dusted in new snow, and all was at peace in the Swiss Alps hamlet. After the speech and a remarkable lunch, we stepped out into the crisp air. Our new mission was a little Christmas shopping. Suddenly, a young man about twenty steamed past us with a stolen valise in his clutches, locals running after him. I had just given a speech on the new crime and here it was! Instinctively, Monika gave chase. I shed my overcoat and took off after her.

A cross-country skier, Monika ran him down, and as she manacled the thief, I kept the gathering crowd at bay, even though I couldn't speak Swiss German. Rapid-fire profiling came in handy as some of the crowd became hostile. They thought we were mugging the thief as Monika was in plain clothes! That's when I turned my palms up and tilted my head in a non-threatening, NONASSERTIVE position and gestured to Monika as I said, *polizei, polizei.* You never know when profiling will come in handy, even when you have a foreign accent.

My experience is when traveling abroad or interacting with new cultures in their own country, those who can't profile will often stereotype out of ignorance. I've been in many situations where profiling and being culturally astute were vital to communicate issues, establish rapport, and work with a diversity of performance perspectives. In Winterthur, in the space of just an hour, I used cross-cultural profiling concepts to convey an important issue, establish rapport from a Swiss business perspective, and keep a crowd under control. Profiling opens our eyes and has been an invaluable tool for me.

It's what I call *being color blind but culturally astute.* We don't stereotype, but we do recognize and respect that cultures are different and treat them uniquely.

In Warsaw, Poland, I addressed over two hundred young rising entrepreneurs at the invitation of the local government to encourage truthtelling in business. It was at a time when no one believed it was possible to successfully build a business without bribes. During the days of communism the only way to own a business was to pay bribes. In another setting, during the 1990s Bosnian-Serbian war, I gave a speech at the University of Belgrade encouraging students, who were desperate for the truth, to be discerning. For books and documentaries, I've interviewed Polish skinhead youths explaining why they hate, and mothers in Kiev, Ukraine, describing the transitions in their daily lives brought on by the fall of communism. I'm certain I wouldn't have been able to tackle these varied situations if I couldn't profile across cultures.

The reason it's possible to profile people from cultures that are significantly different from ours is that the core traits of human behavior are consistent cross-culturally. Stripped of our cultural facades, we are all made of the same stuff.

In this short section, we'll look at the three critical steps required to successfully profile people across cultures. (Additional concepts are found in the chapter on cross-cultural profiling in *Snapshot*) The three steps are:

1. Identify the cultural behavioral profile—how people prefer to act in public (the traits they prefer to use).

2. Identify cultural expressions and customs that can create the appearance of a trait.

3. After identifying Steps 1 and 2, identify the person's actual profile.

I recommend compiling Steps 1 and 2 on a small reference card that you can carry in a passport pouch, foreign pocket dictionary, or your travel planner. Collectively, they will serve as a safety check and reminder to take more than one read with cultural sensitivity. Your effort will be appreciated by those you meet and will distinguish you from those who stereotype.

Step #1: Identify the cultural behavioral profile—If asked which people as a culture are more ASSERTIVE when they communicate in public, the Swiss or Americans, it's easy to state Americans, because the Swiss are generally more reserved in public. This isn't stereotyping all Americans as ASSERTIVE, but as a country that's our public persona.

If we compare the Swiss to the French and ask who is more EXPRESS, the French would easily come to mind as more expressive when we reflect on their art and lyrical language—as well as observing them in public.

Obviously there are differences in regions in a country and there is a difference between big cities (more ASSERTIVE and EXPRESS) and small towns (more NONASSERTIVE and CONTROL). What we are after is the big picture trait for each country or culture. Listed below are several countries and the CONTROL–EXPRESS trait people usually display in public as compared to other countries.

- United States (EXPRESS—think of our media)
- Mexico (EXPRESS—warm and expressive)
- China (CONTROL—more reserved)
- Italy (EXPRESS—think of how they communicate)
- France (EXPRESS—think of their art)
- Switzerland (CONTROL—think of their banks and precision clocks)

The reason you must first identify the traits people typically display in public is because a person's actual profile that he uses privately, in small meetings, and so on, may be different. This is very common across cultures.

Once you identify the cultural traits, just accommodate the traits you observe just like you would in an individual. So if a culture is more NONASSERTIVE, be a bit more restrained when communicating. Or, if people are more CAUTIOUS/FEARFUL, allow more time to process a decision. Also, if you are in a country, like Italy, where the cultural profile is EXPRESS, you may find that people are less EXPRESS in small towns, so be prepared to adapt.

On your reference card, list each trait that is commonly displayed in that culture and a couple of suggestions, based upon your profile, how you can better interact when first meeting people in a public setting.

Step #2: Identify cultural expressions and customs that can create the appearance of a trait. Identifying cultural expressions and customs that can be confused for traits is different than identifying customs, such as whether you should or shouldn't cross your legs when seated or which hand expressions to avoid. In some Middle-Eastern countries, for example, it's an insult to cross your legs and let the sole of your shoe be seen, while in some Latin American countries making the "A-OK" sign with your thumb and index finger joined in a circle is a severely insulting gesture. These kinds of customs, while important to observe, will not help you identify someone's profile.

What we are identifying in this second step are specific cultural customs which might be confused for a trait. Here are two examples:

Japan—A Japanese manager is asked by a salesman: Would you like to purchase this machinery? In response, the manager politely bows low at the waist and says, *Yes*. In fact, what he means is: *Yes, I will consider your request.* It is simply a courteous response. To the uninitiated, one might mistakenly believe that this potential Japanese customer is NONASSERTIVE, because of his agreeable style of communicating, when in fact the manager might be strong ASSERTIVE, who is simply displaying a cultural custom.

Hungary—It is common for many Hungarians to use broad sweeps and slashes of their hands when they communicate. Even those with a strong CONTROL trait often communicate in this manner. It is the cultural facade. To the uninitiated, this might lead one to conclude that most Hungarians are EXPRESS or ASSERTIVE.

If you don't *separate* these customs from your read of someone, you will think this is a person's actual profile. So you first identify the cultural profile (Step 1), second identify *specific* customs that appear to be a trait, and then you profile the person *separate* from these two steps.

On your reference card, as per the Japanese example, you would note "response to a request could be misinterpreted as NONASSERTIVE." A cultural trait (Step 1) is CONTROL.

For Hungary you would note that the free use of hands can be confused for EXPRESS or ASSERTIVE. A cultural trait (Step 1) is EXPRESS.

Ideally, you should identify cultural expressions and customs which can be confused for traits before entering a new culture. Many companies offer training for staff members who travel internationally. Additionally, independent workshops are taught on this subject. Other places to find recommendations for source information are the major international airlines and embassy offices. (If you look online, be careful as there is also a lot of misinformation.)

When possible, review your list with someone from that culture who is observant and fluently speaks your language. Next, point out the cultural traits you have observed in public interactions. Then, detail the kinds of interactions you expect to have and the context. Finally, ask for cultural customs that might be confused for a trait.

Step #3: Identify the person's actual profile—After you've identified the cultural profile and customs/expressions which can appear to be a trait, you are now ready to use the *KPS* and identify someone's profile. The first two steps allow you to have greater accuracy because you won't confuse the public cultural façade and customs for their actual profile. If possible, it is recommended that you allow yourself at least two or three days in a new culture before attempting to identify profiles.

Be prepared with two approaches—Once you've identified someone's profile, it's best to interact based upon whether you're in a public or private setting. In a public setting, you'll interact based upon the cultural profile, and when in a more private setting, interaction is based upon the person's actual profile. For example, in Switzerland, it's best to be reserved in public, but if your host is a SALESMAN type, it's okay to be more ASSERTIVE and EXPRESS in their home or more private gatherings.

Use unobtrusive reads—An extension of what you learned about unobtrusive reads in Chapter 7 is that they can be the window into the heart of a culture, enabling you to read people without your "foreign influence" artificially affecting their actions. The following are suggestions for when and how to make unobtrusive reads.

Observe response during translation—If using a translator, first identify your translator's profile. This will provide you with a cultural reference point, enabling you to gauge how other profiles are likely to react or respond to him as he translates. Next, after you have spoken a phrase that must be translated, observe how the person to whom you are conversing reacts during the translation. There is often transparency when this person is listening to your foreign words being translated, especially if he asks your translator to clarify a thought.

The reason people are often more transparent than normal is that, out of courtesy, they are trying to make sure that the nuances of their thoughts are clearly communicated to you, or that they fully understand what you are communicating. Believe it or not, when giving a speech, you will often find that your delivery in a foreign culture will be clearer than in your own country. Why? First, because you have a chance to think about your next thought during the translation. Second, you are able to read your audience unobtrusively and modify your thoughts during the translation, resulting in a more focused and sensitively delivered presentation.

Learn how people respond to you—Before entering a culture, consider the context in which you will be interacting with people. If you will be making presentations, consider how people with different profiles in your city or town typically respond to a particular story, proposal, or joke. Surprisingly, you will find that people with similar profiles in another country may respond similarly. This can provide an excellent opportunity for making unobtrusive reads. Be sure to review Tip #9 (Chapter 7) regarding how opposites respond to you.

Observe people engaged in commerce—Much can be learned by just strolling the streets surrounding an open-air square (often called a platz in Europe), observing people at ticket counters, watching someone discover a parking ticket on a windshield (a source of stress), observing clerks in a bank, or watching people haggle over the prices of goods. Be creative with the time you have and observe people in as many types of situations as possible.

Profiling in new cultures
gives you the ability to be color blind
but culturally astute.

Tone of speech—In cultures in which you can't understand the language, it's possible to make reads based upon the tone of someone's speech and the reaction others have to someone's dialogue. This is primarily useful when watching others communicate, and not when someone is communicating with you.

A helpful exercise—Foreign cable television is usually available from your provider, and you can watch stations and try to profile the characters of a weekly show, those interviewed in news broadcasts, game show contestants, and so on. You will be surprised how quickly you will catch on to nuances that will enable you to read traits. Just be careful of stereotypes, which are present and often exploited by media in all cultures.

When possible, enlist the help of a neighbor or student at a local university who can point out examples of people who might represent the extreme ends of each gauge. It's best if your examples are from television programs you have recorded or video clips you have shot on a previous trip, so that you can review them. Reviewing clips is especially helpful as a reminder of trait connections when preparing for a return trip to a culture.

Some Confusing Traits—When you are interacting with someone directly, there are traits which are commonly confused for others. This often occurs when people are listening to you or to your translator. This is especially pronounced if someone is only partially fluent in your language. One of the reasons that people may temporarily operate outside of their actual traits is that they aren't quite as confident when interacting with you, which can manifest itself as uncertainty and hesitancy. The tendency is to be a bit more courteous and reserved than usual. Together, these two tendencies can create some of the following inaccurate reads.

- **ASSERTIVE misread as NONASSERTIVE**—When people aren't fluent in a language, they often take on a more NONASSERTIVE persona. This occurs because a person is inquiring about what you are communicating. Therefore, people who are ASSERTIVE can be misread as NONASSERTIVE, or people who are low NONASSERTIVE misread as high NONASSERTIVE.

- **EXPRESS misread as CONTROL**—People tend to tilt toward the CONTROL end of their range when intently trying to process what you are saying (facts). Therefore, people who are EXPRESS can be misread as CONTROL, or people who are low CONTROL misread as high CONTROL.

- **CONFIDENT misread as CAUTIOUS/FEARFUL**—This is due to the hesitancy that people display when taking longer than customary to process the content of a conversation before responding, making a decision, or taking action. Therefore, people who are CONFIDENT can be misread as CAUTIOUS/FEARFUL, or people who are low CAUTIOUS/FEARFUL misread as high FEARFUL.

The remedy for each of these sources for misreads is to make more than one read and use unobtrusive reads, such as observing how someone interacts with his colleagues, friends, or family. Also, these misreads usually won't apply when people are solely interacting between themselves, because you are not a factor affecting their dialogue.

Final tip—You can use these same concepts in your own country where people speak your language but have a different cultural orientation. Chief

Ralph Mendoza, the former Fort Worth, Texas, police chief, said that when he was a new recruit, his training officer misprofiled those living in a specific neighborhood when they responded to a call. He said this particular cultural group was more ASSERTIVE than surrounding cultures. At the scene, his training officer misinterpreted their assertiveness with a potential to be violent. Mendoza didn't see it that way at all, didn't exert force, and successfully subdued the situation.

Team Profiling: Producing Measurable Results

Team profiling is when people on a team/organization pool their resources and profiling reads in order to profile people before interacting with them. They then use their insight to more speedily produce measurable communication and productivity objectives. Here are some examples:

Coaches—Identify profile of athlete and parents/caregiver before meeting them on a recruiting trip to pre-prepare presentation of why the coach's program is the best fit for the athlete—athletically and academically.

Sales—Identify profile of key players, develop strategies for presentations, identify "champions" who will support and internally advance your service/product staff, predetermine closes, etc.

Consultants—Predetermine consultant strategies so client is more likely to act on and sustain recommendations.

Educators—Teachers can share profiles of students from a previous year with new teachers so they can effectively customize instruction and produce better retention, comprehension, and grades.

Audit—Reduce the time required for fact-gathering interviews.

The idea is common sense: reads from several minds and perspectives are better than one, which will increase profiling accuracy. In addition, there are more resources and opportunities to draw on to make those reads.

For team profiling to produce measurable results, concrete objectives must be identified where profiling will produce quantifiable and timely results. In the example of the football coach in Chapter 1, a measurable goal was to increase the number of blue chip recruits signed as a result of better understanding the athlete and his family. Reads would then be made by his team of coaches/contacts within NCAA regulations, rather than the coach trying to make those reads solo.

In a competitive environment, team profiling directed at targeted objectives is a distinct internal and external advantage over organizations that don't use this strategy. Teams that use it will accurately engage more quickly and with greater effect. Regardless of the application, there are two big-picture objectives when applying team profiling.

1. Increase the frequency and accuracy of profiling people before meeting them to increase insight and profile-specific interaction while reducing the time to effectively engage.
2. Achieve targeted communication and productivity objectives that produce measurable results.

My experience is that for team profiling to be part of an organizational fabric, management must:

1. Require that team members develop profiling proficiency.
2. Identify specific applications where profiling will deliver measurable results and staff is rewarded for producing those results.

A Hiring Strategy

The following is a strategy for using rapid-fire profiling when hiring personnel, which can reduce the screening and interviewing process by as much as one-third. Additionally, it can be used along with a reliable self-assessment test. The steps for applying this strategy are as follows:

Step #1: Team develops the profile—One of the most important elements for successfully onboarding a new staff member is that the rest of your team believes someone will be the right fit and will contribute. This first step ensures this happens as they make a case for which profile is best suited for the job and why.

To begin, type a list of the PERFORMANCE and COMMUNICATION actions for *each* type, but *don't* include any of the identifiers like MANAGER. Be sure to include positive, negative, and other tendency actions. You only want them to see the four sets of actions associated with the PERFORMANCE and

COMMUNICATION types.

Then, during a team meeting, first show them the list of actions for the four COMMUNICATION types and ask them which *set* of type actions is a better fit for the new position. Be sure they engage in a healthy probing discussion of *why* the specific group of actions will work better than the others. Then have them articulate which specific positive actions from that type are essential for the position and which negative actions *cannot* be present. It's common, as the pros and cons are discussed, that they'll realize they've selected the wrong "list."

As they debate the positive and negative actions, emphasize that no candidate will have the entire list of positive actions in the type list or none of the negative actions. We all have a mix of both. What you want them to define, however, are those "must have" and "can't have" actions.

Now repeat the same process and select one of the PERFORMANCE types, and which positive actions are essential and which negative actions are deal killers.

Step #2: Identify the ideal strength of each trait—Once they've selected the two types, show them the two gauges/traits associated with each type. Then lead the discussion regarding the strength of each trait and what is the optimum strength and why. For example, if a team has a NONASSERTIVE trait, someone who is low ASSERTIVE might be a better fit than someone who is high ASSERTIVE because they'll have an easier time restraining assertiveness when necessary, while still having a more commanding communication trait.

Step #3: Other non-profile attributes—This step is facilitated as a part of your process. Here you detail the other non-profile factors that must be considered. These include:

- Knowledge
- Skill
- Ability
- Experience
- Culture Fit
- Other relevant factors

Believe it or not, these factors are usually the easiest to determine, while consistently identifying the best-fit profile is the hardest for most organizations. This is based upon having trained over 2,000 human resource professionals through the chapters of the Society of Human Resource Management. After learning how to profile and having an on-the-spot check of their assessment tests, the HR professionals said they could spend more time on the competency/fit part of the process than trying to discern if the "person" was the right fit.

Step #4: Identify when you can make reads—Depending upon your hiring process, there are usually several opportunities to make profiling reads of a candidate.

The first is of course the resumé. While many are created by automated programs, they provide initial reads that can be tested during an interview. For example, if you are looking for an ACCOUNTANT type, but past work history suggests that a person might be a SALESMAN type, you carefully test your NONASSERTIVE–ASSERTIVE and CONTROL–EXPRESS reads.

A second read is by phone during a follow-up call to the candidate to reaffirm they're interested in the position, set an appointment for an interview, and so on. Here, unobtrusive reads can be made. (As with each of the suggestions in this book, please consult with your legal counsel to be sure that you are faithfully complying with local, state, and federal laws and guidelines.)

A third read is of course during the interview.

One client uses a fourth read made by the receptionist, who was trained to use the *KPS*. While candidates waited for their appointment, she engaged them unobtrusively in dialogue, and any important insight was then passed along.

Step #5: Select who will do interviews and where—When possible, select people who are adept at identifying the traits you are looking for in a candidate. If there is uncertainty regarding a trait, have a colleague who is proficient at identifying the desired trait conduct an additional short interview. For example, in an engineering group, Elizabeth might be more adept at reading CONVENTIONAL–UNCONVENTIONAL, while Chris might be more adept at reading COMMUNICATION types. For a change of environments, Elizabeth interviews a prospect in her office, but Chris conducts his interview over lunch at a nearby cafe. Different environments create more opportunities to make reads and are recommended.

Below is a short sample list that details traits, desired strength of traits, and positive actions for a position. Negative actions that *aren't* a fit for the position should be listed as well.

Project Coordinator
Desired Profile: ACCOUNTANT–MANAGER

▲ Review on the phone   ■ Review during interview   ● Review resumé

Ideal Traits

____ NONASSERTIVE—3 or lower with good verbal skills

____ CONTROL—about 2 or 3

____ CONVENTIONAL—3 or higher

____ CONFIDENT—3 or higher

Communication Actions/Skills

____ ▲ ■ ●	Detailed
____ ▲ ■	Easygoing
____ ▲ ■	Efficient
____ ▲ ■	Inquisitive
____ ■	Discreet

Performance Actions/Skills

____ ■	Organized
____ ▲ ■	Goal-oriented
____ ▲ ■ ●	Precise
____ ■ ●	Stable/Dependable

Format ad to appeal to profile—When advertising for a position, use language that will appeal to the profile of the person you hope to recruit. For example, if you're looking for an INNOVATOR, use language that is idea driven; if you're looking for a MANAGER, use bottom-line language.

Resist opposite trait (diagonal) accommodation—There is always a possibility that a candidate may not fit your profile but may still be a fit for the position. For example, you might be seeking a SALESMAN type, but you find a SERGEANT who is low ASSERTIVE who can do the job. Rarely, however, will you find someone who is *opposite* the type that you are seeking who is the right fit, unless you miscast the position. For example, if you're looking for an ACCOUNTANT the diagonal opposite is a SALESMAN. We say they are "opposite" because they are diagonally positioned from each other, as you seen in the graphic representation of COMMUNICATION types (Chapter 6) or PERFORMANCE types (Chapter 9). They are opposites because they don't share a common trait.

An exception to the diagonal rule, though, might be someone whose traits are 2 or less, allowing them to more easily operate in the direction that is best suited for the position. This is similar to the development concept discussed at the end of Chapter 9.

Behavioral interviews and rapid-fire profiling—A common best practice when hiring is the behavioral interview. During behavioral interviews, candidates are asked questions about how they handled a past situation, because past behavior is one of the best predictors of future behavior. Thousands of HR professionals have used the *KPS* as an on-the-spot check for self-assessment tests. Also, once a person's profile is confirmed, which is usually in just minutes, the interviewer presents all remaining questions based on the candidate's profile, which provides two positive benefits.

First, it reduces the length of an interview and increases the quality of information obtained. Second, the combination of written tests (quantitative information) and interviews or observations (quantitative and qualitative information) increases your ability to make a sound decision.

CHAPTER 17

FIVE CLUE SOURCE CATEGORIES

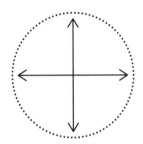

Beginning with the first wire, CONTROL–EXPRESS, you learned that the quickest way to accurately profile is to observe a person's whole persona, compare them to the extremes of the gauge (like Jim Carrey and Queen Elizabeth II), and make your reads within ten seconds. Your observations may last seconds or minutes, but the read must be done quickly, unless, of course, there is nothing to observe. Statistically, if you aren't decisive once you've made your reads, your accuracy drops several percentage points every few seconds, as noted in Chapter 4.

This chapter is placed near the end of the book for one reason. I found that if the clue sources are presented *before* someone learns the proven progression for accuracy, the tendency is to look for very specific actions/ behaviors instead of observing the overall persona, which results in a significant decline in accuracy.

However, there are situations where focusing on a specific source of actions can produce results. That's what is provided in this chapter: common sources for making reads broken down into five categories. Do not, however, overuse these sources. If you directed someone to walk into a conference and profile people solely based upon one of the five clue sources, such as attire, this will usually result in stereotyping.

The clue sources aren't gimmick solutions, but properly used can produce sturdy results. If you've skipped to this chapter and haven't learned the *KPS*, this chapter will only put you behind.

Organizing Clues

In grade-school science classes, teachers use a recall game with a cloth-covered tray of objects. When the cloth is removed, everyone looks at the objects on the tray for 30 seconds and tries to remember as many as possible. Then the teacher replaces the cover, and the students list all the items they can recall. Usually one or two people in a class can list everything, while the rest wonder how it's possible to absorb so much information in such a short period of time.

For the top performers, they're able to see patterns or "common elements" in the objects or in their arrangement that allows them to focus their memory on a smaller set of facts. For example, they may "see" that the tray is arranged in four sections or corners and then memorize the key items in each corner. Or they may make quick associations between certain objects on the tray. Regardless, they see similarities or common features that allow them to remember several items by remembering only one or two common characteristics. Using this strategy, they aren't forced to remember every item. They simply let one item or relationship trigger their recall of another one.

The same principle of "seeing patterns" applies to profiling and making accurate reads. The best profilers are people who can quickly see patterns in another person's actions. This is one of the reasons why the *KPS* was constructed using just four gauges. You can quickly organize the actions that you see in others by simply answering four questions, which then reveal types and profiles.

In this chapter we'll look at five categories of clue sources that will enhance your ability to focus your reads and will remind you where to look in order to identify a specific trait.

The Five Clue Sources

When observing a person's full persona, the specific things we see, consciously or unconsciously, that allow us to decide *Is he more like Jim Carrey or Queen Elizabeth II?* are found in five categories.

- Attire and grooming
- Speech
- Actions
- Nonverbal actions and reactions
- Background information/observations by others

Attire and grooming are regarded as *actions* because in most situations people choose what they will wear.

You'll use the five sources to help you see the common patterns in actions that reveal traits. This reinforces the first part of Rule #1 that promotes systematic accuracy: *People typically act in consistent, similar ways called traits.*

For example, if you must identify if someone has the NONASSERTIVE trait, you'll learn which clue categories and specific actions are most likely to reveal a NONASSERTIVE action.

The emphasis will be on observations that come naturally, so you won't have to worry about looking for an obscure set of clues. Insights for each observation/clue category will include:

- The traits each category is most likely to reveal.
- Why each category is useful.
- Which actions reveal which trait. (Example: People who demonstratively use their hands when they communicate are often ASSERTIVE and/or EXPRESS.)

The relationships between specific clue sources and traits won't apply in every situation—they are just likely possibilities. For example, some men who wear loud ties are EXPRESS, while another may wear a loud tie, which isn't his preference, because his daughter gave it to him for his birthday. To retard stereotyping, resist the temptation to simply look for clues to confirm your first hunch. Rather, as per Rule #3 that promotes systematic accuracy: *Anything worth measuring once is worth measuring at least twice.*

Attire and Grooming

Attire and grooming (appearance) can be a source for identifying the following two traits:

- CONTROL–EXPRESS
- CONVENTIONAL–UNCONVENTIONAL

When making reads in this category, be certain that you're familiar with the culture in which you are operating. In some cultures, for example, bright colors are indicators of EXPRESS, while in others, bright colors are normative, and not related to a trait.

In some situations it's helpful to read attire and grooming separately. For example, Judith, who is UNCONVENTIONAL, may wear conservative attire because of her professional environment, but she chooses to show her individuality through grooming subtleties in her makeup or hairstyle.

Controlled v. individual appearance—Appearance is one of the easiest observations to make. Controlled attire and grooming often indicate CONTROL and/or CONVENTIONAL, while those who adopt an individualistic persona are often EXPRESS and/or UNCONVENTIONAL. Be careful, though, as much is written about altering attire and grooming to convey an impression. Identifying targeted impressions, however, may tell us something about who a person is trying to impress. A person who is an ARTIST, for example, who is normally casually attired, puts on a conventional suit to make a favorable and CONVENTIONAL impression for a banker. To avoid stereotyping or being fooled by an altered appearance, make reads from the other categories as a cross-check and test your reads.

Corporate uniform—When someone wears a corporate "uniform" (any standard business attire for a specific type of work), there is a tendency to assume that the person is CONVENTIONAL. This may or may not be true. The continuity of attire and grooming may be a requirement, thus sending a false clue, like those who work in financial districts, or advertising executives, who are UNCONVENTIONAL, who wear CONVENTIONAL attire when meeting with conservative clients.

Elements of individuality that can reveal traits are ties, jewelry, scarves, interpretations of the "uniform," hairstyle, condition of nails. They can be the subtle or not-so-subtle layer that reveals culturally suppressed traits.

Over the past few years, corporate/organizational attire in specific industries has become more UNCONVENTIONAL, like software and graphic design companies. Here, it's not uncommon to find people who are CONVENTIONAL that dress unconventionally to fit in.

Specific action-trait relationships—This list shows common relationships between observable attire/grooming choices people make and traits that can be revealed. For example, someone who is CAUTIOUS/FEARFUL might display the action of being insecure. Insecurity, however, can be displayed in many ways. As noted below, a person who is CAUTIOUS/FEARFUL might display insecurity through the specific action of poor grooming, which can be reflective of a poor self-image. As already cautioned, these are just possible connections and aren't necessarily determinate.

Poor Grooming
- CAUTIOUS/FEARFUL—reflects a diminished self-image.
- NONASSERTIVE—nonassertive, not concerned with one's representation to others.

Meticulous Grooming
- CONTROL—every hair must be in place.
- CAUTIOUS/FEARFUL—afraid if things not in their place.

Individualized Attire
- Low CONFIDENT—desire to be noticed.
- High ASSERTIVE—desire to make a statement.

Nonindividualized Attire
- CONVENTIONAL—desires uniformity.
- CONTROL—prefers not to express oneself visually.
- CAUTIOUS/FEARFUL—especially for LOYALIST type who doesn't want to stand out.

Speech

In this category, we are principally identifying COMMUNICATION traits—the talk—through speech content/pattern and tone. As noted in Chapter 16, how someone handles *people* reveals COMMUNICATION traits—the talk. It is possible, though, to get a *first* read on PERFORMANCE traits if a person talks about what he likes to *do* or how he makes decisions. These reads, though, must be rechecked because talk isn't always walk.

The third clue source category, *non-verbal actions*, may also tie to speech, such as the arching of an eyebrow, the turn of the head, always keeping one's hands in the lap. While these are actions that relate to speech, they are kept in a separate category to reduce confusion.

Here are examples where speech content and tone can reveal a trait:

- Patricia speaks confidently during a speech. (ASSERTIVE)
- Marc is dispassionate during a two-day negotiation. (CONTROL)
- Louisa says she's unwilling to accept change. (CONVENTIONAL)
- Erik says he needs more time to make a decision. (CAUTIOUS/ FEARFUL)

Content—These are a person's actual words. If somebody always uses qualifiers, like *perhaps,* a person is more likely to be NONASSERTIVE while someone who uses demonstrative words like *give me, show me, let's do it,* etc. is more likely to be ASSERTIVE.

Content can also provide insight into what a person might *do*, which can reveal PERFORMANCE traits.

Regardless of what might be revealed, test your reads with additional reads and make unobtrusive reads when possible as they are more reliable. This also applies to reviewing audio or video recordings.

Tone of voice—The *quality* of a person's voice usually has little to do with traits, except when that quality is artificial or affected. The tone of someone's voice, though, can reveal a COMMUNICATION trait. What you're looking for is consistency that doesn't sound forced or stunted.

For example, let's assume that you are EXPRESS. You meet with Teri, who in the past appeared to be CONTROL. She has a proposal for a new project. In this meeting, though, Teri's voice tone seem to be artificially EXPRESS. Perhaps she intuitively knows you express emotions, and she is trying to share your enthusiasm. But, your past and present reads don't match; you may need to make another read. What's important is that you don't let her well-intentioned effort confuse you when profiling.

Specific action-trait relationships—The following are common relationships between speech content and tone as the potential to reveal traits. The first two categories require that *both* content and tone or tone and language be present *simultaneously* to increase the odds of an accurate read.

Reserved Speech Content and Tone

- NONASSERTIVE—prefers to be in the background.
- CONTROL—indicates lack of expressiveness.
- CONVENTIONAL—desires uniformity, resists change.
- CONFIDENT—doesn't feel he has to make his point with words.
- CAUTIOUS/FEARFUL—doesn't say much because of fear.

Inquiring Tone and Language

- NONASSERTIVE—indirect approach preferred when seeking a response.
- CAUTIOUS/FEARFUL—questions used to avert making decisions or taking action.

Forceful

- ASSERTIVE—is directive using language, set of the jaw, etc.
- EXPRESS—can aid ASSERTIVE person's ability to sell an idea.
- CONFIDENT—reveals commitment to carrying out an agenda.

Monotone

- CONTROL—lack of expressiveness.
- CONVENTIONAL—resistant to change.
- NONASSERTIVE—desire to be indirect, not noticed.
- CAUTIOUS/FEARFUL—afraid to reveal oneself.

Effusive

- ASSERTIVE—prefers to drive across one's point.
- EXPRESS—expressive nature is a part of how he communicates.

Actions

In this category we are looking for observable actions that will reveal PERFORMANCE traits—the walk. Some examples:

- Pat confidently moving forward on a high-risk project. (CONFIDENT)
- Marc working to create a predictable environment. (CONVENTIONAL)
- Erik's rebellious attitude. (UNCONVENTIONAL)
- Jacqui unwilling to accept change. (CONVENTIONAL)

As noted in Chapter 16, how we handle *situations* or tasks reveals PERFORMANCE traits.

Suggestions for Observing Actions—When observing actions, such as someone making and carrying out a decision, remember to apply the two ideas that were addressed in Chapter 7:

- Look for clear consistencies and breaks in consistency (leakage).
- Unobtrusive observations are usually the most reliable.

Specific Action-Trait Relationships—These are some of the most common patterns when reading actions.

Decisive When Taking Action
- CONFIDENT—decision to take action based in confidence.

Waivers When Taking Action
- CAUTIOUS/FEARFUL or low CONFIDENT—lacks sufficient confidence to take action.

Resistant to Change
- CONVENTIONAL—prefers predictability, uniformity.
- CAUTIOUS/FEARFUL—afraid of unknown.

Welcomes Change
- UNCONVENTIONAL—comfortable with ambiguity.
- CONFIDENT—although some people may be CONVENTIONAL, their CONFIDENT trait enables them to move past their desire for predictability when a specific opportunity is presented or change is needed.

Nonverbal Actions and Reactions

The popular term for nonverbal actions and reactions is "body language." They are a moderately effective source for identifying the following three traits:

- NONASSERTIVE–ASSERTIVE
- CONTROL–EXPRESS
- CONFIDENT–CAUTIOUS/FEARFUL

As already noted, speech can be helpful for identifying COMMUNICATION traits, while physical actions, like performing a task, are more helpful for identifying PERFORMANCE traits. Nonverbals are like "silent" speech, which is why they can identify COMMUNICATION traits. However, because nonverbal reactions are tied to a person's actions, like performing a task, they can also be of some help, though more limited, when identifying PERFORMANCE traits. The difference between a nonverbal action and a nonverbal *reaction* is that a nonverbal action is *not* prompted by an external influence.

For example, some people who are ASSERTIVE or EXPRESS will point their finger or wave their hand when communicating. They might do this regardless of whether or not there is an external pressure or influence present. Or, they can be driven by a cultural custom, such as the Hungarian example in Chapter 16.

Nonverbal reactions, however, are actions that appear because someone is *reacting to a situation—an external influence.* This includes a reaction to a question or statement, a response from an audience during a presentation, a response to a pleasant or stressful situation, and so on.

For example, a person with a strong ASSERTIVE trait might use a hard gaze in response to being affronted. Or a grandmother, who is EXPRESS, might display an open, expressive smile that extends to her eyes and forehead when she is asked to retell the moment her granddaughter was honored during a graduation ceremony.

This means that *nonverbal reactions are more likely to reveal a trait* than nonverbal actions because reactions are a response to some kind of positive or negative influence or pressure.

Some typical sources to make reads of both types of nonverbals are:

- Eye contact
- Facial expressions
- Use of hands when talking
- Body movements and posture

Some nonverbals may be tied to speech, such as sighing or rolling of the eyes.

Questions that can be helpful when observing nonverbals are:

- Is the nonverbal action or reaction consistent with the situation?
- What are the person's nonverbal patterns and consistencies?
- When do breaks occur in the nonverbal patterns?

Specific action-trait relationships—The following lists common nonverbals and the traits they can reveal.

Forceful Use of Hands
- ASSERTIVE—used to drive home one's position.
- EXPRESS—extension of expressiveness.

Retreating Use of Hands (If Henry is asked, "Did you do this?" a retreating action would be Henry bringing his open-palmed hand against his chest, as he responds, "You mean me?")
- NONASSERTIVE—a nonassertive response.
- CAUTIOUS/FEARFUL—an insecure reaction to being asked a question.

Hard Gaze (more than just staring back)
- ASSERTIVE—used to increase forcefulness.
- CONFIDENT—unwilling to move on a position.

Empathetic Expression (Example: When the inside of the eyebrows move upward, causing the eyebrows to form an upside-down "V." This involuntary action usually indicates sadness—only about 10% of the population can do this at will.)
- EXPRESS—expressively relating to someone or a situation.
- NONASSERTIVE—an agreeable-curious response.

Stiff Posture (Be careful that someone doesn't just have back problems!)

- ASSERTIVE—means of being forceful, directive.
- CONTROL—an expression of emotional control.
- CONVENTIONAL—not as common, but can indicate need for predictability.

Casual, Open Posture
- EXPRESS—venue for displaying expressiveness.
- NONASSERTIVE—can indicate desire to be indirect, laid back.
- UNCONVENTIONAL—not confined to convention.

Background Information

Background information—Reading past actions is a compilation of the four previous clue categories, which means that any of the four traits can be revealed. The only difference is that the PERFORMANCE or COMMUNICATION actions occurred in the *past*.

Developing background information increases the accuracy of our reads because we are making an unobtrusive read of past behavior which is one of the best predictors of future behavior. The exception to this principle is when a person is undergoing some kind of significant, life-changing event or experience. Because large portions of the population in the US and other countries are experiencing these kinds of events, it is wise to inquire if a person's past actions were due to a life-changing event. Additionally, it can be helpful to identify if present actions are being influenced by a life-altering situation.

Sources for information—Sources for developing background information can include:

- Professional associates
- Friends and acquaintances
- Adversaries
- Media
- Resumés, memos, correspondence, etc.

While it might seem difficult to develop reads from media accounts, memos, and so on, consider these four examples that reveal the traits of both individuals and a group.

- When an internet provider's services went down in the early days of the internet, a news report wrote: "Many subscribers are pioneers. . . . These are the kind of people who are more accepting of growing pains."[1] The descriptor, *pioneers*, points to those who are more UNCONVENTIONAL, a common trait for early internet users.

- Bill Moyers, noted journalist and press secretary to President Lyndon B. Johnson, was interviewed and made remarks that revealed his NONASSERTIVE trait. In 1965, at 31, he was featured on the cover of *Time* and *Newsweek* magazines for his intellectual wizardry, and he quipped: "This is the truth. I didn't want to go on the covers. LBJ wanted me to go on the covers. It didn't go to my head. I had a contrary response to it, and regretted the visibility I was gaining. It limited my capacity to do good work for him."[2] When Moyers was asked to identify his "trademark expression" when responding to others, he replied, "Is that right?"—an open-ended response by an NONASSERTIVE person.

- Unabomber Ted Kaczynski, who killed and maimed with letter bombs, lived like a misfit hermit in Montana and wrote letters to his family during the several years prior to his arrest. His brother, David, illuminates his ACCOUNTANT–RANDOM ACTOR profile: "Through the years, the letters have shown sudden and unpredictable mood swings [UNCONVENTIONAL], a preoccupation with disease, extreme phobias [FEARFUL], compulsive thinking and an inability to let go of minutiae [ACCOUNTANT type absorbed with details].[3]

- This is an excerpt from an American missionary's letter to supporters who sent him on a missions trip to a small town in Russia. Note the clearly EXPRESS tone: "Well, I made it back alive. Not only alive, but changed from the inside out!!! I have so many stories to share that glorify God, but before I share them, I will explode if I don't first thank you (*spaceeba*, in Russian). I thank you from the bottom of my heart for your exceeding generosity."

A stimulating exercise is to read a number of articles and practice identifying traits. Not every read will be accurate due to the bias of a reporter, the accuracy of the report, or the image someone is trying to project to the media. Articles and correspondence can provide a starting point for identifying traits or for confirming reads from other clue sources.

When discretion is imperative and avoiding any direct contact with the person you are profiling, consider having someone else gather information, such as a colleague or trusted friend. Discretion not only aids your reads, but also protects the person whom you are reading from needlessly feeling threatened. In a professional context, profiling someone before direct interaction, as described in Chapters 16 and 17, can enhance effective communication and interaction. For those who have investigative/security responsibilities, it is the backbone of the job.

Strategy for gathering background information—The following is a simple and direct strategy for developing background information that can reveal someone's profile:

1. Prioritize which trait(s) is the most important to identify.

2. Identify the likely places where you can obtain reads of each trait.
    - For PERFORMANCE traits, use sources that focus on how someone handles situations/tasks. (Chapter 16)
    - For COMMUNICATION type, use sources (like social contacts) that focuses on how someone handles people. (Chapter 16)

3. Organize information gathered broken down by traits.

4. Test reads and get more than one opinion. Remember, you are getting filtered information that may have a spin on it.

5. Look for patterns from those who are supportive as well as those who have had confrontations with the person you're profiling.

6. Inquire about actions and reactions in stressful situations.

Short list of common relationships between clue categories and traits—This list points out clue categories that are more likely to reveal a trait when reviewing past history.

NONASSERTIVE–ASSERTIVE
- Speech
- Nonverbals
- Actions

CONTROL–EXPRESS
- Attire and grooming
- Speech
- Nonverbals
- Actions (only moderately helpful)

CONVENTIONAL–UNCONVENTIONAL
- Actions
- Attire and grooming

CONFIDENT–CAUTIOUS/FEARFUL
- Actions
- Speech
- Nonverbals (only moderately helpful)

Checklist for Accurate Profiling

The following is a summary checklist to help you remember the key ingredients for accurate profiling with chapter references.

- Read people by comparing them to the examples at the extreme ends of each gauge. (Chapter 4)

- Take more than one read and test reads. (Chapter 3)

- Use your two safety checks. (Chapters 6 and 12)

- Make unobtrusive reads. (Chapter 7)

- Make opposite assumptions and test reads. (Chapter 7)

- Consider someone's range. (Chapters 4 and 11)

- Past behavior is the best predictor of future behavior. (Chapter 7)

- Under pressure, actual traits are often revealed. (Chapter 7)

- Review COMPREHENSIVE PROFILE to see if it matches the cumulative effect of your reads. (Chapter 12)

- Consider cross-cultural idiosyncrasies. (Chapter 16)

- Consider suppression of traits by culture or choice. (Chapter 11)

- Consider if someone has learned a specific action. (Chapter 11)

- Consider if you have confused one trait for another. (Chapter 11)

- When you need to identify COMMUNICATION traits, observe how a person handles people. (Chapter 16)

- When you need to identify PERFORMANCE traits, observe how a person handles situations and tasks. (Chapter 16)

CHAPTER 18

OUR FUTURE

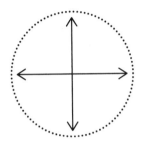

There are shortcuts for reading people accurately and identifying the best way to interact with them. There are no shortcuts, though, when *treating* people based on their profile. It takes time, care, and effort.

Sometimes our response can be immediate, like being a little less ASSERTIVE with a person who is high NONASSERTIVE. A quick read, and a quick response. Other times, though, our read requires thoughtful and sustained action. If a person is UNCONVENTIONAL, you may need to mentor her how to innovate with discipline between the lines. Or, he might be FEARFUL, which requires coaching him on making CONFIDENT decisions separate from his area of competency.

People are precious and require time. The challenge is that we live in a strange and contradictory age. It's an unprecedented era.

Today, technology provides the ability to communicate and make ourselves known to as many people as we desire. It doesn't cost millions—just a few keystrokes. It's now replaced face-to-face contact, with so many always looking *down*, reading and tapping out messages on cell phones.

Look up!

Profile someone. Reach out to people based upon who they are.

We talk about respecting and understanding people of all cultures—

those who are different from us. But what do we do? We barricade ourselves in front of a screen, reading posts on social internet networks, reducing meaningful in-person interactions.

Social networks do have value, like keeping family and friends informed about nonsensitive matters, or even inspiring people living under oppression to form democracies. But, electronic networks are thin veneer interactions. They don't replace authentic human communication. Instead, they promote illusions—stereotypes—like everyone who signs off on an email with *Thanks!* is seemingly EXPRESS.

If you need a reminder of what it's like to be stereotyped, recall your last trip to the airport, where, because of sustained security concerns, governments resort to stereotyping. They don't have the time or the money to recognize or treat you as an individual. You're simply put in a threat or no-threat group. And even then, their systems don't work. From 2007–2010, the General Accounting Office reported that TSA wasted *half a billion dollars* on its SPOT program (Screening Passengers by Observation Techniques), aimed at catching terrorists. Airport security team leaders regularly complained to me about the lunacy of the program, which failed to spot a terrorist, arrested 427 illegal aliens (stereotyped as if they aren't human, rather than identifying them as *illegal residents*), and most people who received attention were false positives. Six-year-olds picking people out at random could have produced better results.

To resist stereotyping and to treat people uniquely not only affects our quality of life, it can be a matter of life or death, like the following story.

They were frightened, but vicious. Even more frightened than their hostages. Us-against-them stereotypes were thick in the air.

Talladega prison. Alabama. Summer of 1991.

The prison population had taken over everything but their own fears, which jackknifed in the minds of angry inmates.

Clint, what did you do before you went in?

Clint Van Zandt was one of the original members of the FBI's esteemed Behavioral Sciences Unit. A criminal profiler, he developed and confirmed the profile of the "Unabomber," Ted Kaczynski in 1996. In 1985, as the FBI's chief hostage negotiator, Clint led negotiations when a militaristic group of families, who called themselves The Covenant, the Sword, and the Arm of the Lord, threatened violent action from their Arkansas compound.

He brilliantly suggested that the men come out first "so that you can see that your women and children are treated with respect." He didn't want to risk the men changing their mind after their families were safe and then hunkering down for a firefight.

It worked. Everyone came out.

After this kind of incident, you look for closure. Something to help put the hammer of stress behind you. But Clint never found closure.

As the special agents were looking for holdouts in the compound, Clint offered his hand to a young, ten-year-old boy in fatigues. The boy swatted away Clint's warm handshake, and glared, "We could have beaten you. We could have killed you. If Jim Ellison [the leader] hadn't heard from the Lord, you'd be dead. I'll get you when I'm older." The boy had already learned to stereotype another human being to death.

Looking at the youngster, Clint thought, "I've seen the face of the future. Here is the next generation. And he has already learned to beat, kill, and hate the government."

Clint was also in Waco, Texas, in 1993 when David Koresh followers torched their compound and eighty men, women, and children perished in the blaze. There was nothing that Clint or his colleagues could have done that would have altered the outcome. Another law enforcement agency made the regrettable mistake of assaulting Koresh's compound while he was with his group. Clint and his group simply tangled with an inevitable outcome plotted in Koresh's twisted mind.

As a hostage negotiator, Clint has experienced liberating victory and life-ending defeat.

I first met Clint during the fall of 1993 when I was invited by his unit to lecture for two days at the FBI National Academy. We spent half a day together. I dubbed Clint and his colleagues "the boys of the bunker." I told Jana Monroe, the lone female profiler in the unit, about the nickname. She good-naturedly smiled and said, "Yeah. That's about right."

When the first FBI director, Edgar J. Hoover, built the FBI National Academy on the county-sized grounds of the Marine base in Quantico, Virginia, he wanted his brightest to be able to survive a nuclear attack. So he encased the two basement floors of the Academy in steel. There are no windows. Office walls are painted cinder blocks. The offices of Clint's unit were ten feet further underground than people are buried.

I'll never forget Special Agent Al Brantley showing me pictures of a logger who used a chainsaw to take his own life. The case set off a panic in Washington State. As I looked at the photos of the nearly decapitated man lying next to a pickup, I kept thinking, *They deal with all this and they don't even get a window!* It was from this sparse command post that Clint and the rest of his colleagues operated.

At Talladega Prison, there were eleven hostages. Ten days deep into the siege, they just wanted a chance to go home.

Clint wanted the same. So he met the inmates face to face. No flak jacket. No concealed weapon. Just a refined understanding of people and how they respond under pressure. Some colleagues thought it was too risky—foolish to go in without at least minimal protection.

"Look, these guys are armed with swords and knives. They're afraid. I have to face them equally stripped down to show them that I am not afraid."

So Clint, what did you do before you went in?

I asked the question hoping to get a nugget of insight. Hostage negotiators don't write textbooks. They can't. Information is typically shared in closed-door conferences and in cubicles.

"I prayed." We looked at each other and both nodded.

That's what you do when you get ready to apply your knowledge for the benefit of others in an extreme situation—labeled a critical incident by those in law enforcement. Nothing cavalier. You acknowledge that you can't control all situations, predict everyone's behavior, or that you have all of the needed insight. People are precious. So you study. You observe. You share ideas. You care. And, you pray.

The best profilers are people who care about others when it's really important. Their eyes are clear. Motives are others driven. And you pass on what you've learned to the next generation who will face the same struggles, just with different names and places.

There were over 150 kids and only two adults, who were clearly overwhelmed.

"Need some help?" I innocently asked, as I peeked my head in the room.

"Yes, you take that half," the exasperated teacher pointed.

That day in 1986, changed my life.

The kids, 6 to 17, were from an inner-city community a few miles from our church. We bussed them in for Sunday School. A third had seen somebody shot, stabbed, or murdered. Some had cigarette burns, some had lice in their hair, and others slept on the floor at night to avoid an errant bullet from a gang. Many were struggling in school.

My innocent *Need some help?* turned into six years of joyful labor with over 400 kids. It was also the first group of youths for whom we applied a strategy I developed that stops at-risk behavior in high-risk kids (the *Missing Protector Strategy*, which I later detailed in *Rage of the Random Actor*).

I watched those kids baffle their teachers—beating the odds—excelling at school. They learned that the Lord who created the universe, uniquely and wonderfully created each one of them. For the first time, they also experienced adults who unconditionally were always in their corner.

Out in their neighborhoods, their eyes were always wide open, alert for danger, but not paralyzed by fear. For six years, none joined a gang or did drugs—and not one teenage girl became pregnant. About 75 percent were African-American, 15 percent were new immigrants from Mexico, and the rest were Asian and Caucasian. Even though some couldn't speak English, others could translate. As we recruited more teachers, they learned to trust us. When they called for help, we showed up, and we all grew stronger together.

Not everyone at church, though, welcomed them, and the kids knew it.

Even a deacon's wife cornered me and offered me a few of her *thoughts*. One day, I brought this up with the kids.

"Do you ever feel that not everyone wants you here?" The kids stiffened.

"Well, I want to tell you a story. Have you ever sung the hymn, *Amazing Grace*?" Most nodded.

"Do you know who wrote that hymn?" Blank stares.

"It was a guy who used to be a slave trader, Jonathan Newton. One day, he realized that what he was doing was wrong, he repented, became a preacher, and he did something else.

"When he returned to England, he and other white men decided that slavery should end. They worked hard so your ancestors, who were brought from Africa, would be free," I added, looking at those with darker faces.

"Now if you and I were God, we'd probably pick black men to free the slaves, but He didn't. He picked a man who was the worst of the worst. He changed his heart and look what happened. He knew that there really was grace—forgiveness. That's how he wrote the hymn, *Amazing Grace*, and then worked to free those he carried into slavery.

"So, when an adult gives you one of those looks, don't hate them. Pray that God will change their heart. Treat them uniquely like you would like to be treated. You never know. You might be looking at another Jonathan Newton. Let go of that anger in your heart, or it will eat you alive."

One of the teachers came up to me afterwards and said, "You know, I was brought up to think that blacks and others were inferior to me. I didn't hate them, it's just what I was taught. But having worked with these kids for over a year, I realize that my prejudice was irrelevant."

She paused, then added, "I have no idea how I believed that nonsense for over forty years."

As we treated each child uniquely based upon how they were created, those who stereotyped learned there is a better way to respect God's creation.

> *For you created my inmost being; you knit me together in my mother's womb. I praise you because I am fearfully and wonderfully made.*
> *Psalms 139:13–14*

SOURCE NOTES

CHAPTER 2

[1] Average accuracy typically drops several percentage points every 5–10 seconds. If someone is trained to use the *KPS* and demonstrates 75% accuracy, but is provided an indeterminate amount of time to make a read, accuracy can drop to as low as 35–50%.

CHAPTER 3

[1] The gauges identify traits found in everyone. They are universal. Specifically what some of the gauges identify, though, was modified within a few years of the release of the 1st edition. Originally, the ASSERTIVE–NONASSERTIVE gauge was the ASK–TELL gauge, which was adapted from a gauge proposed by David Merrill and Roger Reid in their book, *Personal Styles and Effective Performance* (Chilton, 1981), which was derived from the research of Dr. James W. Taylor. The problem was that the gauge's identifiers, "ask" and "tell," were confusing, seemingly suggesting that one was trying to identify whether or not a person asked questions. Additionally, the gauge was not *specifically* focused on how someone *communicates*. I modified the gauge to its current state which identifies whether or not a person is assertive or nonassertive when communicating. It does not identify assertiveness when performing a task.

Another gauge in the first edition, PREDICTABLE–UNPREDICTABLE, also caused confusion, leading some to think that one was trying to identify whether or not a person was "predictable." Psychologists whom I originally consulted thought this gauge was in the same arena as the Dependability v. Undependability gauges identified by researchers, such as Michael K. Mount, Murray R. Barrick, and J. Perkins Strauss (who did extensive research regarding core personality factors—that some refer to as the "big five"). I disagreed as I could point to those with any of the traits who could be described as dependable or undependable. So I modified its use in the 1st edition to specify whether a person preferred to be "in-the-box" or an "out-of-the-box" when performing tasks. In practical use, though, it became apparent that CONVENTIONAL–UNCONVENTIONAL was much easier for people to grasp and apply for rapid-fire profiling.

To my knowledge the combination of the four gauges used in the *KPS* is unique to the literature. Additionally, I know of no other body of research regarding the use of these gauges in a rapid-fire profiling environment where accuracy is tested, as is facilitated in our training, thus making it a uniquely accessible system.

CHAPTER 5

[1] As noted in the Chapter 3 source note.

CHAPTER 7

[1] "Development of Personality in Early and Middle Adulthood: Set Like Plaster or Persistent Change?" Sanjay Srivastava and Oliver P. John, Samuel D. Gosling, Jeff Potter, *Journal of Personality and Social Psychology*, American Psychological Association, Inc. 2003, Vol. 84, No. 5, 1041–1053.

CHAPTER 8

[1] A 2009 United States Preventive Services Task Force study reported that over 6% of all students have been clinically depressed. When you look at their CONFIDENT–CAUTIOUS/FEARFUL trait, most are FEARFUL. In dozens of schools districts across North America, I surveyed school counselors and behavioral specialists who work with schools and they agreed that 6% is a conservative estimate. In the case cited in Chapter 1, the student intuitively knew what most educators now know is fact.

[2] As noted in the Chapter 3 source note.

CHAPTER 9

[1] The reason for the severe increase is noted in Chapter 14 and in more detail in *Snapshot*. Briefly, though, the increase in the UNCONVENTIONAL trait is due to the injection of technology and the many options people have in their personal lives. Our traits are typically formed by genetics, how we are brought up as children, and our responses to life's circumstances. While we can't control genetics, both parenting and the forces in our day-to-day lives encourage us to "do our own thing" with these new tools—which

cultivates more innovation and movement toward the UNCONVENTIONAL trait. Even those who are COVEN TI ON AL trait have an easier time relating to the UNCONVENTIONAL trait than their predecessors just thirty years ago because more people are now UNCONVENTIONAL.

The increase in the CAUTIOUS/FEARFUL trait is due to deterioration of stable families, on which I've written extensively in *Suburban Gangs—The Affluent Rebels* and *Rage of the Random Actor—Disarming Catastrophic Acts and Restoring Lives.*

Presently, it's not uncommon to find 20% or more of the students in a classroom with the CAUTIOUS–INNOVATOR profile. This has then translated to more people with this profile in the workplace.

CHAPTER 15

[1] Robert D. Hare, *Without Conscience* (New York: Pocket Books, 1993), pp. 23–24.
[2] Robert Hare, "Comparison of Procedures for the Assessment of Psychopathy," Journal of Consulting and Clinical Psychology 53 (1985):7–16. In J. Reid Meloy, Ph.D., *The Psychopathic Mind* (Northvale, NJ: Jason Aronson, Inc., 1988).

CHAPTER 17

[1] Bruce Horowitz, "AOL takes right approach offering mea culpa, rebate, *USA Today,* 9 August 1996."
[2] As quoted in *Dallas Morning News,* 12 January 1997.
[3] Associated Press wire service.

ADDITIONAL RESOURCES

COACHING, TRAINING, AND CONSULTANT SERVICES

Korem and Associates provides assistance to presidents of companies, entrepreneurs, and professional and collegiate athletic coaches. Interactive training classes that validate profiling accuracy are available for organizations. For more on additional services and open-registration workshops, see: KoremAssociates.com

RAGE OF THE RANDOM ACTOR
DISARMING CATASTROPHIC ACTS AND SAVING LIVES
Dan Korem

- Suicide terrorists
- Serial killers
- Columbine-type school shooters & bombers
- Postal & company shooters

Most have the RANDOM ACTOR behavior profile identified by Dan Korem in this classic text. Learn how to identify this profile by answering two questions, and how to apply a three-point strategy that guides someone out of the profile. Has been used successfully to prevent catastrophic acts in schools, companies, organizations, neighborhoods, and in combat. Can also be applied with anyone who has the profile, even if not violent. **$28.95 • Hardcover, 173 photos and illustrations, 523 pp. • ISBN-13: 978-0963910356**

"Powerful hope. Practical solutions that work. Must reading for every team leader — corporate, government, and education . . . and citizen in the neighborhood."
Bob VandePol, President, Crisis Care Network, nation's largest crisis responder

"Dan Korem's strategies save lives. I used them in Iraq to protect those in my charge and even save the lives of over 50 suicidal-led insurgents who wanted to kill."
Maj. Pedro Rosario, U.S. Armed Forces

"Extraordinary, Compelling, Urgently Applicable to All."
Amazon 5-Star Top-50 Review

PSYCHIC CONFESSION
Dan Korem

This classic 1983 documentary, seen by over 200 million people worldwide, is the first on-camera confession of a cult-like leader who claimed to have powers. It was Dan Korem's first RANDOM ACTOR case. In 1981, three years after the Jonestown Massacre, James Hydrick, 22, developed a cult-like following in Salt Lake City. He appeared on national television, fooling millions with his claims of psychic powers and alleged healing miracles. Investigative journalist Dan Korem not only exposed on camera how each of Hydrick's tricks worked, such as moving objects without touching them, but his eighteen month investigation also resulted in obtaining a thought-provoking confession of a cult-like figure. After the broadcast, the Department of Health and Human Services purchased the program, as it was the first documentary that traced the effects of child abuse through the eyes of an adult. **$24.95 • 48 minutes • DVD format**

> "It's an altogether fascinating study that transcends the somewhat exploitive subject matter." *Los Angeles Times*

SUBURBAN GANGS—THE AFFLUENT REBELS
Dan Korem

In the mid-1980s, Dan Korem predicted gangs would appear in affluent communities for the first time in US history. By the late 1980s, his prediction was a fact. By 1994, the typical suburb of 50,000 had 250–500 gang members. Based upon seven years of research in eleven countries, Korem produced the first hard-hitting guide to counterattack this unprecedented trend. Laced with riveting accounts and lucidly written for professionals and laymen, *Suburban Gangs* answers the whys while giving real solutions and identifying the following critical information:

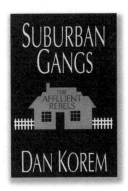

- The Missing Protector Strategy: Stops most at-risk behavior, including gang recruitment, suicide, chronic drug use, teen pregnancy, and truancy. The strategy works effectively in both affluent and inner-city communities. (Korem applied this strategy to over 400 inner-city youths, and not one joined a gang in six years.)
- The profile of the youth recruited by gangs.
- Gang types and activities found in affluent communities.
- Disengagement strategy—eleven reasons why youths disengage from gangs.
- Why skinhead and occultic gangs mysteriously appeared simultaneously in the US and Europe—unique survey of skinhead gang members.
- European parallels that foreshadow gang trends in the US.
- Over 70 photographs show how youth gang cultures in the US and Europe influence each other for the first time in modern history.

$29.95 • 285 pages • Hardbound • ISBN: 0-9639103-1-0

- Over 70 photographs show how youth gang cultures in the US and Europe influence each other for the first time in modern history.

  $29.95 • 285 pages • Hardbound • ISBN: 0-9639103-1-0

  "Recommended strongly for professionals, academics, and the general public."
  Library Journal

AUTHOR

Dan Korem has worn some pretty diverse hats that together have helped people in so many situations...

Best known for developing the *Korem Profiling System*®, he and the Korem and Associates faculty have trained over 40,000 people how to rapid-fire profile—more than any other firm. His consulting clients globally include: professional and collegiate athletic coaches, corporate executives and professionals, entrepreneurs, educators, law enforcement, and military units. He also spends time showing people how to use profiling to enrich their personal lives and retard stereotyping. Each year he trains high school and college student leaders how to profile and use their skill to improve campus academics, lead students, reduce behavioral issues, and more.

As an investigative journalist, he produced the documentary *Psychic Confession* (1983), in which he obtained the first confession of a suicidal cult-like leader who claimed to have psychic powers—viewed by over 200 million globally. The *Los Angeles Times* wrote: "It's an altogether fascinating study..."

A frequent keynote speaker and distinguished lecturer for groups in over thirty countries, he uses these opportunities to hunt for answers to all kinds of issues and uncover the unexpected.

Before 1981, he was a professional sleight-of-hand magician who used his skills to educate and protect the public from threatening deceptions and was often called by law enforcement for assistance. It's how he transitioned to investigative journalism, and he often times uses effects he has invented in speeches and lectures.

For thirty years he has worked with at-risk youth as an expression of his Christian faith to "care for the widows and the orphans in their affliction." While researching his 1995 book, *Suburban Gangs—The Affluent Rebels*, he developed and applied the "Missing Protector Strategy" to over 400 inner-city youth. For six years, not one student joined a gang or became pregnant. The strategy has been used to stop gang formation and suicide—including suicides in the military during the wars in Iraq and Afghanistan.

An avid golfer, he has been married for forty-six years to his wife Sandy, one of America's premier caterers and owner of The Festive Kitchen®. They have three children, five grandchildren, and reside in the Dallas area.